Beyond the Light

A Personal Guidebook
for Healing, Growth, and Enlightenment

by Ginny Katz

Golden Age Publishing
P.O. Box 3217,
Gresham, Oregon USA 97030

Beyond the Light

Printed in U.S.A.

ISBN: 0-924700-00-9
Library of Congress Catalog Card Number: 91-058333

Chief Editor: Suzanne Alexander
Cover Art: Edward Clay Wright, Jr.

Dedicated
to the Wayshower
and all who accompany him
in the Light and Sound of God

A Special Appreciation

Many have helped and supported me, both physically and inwardly, as I manifested this book. My children, family, friends, and co-workers have each demonstrated great measures of patience, love, and understanding through the many stages of writing and editing. I thank them dearly.

However this book could not have been written without one special individual, who gave from the depths of both heart and Soul. During my inner-world explorations, while I was recording the discourses collected in this book, he was there protecting me from physical disturbances. He also shielded me from any non-physical negativity that would compromise my mission by constructing a vortex of golden light around me.

Afterward, throughout the time-consuming process of translating my recordings into literary English, he respected, supported, and encouraged my work. Often our relationship came second. He also offered an objective ear during the final stages of editing, and took the responsibility for the many business aspects of publishing this book.

To my husband, Michael, I am deeply and everlastingly grateful.

Table of Contents

Note to the Reader

*B*eyond the Light is a series of personal discourses from various spiritual Masters. They were a blessing that transformed my life, catapulted me to a higher consciousness, and revitalized my inner health. There is no doubt in my mind that the wisdom and practical exercises these Masters shared can affect your life just as profoundly.

To experience the full benefits of this book, I suggest you practice the exercises given at the end of each chapter before moving on. This way, you'll be prepared for the discourses to come, and your experience will unfold according to the natural process intended by the book's contributors.

You will probably find several exercises that are particularly rewarding. Incorporate at least one or two of these into your daily schedule. Be sure to give yourself time to feel their effects. After a while, try other techniques.

By practicing these exercises, your daily and nightly experiences will become more alive, uplifting, and rewarding. Therefore I also suggest that you pay close attention to your dreams and daily life as it unfolds around you. You may be pleasantly surprised by how much things begin to change.

This was my experience. It was deeply personal. Though the information was tailored to me, the Masters had you in mind too as it was presented. I did my best to translate those experiences which language cannot fully convey and describe the concepts for which words have not yet been invented.

You may read this book simply to broaden your knowledge. Or, join me on the adventure of mastering your inner dimensions. Together we can listen to the God-Realized Masters who share their wisdom.

I invite you to make this a personal experience, uniquely yours. You too can be transformed!

May the blessings be.

Ginny Katz
9/17/91

Chapter 1

The Journey Begins

Are you ready? *asked a familiar voice in a soft, Southern accent. I couldn't ignore the compelling inner call. I turned off the computer, closed my eyes, and sang 'HU', an ancient name for God. I had no idea what awaited me. But the HU-song would calm my outer senses and help me be more receptive to the spiritual experience I hoped would follow.*

Within moments, a gentle inner wind blew into the room and began swirling around me. It increased in speed until my awareness was lifted from my body. The sound of HU faded from my lips as I rapidly floated higher and higher. Watching with fascination, I saw the back of my head, then the rooftops, countryside, and finally the Earth herself fall away.

Suddenly, I was cast into a realm of brilliant light. In a moment of split attention, I realized it even made my physical eyes squint and water. I tried to close my inner eyes against the overwhelming brilliance, but it didn't seem to make any difference. It was just as luminous and clear.

A pure note of an invisible flute flooded every atom of my heart, mind, and body. The soft voice spoke again, beckoning me through the blinding light. Slowly I emerged into a golden world of unspeakable intensity and boundlessness.

Soon, images began to form from the golden liquid brilliance. Gradually, I became aware I was standing at the foot of an enormous throne made from a concentration of the same light-substance that filled the atmosphere.

Sitting in quiet contemplation upon the towering throne was a magnificent bronze-skinned man. He was dressed only in a loincloth and a golden band which encircled his left arm. He had no hair on his head. His body was as immense as his throne, giving him the appearance of a serene statue several stories high. Yet a vital, dancing light emanated from his every atom, convincing me he was more alive than any being I'd ever encountered.

This is the Lord Sat Nam, my spiritual guide informed me, as he gradually manifested at my side. I turned my attention toward my mentor as his beloved features gently came into focus. He was a few inches shorter than me and wore a neatly pressed suit of light blue that matched his twinkling eyes. He is known by many names, but I call him Peddar.

Sat Nam is the first pure manifestation of God, Peddar continued. He is the Lord of this Kingdom and the ruler of the lower worlds—the realms of matter, energy, space, and time.

I gazed in awe at this great being who sat quietly contemplating. Suddenly, his eyes opened wide and peered down at me. A thunderous voice rolled from his lips like a storm moving down a mountain.

Love and power! *he said.* What do you know of each?

The vibration of the words reverberated in my heart, echoing throughout my entire being. My mind sped through all I had learned about love and power during years of spiritual study. But no answer seemed worthy of the occasion.

Answer the question put forth!

I quickly thrust my mind aside and spoke from the heart. "Of power I know not much other than it clouds love. And of love, I know even less. Yet I know when I feel love, and my goal is to receive and express it more and more."

Can you do this without power? *he asked.*

"Yes, I believe I can, if I acknowledge the power's presence and respect it," *I replied.*

Very well. You have answered correctly for who you are now, but incorrectly for who you will become.

Then Sat Nam continued with a more gentle voice: I have called you here to assign a special mission. More than anything you have yet experienced, it will help you realize who you truly are. When this assignment is complete, I will again ask what love and power are. Your answer at that time will be an expression of the new state of being you have earned.

My eyes wandered the room, as I stood silently absorbing his words. More of the palatial throne room was now visible to me. Its tall ceiling and arched walls were made of the same concentration of golden light as Sat Nam's throne. The floor reminded me of a single facet of a diamond, polished to perfection and sparkling with a clear, reflective brilliance.

A splash of color in the floor made me look up again, and I saw that the ceiling was decorated with intricate mosaics of glittering, faceted jewels. Their myriad colors projected sparkling images on the shiny walls and floor. These images hinted at places even more magnificent, a subtle reminder that there is always another world beyond—another step to take on the path to God.

I wondered about the great being who sat regally on his throne. I thought about using a technique which once allowed me to better know and understand other spiritual beings, who guarded the healing secrets of gemstones. Upon meeting each guardian in the inner worlds, I would ask permission to enter his or her aura, a communication method not possible in the Physical World. Inspired, I turned to Peddar. "Should I enter Sat Nam's aura to know him better?"

Peddar simply smiled. Warm ripples of joy burst from Sat Nam and washed through me with love as he replied softly, You are already in my aura, Dear One, which encompasses this entire dimension.

Then his tone changed again. Spark of God, *he thundered,* you are Soul, unique and unlike any other. Do not compare yourself with your fellow creatures. Each Soul is unique, though there may be a shared similarity of physical bodies, mental patterns, and emotional expressions. Soul Itself is the only true identity. Its true home is in this world, which you call the Golden Kingdom. This is the first pure spiritual plane beyond the lower worlds of time, space, and matter. It is only the first of innumerable realms that extend from here into eternity, into the very heart of God.

Each uneducated Soul must leave Its home in the Golden Kingdom and enter the material worlds for learning. Before each Soul begins Its great journey, It is given certain innate abilities in seed form. These gifts to Know, See, and Be, are Soul's guarantee It will one day return to Its home in the Golden Kingdom.

Soul experiences many lives in the lower worlds, each time learning a little more about Its innate gifts. Gradually the seeds emerge and blossom, and Soul earns re-admittance home.

At the core of these gifts is God's abiding love. It is constantly showered upon Soul. As you become ever more aware of this love, Soul discovers and experiences Its own beingness. Divine love is different from the emotional love Soul expresses through Its human self.

Emotional love is a pale, dilute reflection of divine love, and is limited by the laws of the Emotional Plane. Unconditional, divine love exists on all planes and originates in the very heart of God. It is the essence of God, or Spirit, and the most fundamental component of Soul Itself. Thus, Soul learns that It exists because of God's love for It.

As Soul moves and lives in the darkness of the lower worlds, it is challenged by the problems and experiences of life. Eventually It learns to open Its heart, identify God's gift of love within, and then express this love. This expression awakens a driving impulse to return to the Golden Kingdom. Only here can Soul fully know and express Its true beingness.

4

Once Soul becomes aware of Its true identity and divinity, It gains the opportunity to know and experience innumerable worlds beyond the Golden Kingdom. Each is of an increasingly finer vibration and brilliance than the last. Soul's desire to unite with more of Spirit—as love—draws It further and further into the heart of God.

As if on cue, a young boy dressed in princely clothes ran up and handed me a glowing book. It was made of the same golden essence as the walls. I bowed my head in thanks as he dashed off to perform another divine errand.

I hugged the book close to my heart. It not only symbolized God's gift of divine love, but also my work in this present life as a writer.

The book also has a more specific significance, *Sat Nam replied, as if my thoughts had been spoken.*

With a graceful movement, he stepped down from his throne. As he crossed the room, his tall, statuesque appearance diminished. By the time he reached Peddar and me, he was only a few inches over six feet. I was amazed. He no longer appeared aloof, like a deity to be worshipped. He was simply a loving co-worker with God. As his brown eyes looked into mine, I felt respect for the being I truly was—a Soul worthy of learning, growth, and unfoldment.

Sat Nam continued, Your presence here marks the first chapter of a special, three-part assignment to write a book. First, you must learn more about Soul's journey into the lower worlds. Second, you will share a study of the five sheaths that protect Soul there. And third, you will explore how Soul may follow God's call of love, freeing Itself of the lower worlds forever. All this will be recorded on tape, transcribed, and written down for other Souls to experience.

After I share a few beginning discourses, Sri Peddar will continue your lessons. He will also arrange meetings with other spiritual masters to add to your understanding. As you learn from these spiritual adepts, your mind, emotions, and physical body will be purified and adjusted so you can absorb this high spiritual knowledge. The same will be true for your reader. At times, you may feel stretched or torn apart.

In fact, your very atoms are being rearranged and transformed. This process will continue throughout the assignment, and be supported through the practice of certain exercises.

Sri Peddar, the masters you meet, and I will each describe unique spiritual visualizations and exercises to try. These will ease your transformation into a new being, and help you understand and assimilate what you have learned. The exercises will also prepare your consciousness for the discourses that follow.

The significance of Sat Nam's assignment began to seep into my consciousness. I was already aware of the existence of Soul's five protective sheaths: the physical, astral, causal, mental, and etheric bodies. But information on these wrappings of Soul was scarce. Available esoteric writings had left me with scores of questions.

The prospect of interviewing several spiritual adepts on man's subtle bodies was exciting indeed. Perhaps they would show me how to heal and align my own inner sheaths, and unlock many puzzles I'd encountered in my struggle to be a fully conscious Soul.

Nurturing Seeds of Love
and Recognizing Them in Others

Sat Nam interrupted my reverie. I will give you your first exercise now, *he announced.* It consists of two parts.

The first is designed to awaken and nurture the dormant gift of love within. This love is the very heart and essence of all Souls. The second part will help you see and recognize this same gift in others.

To awaken the seed of love, imagine there is a beautiful container within your heart. It can be made of gold, crystal, wood, or any other substance of meaning to you, of any shape and color.

Slowly open the container. Inside, you will find a gift, manifested as a flower. Remove the flower from the container. Notice that it is immediately replaced with another, similar bloom.

Examine your gift. Is it a bud or a full bloom? Is it a rose? A dahlia? A summer lily—or a lotus? Observe the nuances of color and texture in its petals. Enjoy its fragrance, the softness of its petals, and the purity of its beauty.

Now, feel and imagine the presence of someone you love as he or she joins you. Give him or her your flower.

Follow through by manifesting this gift in the Physical World. You can present your loved one with a blossom or find another way to 'give them a flower' by performing an act of kindness, a service, or expressing your love in some other way.

While doing this visualization, if you are unable to imagine a flower, you can draw one on paper or look at one physically manifested. This may help you visualize it with your inner sight. Or you might visit a florist, either in the Physical World or in your imagination, and browse through the flowers. Choose one and give it to the first person you meet.

The second part of this exercise is to help you recognize the gift of love in others. In some people, this gift is still a seed. Others display a delicate bud, while a few carry love in full, glorious bloom. Practice seeing this seed, bud, or flower of love in the heart of each person you meet. Begin with your family, friends, and co-workers. Later, you will be able to recognize love in the hearts of strangers as well.

You can uplift others just by this simple, devotional act of observing a flower of love in each Soul. Drink in the unique fragrance and beauty of each heart bloom. If your mind must give comment on the individual, let it dwell instead on the flower: 'How beautiful it is!'

As Sat Nam's words echoed in the mighty hall, my heart was filled with gratitude. I was indeed honored to be chosen for this assignment.

We shall meet again, *said Sat Nam in conclusion.* May the blessings be.

Swiftly the scene faded. The light lost its brightness, and the sound diminished. Even as I hugged the book from Sat Nam, I found myself returning to physical consciousness. But the first chapter of its flowering love was stored safely within my heart.

The presence of my spiritual guide lingered like a delicate fragrance. Prepare for experiences to come, *he whispered.*

Chapter 2

The Sound and the Light

*A*bout the same time the next day, I was again called into contemplation. This time, I had a tape-recorder ready to describe my experiences. As I chanted "HUUU..." I recalled Sat Nam's assignment, and his promise that we would meet again. A strange mixture of excitement and apprehension swirled about my heart. I was happy to serve Spirit. But what if the project proved too big?

I pushed my thoughts aside and continued singing HU, until a feeling of peacefulness spread over me. Faith, knowingness, and love melted all doubts from my heart. My inner senses cleared, and I became aware of the presence of my spiritual guide.

Once again, I felt as though I was being lifted. But instead of floating serenely into the air, I found myself pulled upward through the eye of a raging tornado of light. I braced myself against its overwhelming energy. Suddenly I passed through it and entered into Sat Nam's bright kingdom.

You are becoming more accustomed to the vibrations of this world, *I heard Peddar explain, as the golden fabric of the God-world swirled into focus.* Next time the transition can be easier, if you effortlessly expand your state of consciousness. To do this, you must completely let go and trust Spirit.

I stored his words in my heart for later contemplation. I had long tried to practice unconditional trust in Spirit. But it had never occurred to me that this trust was also needed

9

beyond the concerns of my physical reality. Although the many worlds which lie between the Physical World and the Golden Kingdom are more refined and 'spiritual' than the Physical, they still contain materiality that can obstruct one's pathway home to God. Only absolute trust would guide me safely through their borders.

When my inner eyes adjusted, I saw that Peddar and I were standing outside the golden palace we had visited the day before. The sound of the flute permeated every atom of my being. I followed Peddar's lead up the many golden stairs to the massive palace doors.

Instead of entering, Peddar strolled out onto the vast terrace surrounding Sat Nam's abode. As we approached the marble balustrade, a panoramic view filled my senses. An expansive valley sloped downward from the foot of the palace, leading to a long chain of iridescent gold mountains on the horizon.

As I gazed into the valley, I saw a unique gathering of millions of Souls. Each was a unique spark of God, shining with a brilliance worthy of this wondrous world.

But something about this gathering was different than I expected. Though Souls mingled with one another, they did not interact. Each seemed preoccupied with Itself, passive and incurious, with no desire to be or do anything else.

Those Souls are awaiting entrance into the lower worlds, *explained Peddar.* Each is a divine spark of God, yet they are still immature and unproven. They are not yet worthy to be co-workers with the Creator. Many lives in the worlds of matter, energy, space, and time will give them the experience, training, and unfoldment they need to serve in the Golden Kingdom as Self-Realized individuals.

As Peddar spoke, the Lord Sat Nam quietly joined us. He smiled warmly and welcomed us to his kingdom. Despite the awesome presence surrounding this agent of God, I felt surprisingly at ease.

We will begin at the beginning, *said Sat Nam.* For your first discourse, I wish to explain how the lower worlds were created. Behold a re-enactment of this process.

He waved his arm from horizon to horizon and instantly the Souls in the valley disappeared. The sound of a soft flute grew louder and sharper, overwhelming my senses. When it seemed as if it could not increase in volume any more, a giant wave broke through the atmosphere. The ground below us shook and undulated in its wake. The valley floor became transparent, and through it we observed the formation of a new world.

This wave was the breath of God as it shot forth from the heart of God to create new worlds, *Sat Nam explained.* The undulating motion was a result of Its outflow. Thus, the Word of God, or Spirit, flows from the pure, positive, undifferentiated completeness of the God Worlds into the differentiated realms of duality, which we call the lower worlds.

During this transition, Spirit also clothes Itself in duality. It is divided into two forms which man can apprehend: Sound and Light. This tangible, measurable, manifested Sound and Light sustains and creates the material worlds, with their duality of positive and negative, light and darkness, male and female.

The Sound, the essence of the Word of God, is imbued with a purpose. The Light is dually manifested with the Sound in order to help fulfill that purpose. Encoded within the Sound are complete instructions for the creation of the lower worlds—the testing ground of Soul. The Light allows the testing ground to be perceived and understood. Thus, the Light is Soul's link to the Sound.

Originally, the Light was only divided into seven simple color rays: purple, indigo, blue, green, yellow, orange, and red. The Sound was likewise given four basic qualities: character, substance, rhythm, and magnetism. Each of these qualities could manifest in a positive, negative, or neutral way.

11

This division into positive and negative polarities was essential. It enabled the Sound to fulfill one of the instructions inherent within it—to find a return path to its source. You will learn more about this return flow and the role of the neutral force later.

We watched as the golden current of Sound tumbled into the darkness, turning, unfolding, and concentrating itself into wave after wave of lower and coarser vibrations. It was clear that all the power of the Creator was within it. Indeed, it originated as the Word from the very heart of God. The Light also spread Itself over each successive wave, following the pulsing Sound into new, more coarse vibratory rates.

Eventually, *Sat Nam explained,* a continuum of vibratory rates formed, stretching from the borders of the Golden Kingdom to the bowels of the Physical Plane. Within this continuum, sections of waves banded together to form planes and sub-planes.

Watch the first band of vibratory rates now forming, *he said.* As the sound matrixes manifest, the seven color-ray frequencies expand in height, width, and depth to create new, non-color-ray frequencies. These frequencies, together with the Sound, form the very fabric of this first lower world and of all that will follow.

In other words, the Sound vibrations combine with the Light frequencies to create each subsequent plane and all that is in it. Again, this process is first orchestrated by the Sound and its four qualities: substance, character, rhythm, and magnetism.

The substance of the Sound organizes the seemingly limitless supply of Light frequencies and defines them into what might be regarded as individual notes. Eventually, when the worlds at the lower end of the continuum are formed, these notes will manifest as atoms.

As the breath of God flows out, the character of the Sound arranges these notes into both simple and intricate melodies. The Sound's rhythm gives cyclical life to the world this music has created. And the Sound's magnetism sets this manifestation into a divine order which feeds and maintains all life.

Thus the music of God—the instructions inherent within the Sound—becomes the matrix for all in the lower worlds. It also provides genetic blueprints for the forms that will eventually house Soul. They are woven out of the seven color-ray frequencies.

This first plane is the highest realm of the lower worlds. You call it the Etheric or Subconscious Plane. It is more of a transition area between the Golden Kingdom and the worlds of matter below, than a world of itself. This is because so much of the Golden Kingdom and its attributes are reflected here.

Still, there are great differences between this area and the Worlds of God above. Perhaps most significant is the element of space. Here in the Etheric Plane, Spirit is manifested in the form of Light and Sound—dual, parallel forces. All exists at every point, and within every point is the all.

In the Golden Kingdom, Spirit is a singular force. It is everywhere but nowhere. It is all, yet nothing. It is here, but not here. All exists but does not exist. Therefore, descriptions of experiences in the Golden Kingdom have one thing in common: words cannot portray their true nature! Mind, memory, and emotion do not exist here, for they are the stuff of the lower worlds.

In surprise, I piped up, "Then how am I able to record this experience?"

You are here in your Soul form, by the grace of God and the action of Spirit. The Golden Kingdom is an area of knowingness that lies beyond the world of the mind. However, your mind is being fed simplified impressions of your experience.

It in turn translates these impressions into words, so you can share your experiences with others. Simultaneous recording of these experiences—instead of writing them down afterward—is essential to report them accurately. Emotion and memory play no part in this process.

I reflected on his description. My mind was picking up impressions which I spoke aloud to the tape recorder. But it was true that I felt emotionally and physically detached from the entire experience. I knew from previous experience that this detachment was necessary to remain in the Golden Kingdom. Feelings, memories, or thoughts could send my awareness hurtling back to the Physical Plane. I refocused my attention on Sat Nam.

All is inherent in the Sound, *he continued,* but certain manifestations only occur within specific bands of vibration. Therefore, each different plane has its unique manifestations of Spirit, its own life forms, experiences, and reality.

Sat Nam motioned for us to look past the Subconscious Plane, deeper into the worlds forming at our feet.

Previous matrixes and blueprints were uncomplicated compared to those whose formation we were now witnessing. Notes and colors combined to form highly developed and intricate relationships. These groups of frequencies would then communicate with others to form complex networks of Light and Sound.

The plane which Spirit is now creating is called the Mental Plane, the World of the Mind, *Sat Nam explained.* The neutral force is present here, but it is not needed by the partnership of positive and negative forces to form this or the Subconscious World.

It is not until the formation of the next realm, which you call the Causal Plane, that the neutral force will become an essential catalyst for creation. Watch how this occurs.

We watched as the Sound tumbled past the farthest borders of the Mental Plane.

Suddenly the Sound and Light exploded!

This explosion was enormous. It occurred everywhere along the Mental Plane's borders. Then, gradually but quickly, the temporary chaos settled into order. The new, lower and more coarse vibratory rates of the Causal World manifested.

"What was that explosion?" I asked.

Sat Nam replied, The vibratory rates at the borders of the Mental Plane became so coarse that the positive and negative forces could no longer remain intertwined. In order to continue manifesting lower vibratory rates, they were compelled to split apart. As a result, the Sound, and the Light that accompanied it, exploded.

As the positive and negative forces tore away from each other, they manifested distinct 'particles' of spiritual energy called protons and electrons. In order to balance this split, the neutral force manifested neutrons.

The manifestation of the neutral force is an integral part of creation. It provides the medium in which all further manifestation is suspended. The third force keeps the positive and negative forces from crashing into each other and causing further explosions.

Atoms, made up of protons, electrons, and neutrons, provide the foundation for all further creation in the Causal World, and the worlds below it. Atoms are formed when the neutral force combines with the positive and negative aspects of the Sound.

The four qualities of Sound, as I have explained, are substance, character, rhythm, and magnetism. Protons, neutrons, and electrons are first given substance out of the Sound. Their character compels them to define their own unique qualities and quantities relative to each other. Rhythm gives them orderly movement and life. This order is made possible by magnetism, which draws atoms into organized molecules, cells, and eventually complex organisms.

From this point onward, Light no longer follows Sound to fill its matrixes. It is now inseparably linked to the Sound.

15

In addition, all further manifestation will occur directly from the atomic matrixes produced in the Causal World. See for yourself.

We watched the Sound and Light as it stepped itself downward through the Causal Plane. I noticed that not all Light and Sound was packaged into atoms. Part of the spiritual force remained unmanifested. In addition, as the atoms and molecules manifested, their vibratory rates expanded into a continuum which extended toward the Causal Plane's farthest borders. Interestingly, many only expanded to a certain vibratory rate before suddenly stopping.

"Why did they stop?" I asked.

Sat Nam replied, Certain manifestations of positive, negative, and neutral energy cannot exist at low, coarse vibratory rates. In fact, the only structures whose continuum will reach uninterrupted into the next world, which is the Astral Plane, and then into the earthly Physical Plane, are certain ones destined to house Soul.

We continued to watch the performance. Soon the vibratory rates that the Sound was forming became highly kinetic. The Astral World was forming. This kinetic energy seemed to radiate from the very fabric of the new world. Once released, it scattered wildly throughout the Astral Universe.

This energy characterizes the Astral Plane as the world of emotions, *noted Sat Nam.* Only the Light will compel these scattered and chaotic energies to organize themselves and become useful and functional.

One day, perhaps in your lifetime, this energy will be harnessed by Earth's scientists for space travel and other great technological gains.

As Sat Nam spoke, the Sound continued to catapult forward, forming new, lower, and more coarse vibrations of Itself. The lower the vibrations, the more densely knit the positive, negative, and neutral patterns became. Eventually these intertwined so closely there was no space for the

16

scattered, kinetic, astral energy to express itself. This density marked the beginning of the Physical World.

Here the essence of Sound and Light was almost completely contained in the relatively tight web of positive, negative, and neutral which comprised the atoms. These limiting vibratory patterns caused the Light and Sound flowing into the Physical Plane to bottleneck.

The resulting pressure made the Sound current rumble and moan, forming the most far-flung and coarse vibratory rates of the lower Physical Plane. I commented on how slowly these new vibratory rates were now forming.

Did you notice how the flow of spiritual energy is restricted on this plane? *Sat Nam asked.*

"Yes," I replied.

That restriction is only temporary, *Sat Nam said.* At this point, it is necessary for the Physical Plane to bottleneck spiritual energy, thus pressurizing it and allowing it to form lower and lower vibratory rates. As these considerably lower vibratory rates build, the negative pole of the lower worlds strengthens.

At some point, the breath and love of God will manifest a positive pole in the lower worlds. When that occurs, the river of Sound and Light will burst the banks of the bottleneck and spread like a flood encompassing the land. Additional Sound and Light entering the Physical Plane will then expand the area covered by the flood.

Gradually this flood will reach upward into the Astral Plane and every other lower world, retracing each pathway the Light and Sound created on its journey toward the Physical Plane. This flood will not add to the frequencies or vibratory rates already in existence, but expand them. This expansion will provide a direct mechanism for the Sound and Light to flow back into the Golden Kingdom. At this point in the reenactment of creation, this return flow has not yet been initiated.

But in the lower worlds today, such a flow back to God does exist. To find Its way home, Soul must first locate the initiator of this return flow. He links Soul with the return wave to aid Its journey back to the Golden Kingdom. The experiences acquired on this journey home teach Soul invaluable lessons. It realizes the full measure of Its strength, stamina, wisdom, understanding, and love. When It reaches my kingdom again, Soul is prepared to become a co-worker with God and fulfill Its highest destiny.

Again, to unfold Its essential qualities, Soul passes through many lessons in the realms outside the Golden Kingdom. To manifest these lower-world school rooms, Spirit had to leave the Golden Kingdom. In doing so, it clothed Itself in Light and Sound and gave birth to the worlds of duality.

What does this mean in practical terms? Without the Sound, Soul could not exist in the lower worlds. Sound is essential. This is why you sing the HU—to resonate with your true essence as Soul and the essence of Spirit.

Without the Light, Soul could not perceive Its presence in the lower worlds. It would be blind and unable to find Its way home. That, of course, is not what the Creator intended. Souls are destined to enjoy the full richness of the lower worlds in all their dimensions. This is why you look for the inner Light as you sing HU. It helps Soul see the potholes on the road home.

Soul needs both Light and Sound. In order for the Light to be perceived, it must reflect off the basic matrix of the Sound Current. At the same time, the Sound must have the Light. For it enables Soul to find and negotiate the returning wave home.

Furthermore, Sound provides the learning experiences for Soul in the lower worlds. Light enables It to see the spiritual lessons or principles uniting these experiences. In turn, this recognition helps Soul find the Sound, the Life Current, which provides a means to return to the worlds of pure Spirit. The light illuminates this path. So you see the Light and Sound weave a divine, upwardly spiraling circle for Soul.

Sat Nam cast his gaze into mine. To open your understanding to the relationship between Light and Sound, you must return to Physical World consciousness. But keep your inner ears open to my instructions. I will lead you through a spiritual exercise.

The image of Peddar, the temple, and all else in my peripheral vision gradually faded. The only thing I could see was Sat Nam's eyes against a background of darkness. The Sound was like an ocean of flutes playing a single note. It maintained its enduring rhythm, and I felt the steadfast presences of Peddar and Sat Nam.

As my physical senses slowly returned, a part of me remained in the Golden Kingdom. I had long sought the ability to be consciously awake in the physical and inner worlds simultaneously. I felt my body shift in the chair as I repositioned my legs for comfort.

Finding the Sound and Light Within

Now, go sit in front of a mirror, *instructed Sat Nam.*

I rose and placed a chair before the floor-length mirror on my closet door.

First contemplate not upon your reflection, but on the mirror itself. It is a piece of glass with a backing that presents a reflection of all who look into the glass.

Now study the reflection of yourself in the mirror.

Close your eyes and think about the different parts of your body. Sense what they feel like from the inside.

For example, think about your shoulders. What do they feel like? How does it feel when you move them in circles?

Now think about your hands. What does it feel like to open and close your fists? Feel your feet and the way they contact the floor. How does your back feel where it touches the chair? Feel your weight on the seat of the chair.

Now, open your eyes and look at your image.

Close your eyes and again feel your body.

Continue to open and close your eyes, each time inspecting and reflecting on what you see when your eyes are open and what you feel inside when your eyes are closed.

I practiced this while Sat Nam waited patiently.

Do you notice a difference? *he asked.*

I did. With eyes closed, I was a subjective being experiencing the chair, floor, and my own skin. They were only an outer 'reality' because my brain said so. With eyes open, I saw proof of my physical form and all that my mind counted as 'real'.

With my eyes closed, I felt the subtler essence of my existence; with my eyes open, I saw only the surface of my physical body and world. This appearance felt like only a small piece of the real me.

After practicing this technique for awhile, I realized I was dealing with three points of view: one with eyes open, one with eyes closed, and a separate one that was observing the entire experiment with detachment.

Open your eyes, *said Sat Nam.* What you see in the mirror is the reflection of Light bouncing off a silvered surface. When you look at anything in the Physical World, what you see is the reflection of Light as it bounces off the Sound. Remember, the Sound manifests and organizes your atoms. The Light fills that matrix and makes the atoms perceivable.

Close your eyes. What you feel is who you are within the framework of atoms, the physical embodiment. Essentially, when your eyes are closed, you feel your own Sound matrix; when your eyes are open you see the Light filling this matrix; the manifestation is complete.

20

The You that is the observer, the one who is performing this experiment, is divine Soul.

When your eyes are open, they serve as tools to perceive the Light as it is reflected off your physical form. When your eyes are closed, your awareness or consciousness can connect directly with the Sound, the organizing matrix of your atoms.

As I listened and practiced what Sat Nam was saying, I felt a renewed link to the Sound, the Light, and to myself as Soul.

It is best that we stop for now and let your physical body rest, *said Sat Nam.*

A part of me was tireless and yearned to continue. But Sat Nam was right, my physical body wanted sleep.

When we meet again, you shall witness the entrance of a wave of Souls into the lower worlds. In the meantime, practice the technique I have given you.

Within moments my conscious connection to Sat Nam and the Golden Kingdom dissolved. Peddar's presence remained, comforting me as the Physical World again became my point of reference.

I had witnessed the creation of the lower worlds. Tomorrow, Sat Nam would show me Souls' movement into them. Had he taken me back to the beginning of time to witness this creation firsthand? If so, did it really happen so fast? It had been less than an hour since I began this spiritual contemplation.

I wondered about the existence of time in the Golden Kingdom, and asked Peddar to explain it.

When we meet again, before you continue your experience with Sat Nam, I will discuss your questions about time, *he said.*

Until then, May the blessings be!

Chapter 3

Entering the Lower Worlds

Within *minutes of settling into my contemplative exercise, I entered the inner worlds. I found myself standing on a beach of fine white sand, bordering a long, crescent-shaped bay.*

As I gazed across the waves, a magnificent city filled my vision. It was an architectural wonder of tall spires and golden domes, incomparable to anything on Earth. The buildings spread for miles. My eyes followed them into the gentle foothills, which fronted a gigantic mountain range with peaks stretching into the clouds.

Turning around, my eyes were swept upward by white, vertical cliffs, thousands of feet in height. I caught my breath in wonder as I leaned back to take in their full stature.

Mighty tall cliffs, aren't they, *said Peddar in greeting, as he materialized next to me. I nodded to him and we stood silently for a moment, watching the circling sea gulls. Some came tumbling out of their cliff-side nests, in full cry, to forage in the sea while others sailed home sporting food for their young.*

Then Peddar began the discourse. Regarding your question about time...

I had forgotten my query until he spoke. Time was a puzzle of burning interest to me, and I eagerly gave him my full attention. With a gesture, he invited me to stroll the beach with him and said:

Time is an illusion. Depending on one's point of view, an event can fill an eternity or conclude in a few seconds. Yet without the illusion of time, the lower worlds could not exist.

When Spirit first flowed out of the gates of the Golden Kingdom, the unfolding of Sound into the lower worlds created space. The creation of space accompanied the movement of Sound from point to point as it extended into lower and lower vibratory rates. This movement was, and is, measurable in time. Therefore, time is a byproduct of space.

Space and time are like a parent and a child who has grown to adulthood. Although time is the offspring of space, each functions independently. One does not govern the other. Space and time are, however, indelibly linked, and work together to form the lower-plane fabric of reality.

Within each range of vibratory rates (which you call worlds), the laws governing the interrelationship of time and space differ. As a rule, the more dense, confined, or physical the vibration, the more closely time is tied to space.

Souls in the lower worlds perceive time because of the Sound Current's continual circulation through space. Time and space become realities for Soul because they provide experiential reference points, or backdrops for learning. Time also offers a useful yardstick to measure how quickly one experiences, learns, and unfolds in the lower worlds.

In the pure spiritual worlds of God, time and space do not exist. These properties are confined to the lower worlds. They are very necessary, because the mind cannot grasp reality outside the context of time and space. The mind is a computer-like machine which can only perceive in the relativity of the lower worlds. To experience the pure spiritual worlds, one must switch his viewpoint to Soul, and let go of the mind.

When you witnessed the reenactment of creation from Sat Nam's palace, you experienced it as Soul. As Soul's impressions flowed into the much smaller receptacle of the mental body, it could only contain a fraction of the larger reality. It interpreted the experiences and made them under-standable by employing the familiar yet limited anchor points of time and space.

I have spoken to you of time to acknowledge it and to answer your question, *Peddar said with a note of finality in his voice.* Now we can put it aside in order to see a greater truth.

As he spoke, the scene around us dissolved. In its place arose the grand view of the valley near Sat Nam's royal residence. I smiled inwardly at my accomplishment; I had achieved a graceful transition to the Golden Kingdom!

Peddar and I stood on the terrace atop the palace steps, watching as throngs of sparkling Souls gathered below to await their destiny.

The huge palace doors swung open behind us, and we moved to one side. The Lord Sat Nam emerged and nodded to us before calmly scanning the teeming mass of Souls below.

He began to speak in a strong, yet gentle voice audible to all. His communication was not in words, but impressions. I experienced it as a glowing stream of wisdom which gently flowed into the hearts of the listeners.

You are here to realize and nurture the bond of love which links your heart to the very heart of God. You are now ready to develop this bond into a unique, two-way com-munication with the Divine One. This relationship will enable you to become a co-worker with It.

This connection will be strengthened and expanded in the worlds outside the Golden Kingdom. There, in the darkest corners of existence, you will be forced to rely on your essen-tial love bond with God. Allow it to be your guiding light and salvation.

I will now share the secret that will aid you in your eventual return passage to the Golden Kingdom. It is this: You are not the bodies you wear in the lower worlds. You are

Soul, a spiritual being, divinely connected to God. You exist because God loves you.

One day, you will learn of the key to your journey home. You will once again see yourself as Soul, and activate the full awareness of your God-connection. After this awakening, you may still dwell in the worlds of matter, but you will not be of them.

By living according to your true, immortal nature and listening to the communication or Sound Current of God, you will become the spiritual co-worker your Creator calls you to be.

Tests and trials will follow one after another. Each will help you realize your connection with God, and provide opportunities to prove you can maintain it. While living in the lower worlds, you will experience love and power—dual aspects of Spirit as it manifests in the material worlds. In the company of other Souls, you will come to understand and overcome the seductive influence of power. You will also experience Spirit's pure love.

One day, you will remember your birthright. You will learn to exercise the qualities of Soul which you share with the all-powerful, all-wise, and all-loving Creator. These qualities include beingness, awareness, joy, and spiritual freedom. But this can only occur after you have remembered your connection to the heart of God and rekindled the divine fire implanted within you.

Sat Nam paused to let his words sink into the hearts of everyone present.

There is more you must know about your journey into the lower worlds. *The God-being slowly swept his hand across the panorama of the valley before him. The valley floor again became transparent, exposing the darkness of the lower worlds to all.*

Whispers rose as the Souls gazed awestruck into the worlds beneath their feet.

First, *resumed Sat Nam,* be assured that these worlds will not appear so dark once you enter them. The brilliance of the Golden Kingdom will fade from memory. The light of your new home will become your standard until you once again remember your inborn divinity.

Second, when you enter the realms below, you will be given a unique link to your home here in the Golden Kingdom. As you leave, you will pass through one of seven doors into the lower worlds. Each door corresponds to a particular color—a frequency band which divides and defines Light in the lower worlds. The door through which you pass will correspond to a color-ray. This ray will later become a homing beacon to locate the Golden Kingdom.

The first stop on your journey will be the Subconscious or Etheric World. It is the highest of the lower planes. As you descend, you will acquire a sheath called the subconscious or etheric body. It will protect Soul and allow you to exist in this realm. The name 'subconscious' merely describes how this body will eventually interact with the physical consciousness.

The subconscious body will not only shield you from the relatively harsh vibrations of the Subconscious Plane, it will also protect that world from your pure Soul essence. Without a sheath, the presence of Soul in the lower worlds would wreak havoc.

This highest and purest realm of the lower worlds is where your individuality will first begin to take form and manifest. The vibratory rates that comprise this plane are relatively narrow in range. The Etheric World serves primarily as a place of transition between the lower realms and the Golden Kingdom.

Although restricted in scope, this plane is still more vast than any of the other lower realms. It is the closest in vibration to the pure, unlimited spiritual worlds and shares many qualities of the planes directly above it as well as the next world below.

Once you have established yourself in this arena, the flows of Light and Sound will gradually reach a balance point within you. Then you will be granted the gift of another sheath, called the mental body. It will allow you to function in the World of Mind.

The Mental World encompasses a wide range of vibratory rates. It may more accurately be considered a collection of many sub-planes. Here you will learn to send out impressions or impulses with your Soul imagination. These impressions will mold the substance, character, rhythm, and magnetism of the Sound Current on the Mental Plane. The Light then automatically fills this mold to create a thought form.

I must caution you to use this ability of Soul wisely. The impressions you send forth will give rise to thought forms, which in turn manifest your reality in the Physical World. You will have to take responsibility for each thought-mold you create. Soul can change, destroy, or live out these forms to make 'reality'. Your fascination with this process may tempt you to believe the mental body is the creator and master of your lower bodies and the planes in which they live.

Nevertheless, when consciously created with love and non-attachment, your thought forms will enable you to master many aspects of life in the lower worlds. If you remember to differentiate between Soul and the mental body, your mind will serve as a very useful tool on the return journey to the Worlds of God.

Upon establishing yourself in the Mental World, you will enter the Causal World. The causal sheath protects both your mental and subconscious bodies on this plane.

This world is made up of patterns and cycles which chart the past and the future. It houses the detailed karmic records of each life you spend in the lower worlds. Your individual causal body also holds many personal memories of these other lives. You will also be able to explore your future probabilities on this plane, based on what you have earned and understood in previous incarnations.

When you are ready, you will enter the Astral World and take on an emotional body. It will encompass the higher causal, mental, and subconscious forms. Here, you must learn how to thrive in the free and chaotic energies characteristic of this world.

The challenges of living in the Astral World will be to maintain focused attention. Despite the alluring call of these energies, mastery will require you to sort, organize and stabilize them to achieve inner balance. Eventually, when you enter a physical body, these rather volatile astral energies will take form and become identified as emotions.

Finally you will reach the all-important, final destination of your journey: the Physical Plane. Your life here will feature a complex and constant interplay between 1) Soul and the other four lower bodies; 2) your individuality and that of other beings like yourself, and 3) your manifestations, meaning what you have created, and the life force itself. Experiences in the Physical Plane will offer many invaluable lessons. Mastery of these lessons will awaken the memory of your true spiritual nature and your connection to God. As you gain command of Spirit's resources in this world, you will earn your passage home to the God Worlds.

The Lord of the Golden Kingdom paused momentarily. You are now ready to enter the Subconscious Plane, *he announced.* Remember who you are and all you have learned— and return!

Sat Nam raised the palm of his right hand in divine acknowledgement of the many Souls gathered before him. May the blessings be, *he intoned.*

At the far end of the valley, seven enormous arches began to materialize. The arches were made of the same golden material that comprised Sat Nam's palace. In the space under each archway, hanging like a curtain of light, shone one of seven vivid colors: red, orange, yellow, green, blue, indigo, or violet. Peddar and I watched as the throngs of Souls sorted into living streams, which crowded their way under one of the brilliant curtains of pure color.

Sat Nam turned to me and asked, Do you know which gateway you passed through as you left the Golden Kingdom?

"No," I replied, "would it help to know?"

Such knowledge would not be significant unless you knew how to use it. Whether or not you know the color of your gateway, it still acts as a homing beacon. It guides Soul through the maze of lower world experiences until its return to the Golden Kingdom. Some call this special hue one's 'main color-ray'.

Visualizing or placing the thoughts on your main color-ray expands awareness. For example, if you are feeling ill, try focusing on the color-ray to explore the cause of your imbalance. It may also help you resolve it.

When frightened, angry, or frustrated, visualizing your special color can renew your inborn sense of spirituality and prompt a change of attitude. Your color-ray can guide you to the next step on your path, and help you sort out important lower-plane issues such as imbalances between power and love.

"If one knew his main color-ray," I ventured, "would he surround himself with that color to the exclusion of all others?"

Every color is born of the Light, which is part of Spirit. Every color plays an important role in helping individuals move through experiences and master the lessons of life. A balance of all colors is essential for health and well-being throughout one's lower bodies.

The main color-ray is simply a homing beacon. Placing attention on this beacon is a tool, another way the individual can reconnect with Soul.

I didn't want to sound persistent, but my curiosity was aflame. "How can one discover his main color-ray?" I asked.

Sat Nam smiled, I can start you on the quest for your main color-ray by sharing a basic technique for the creative imagination. It is one of several methods that can be used to determine your primary color-ray.

A Creative Visualization Technique for Discovering One's Main Color-Ray

For many individuals, this technique brings the true main color-ray to light. For others, the color revealed may only be a temporary stand-in, needed to guide Soul through a complicated set of experiences. When these experiences are resolved, the technique may reveal a different color. Again, it may be the true ray, or simply the color which will help Soul to the next plateau of unfoldment.

Before you begin, collect a sample of all seven colors. Paints, colored pencils, papers, or crayons can all serve as excellent color representatives. Choose a time when you will not be disturbed, and assume a comfortable position. Now hold the color samples or place them in your lap. For the purpose of explaining this exercise, let's say you have gathered seven crayons.

Hold one crayon in front of your eyes, far enough away so your eyes do not strain when you look at it. Concentrate on the essence of this color. Keep your eyes open as you let it enter your body through the eyes. Imagine it filling your entire body. Feel the color frequency as it fills your head, then your shoulders, arms, torso, and legs.

Close your eyes and let the color circulate through your body. At the same time, keep the hue in your inner sight. If your inner eyes 'forget' what the color looks like, open your eyes and look at the color of the crayon again.

Now see if you can imagine the color as a river, which carries you along with its flow. Or see it as a thread or pathway which you can follow beyond your physical body and into the inner worlds.

If you prefer to work with feeling instead of sight, imagine a feeling of expansion in consciousness as you bathe in the hue. This may feel like an opening of awareness, or an overall sense of joy. Allow the feeling to expand to its limits.

Record your experiences or lack of them. Repeat the technique with each of the other crayons.

What you are looking for is a comparatively special feeling or sensation. One of the seven colors should enliven and inspire you more than any of the others. When you think of this color, look at it, or imagine it, you should feel uplifted in consciousness. Perhaps your consciousness may seem to rise or expand beyond your physical body. Or, the color may simply give you the peaceful feeling of overall well-being. If one color evokes these effects more than any of the others, it is likely your main color-ray.

"Thank you," I replied.

Thank you for being here. *Sat Nam bowed and returned to his throne room.*

Peddar touched my arm. It is time to go, *he reminded me.* Sing the HU in contemplation about the same time tomorrow night. I will accompany you back here, for there is still much to learn about Soul's journey into the lower worlds.

"Yes, I know," I agreed.

But I could not return! I felt so profoundly alive in the Golden Kingdom, my physical existence was but a distant dream. In spite of my efforts, a strong yearning rooted me in this heavenly world. I looked to Peddar for help, knowing he would be able to read my heart.

He smiled reassuringly. Where are your children? *he asked with a twinkle in his eye.*

Peddar had chosen the perfect question to ask a mother of three young ones. Hoping his query carried no suggestion of harm, my thoughts raced instantly home.

In less than a second, I returned to physical consciousness. I opened my eyes to my bedroom in the Physical Plane and ran to the kids' room.

Thank you Peddar, *I whispered. I listened to the sound of peaceful breathing as three bundles of blankets lay gently rising and falling. I blessed my soundly sleeping children and went back down the hall to my bedroom.*

Chapter 4

Exploring Soul's Lower Bodies

*T*hroughout the day my thoughts lingered on what I had learned about Soul's entry into the lower worlds. I had so many questions I could hardly wait to meet with Sat Nam again.

Finally I put the kids to bed and the house grew quiet. As I sang HU, Peddar's voice soon joined in. We sang together for a few minutes, then let the echoes of our intertwining voices carry us into the Golden Kingdom.

We arrived near a sparkling lake with a huge, splashing waterfall at one end. Thousands of flamingoes, cranes, and other water birds dotted the shallows and sandy beach. Innumerable smaller fowl perched in the leaves of the plentiful palm trees which completely surrounded the water.

The setting was certainly beautiful, but I wondered why Spirit had provided it for me. I asked Peddar if he knew.

By noticing and enjoying the details of this setting, your attention is focused here. This is necessary for you to stabilize your presence on this plane, *Peddar answered.* As long as you keep your attention sharp, you will remain here. The visual and aural stimuli help you stay alert.

Hoping to anchor my attention in this world, I immediately began a careful study of the birds. Their pastel plumage was more varied and pure than any I'd ever seen. I smiled, for they reminded me of colorful kings and queens, regally parading with heads held high. There was a definite consciousness present in their beady eyes—almost as striking as gazing into the eyes of another human being.

I caught the eye of a large pink flamingo and was about to attempt communication when I heard Sat Nam's voice addressing Peddar. I too greeted Sat Nam.

Welcome dear one, *Sat Nam replied.*

We sat cross-legged on a patch of hardy grass rooted in the sand.

Do you have any questions so far? *Sat Nam asked.*

I lowered my head and grinned. Did he really have any idea how many questions I had?

"Yes," I replied soberly. "When a Soul enters the Etheric World, does it take on a baby's body as in the Physical Plane? And if so, are baby subconscious bodies formed in the same way baby physical bodies are formed—by parents?"

Sat Nam smiled at Peddar, but answered readily, In the subconscious and mental realms, a body or sheath is manifested simply by Soul's desire to enter that reality. Although it may appear Soul is 'sent' into a lower world, its movement stems from inner desire.

This yearning is inborn within Soul's heart. It compels Soul to explore lower and lower vibratory rates throughout the negative worlds. After many experiences and incarnations, Soul realizes it is a divine spark of God. This awareness marks the beginning of its return journey home.

When Soul enters the first of the lower worlds, the Sound is spontaneously compelled to produce a subconscious sheath for It. As soon as Soul directs Its attention toward the Mental Plane, the Sound fabricates a mind sheath to house both Soul and its subconscious body.

The Sound does not manifest these forms in an arbitrary fashion. The substance, character, rhythm, and magnetism of each individual Soul carefully dictates the nature of Its sheaths.

You see, these four qualities apply not only to Sound, but also to the Spirit current. Soul itself is pure Spirit. Therefore each Soul expresses a unique rhythm, substance, character, and magnetism. Furthermore, since matter in the lower worlds is based on Sound, all things also have these four qualities in varying degrees.

When bread is flung into a pool of hungry fish, the fish swarm to receive the nourishment. Similarly, when a Soul first enters the Subconscious World, the Light and Sound rush to greet It. Because the very essence of Soul is Light and Sound, the Light and Sound of the lower worlds instantly merges with it, thereby forming a sheath around it.

As the Light and Sound come together they combine with the Soul's beingness—its unique character, substance, rhythm, and magnetism. Together with Its main color-ray, these forces form the subconscious sheath.

As you recall, Soul's main color-ray is dictated by the doorway through which It entered the lower worlds. Again, Soul chooses a particular door, and therefore a color-ray, according to its individual character, substance, rhythm, and magnetism. Although many Souls choose the same door, each has a different reason for doing so, based on Its unique expression of these four qualities. This is no different than saying that all physical bodies are made up of carbon, hydrogen, and oxygen. The individual expressions lie in how they are organized—according to unique melodies or Sound patterns which make up a singular human form.

The mental body manifests in much the same way as the subconscious body. However, the subconscious body also plays a crucial role in the mind's formation. This body, plus the main color-ray and Soul's substance, character, rhythm, and magnetism combine to make up the essence of the mental sheath.

As Soul moves through the various subplanes of the Mental World, It may or may not need additional sheaths.

Whether or not this occurs depends on how Soul expresses Its four qualities, the types of molds It makes, and how clear a vehicle It is for the Light and Sound.

Now, the formation of the causal body is an entirely different matter. It is a rare occasion for a Soul to simply come to the threshold of the Causal World and collect a sheath around It. Only spiritual masters can do this.

The Causal World is the first plane in which the positive, neutral, and negative forces each manifest as atoms. In most cases, Soul must enter into a form that has been created for It by other causal bodies. This process is similar to the reproductive cycle of parents in the Physical World.

Sat Nam paused and leaned back in the grass for a moment. The birds stirred in the trees, as a light, cool breeze swept the surface of the lake. But still more questions were burning within me. "If Souls are born into the lowest planes, how did the causal, astral, and physical bodies of the first parents manifest? And if the human form did indeed evolve from single-celled creatures, where did they come from?"

The Causal World contains a complete set of seed patterns or matrixes, *Sat Nam replied patiently.* These patterns were carried in the Sound and Light to provide information for the creation of all atoms and combinations of atoms in the Causal, Astral, and Physical Universes. The patterns included elementary blueprints for creation of the bodies which house Soul.

Sheaths suitable to house spiritually conscious Souls require highly-organized blueprints. Indeed, atoms combine to form molecules, which merge to form cells, which form the intricate structures of organs, bones, and tissue for living forms.

The human body did not manifest instantly, for it was not known which forms would best serve the spiritual needs of Soul. Spirit only provided patterns to organize the Sound and Light into rudimentary forms such as molecules and cells. From there, the details and evolution of these forms were left to Nature and trial and error.

I would like to show you another reenactment. You will see what occurred when the first wave of Souls entered the lower worlds. This will also help answer your question.

Sat Nam swept his outstretched hand from horizon to horizon. The trees, the lake, and the birds dissolved to reveal a multi-dimensional view of the lower worlds. It was like sitting on a rooftop looking down into a huge five-story building made entirely of glass.

Each of the floors and their contents were clearly visible: fully formed universes, planets, and stars. Interestingly, the building was empty of plants, animals, and people. Members of the mineral kingdom were the sole occupants.

As I watched, the two upper floors in the glass building below me filled with life. Amorphous forms shone with color and light. They exchanged and shared color-ray patterns and energies with other Souls in the Subconscious and Mental Worlds.

You have already learned how Soul enters the subconscious and mental bodies, *Sat Nam said.* Let's begin our reenactment with Souls in the Mental World, about to enter the Causal Plane.

Many of the Souls equipped with subconscious and mental bodies moved to the lower borders of the Mental Plane and bravely crossed the threshold into the Causal Plane. There they were enveloped by simple molecular or cellular forms.

Driven by their primal desire to explore lower vibratory rates, these forms drifted downward again toward the astral realm. The elementary blueprints of their bodies reproduced forms which encompassed all the higher sheaths of Soul.

Each form is tested in this area, to see if it will survive and evolve, *said Sat Nam, pointing to the borders of the Astral Plane.*

As my eyes followed his direction, I suddenly saw a silent burst of color rays. Another burst occurred, and then another. They were like soundless, multi-colored fireworks. Fascinated, I leaned forward for a closer look.

The explosions occurred as some Souls entered the Astral Plane. Their new astral sheaths could not withstand the energies of the Astral World. The colorful displays occurred as their blueprints burst apart, revealing brilliant color-ray spectrums. These blueprints, and the sheaths they comprised, could not survive in the astral realm.

Souls in these inadequate forms were catapulted upward into the Mental World. Their unsuccessful causal blueprints were given the necessary adjustments. Next time, the Light and Sound could manifest slightly different, and hopefully more effective blueprints to house them.

But most of the forms withstood the coarser vibration of the Astral Plane and continued on their way. They soon entered physical bodies, which were tested further by the vibratory rates of this lowest plane.

Some forms instantly blew apart when met by the intense pressures from the vibratory rates of the Physical World. The blueprints of other forms remained for a while, but could not withstand the test of time. As these physical forms died, their astral and causal blueprints were destroyed as well.

Sat Nam smiled as I shifted my view from the transparent model of the lower worlds towards him. Then he continued his discourse. Souls in forms that cannot survive find themselves back in their mental sheaths, looking for another means to reach their destination in the Physical Plane. This process has been carried out over eons, as atoms, molecules, and cells have combined to form increasingly complex manifestations.

Eventually, the human form evolved in the Causal World. Some time later it also became established on the Astral and, later still, on the Physical Plane.

The complete manifestation of a human body was Spirit's goal for Soul. The frequencies which comprised this sheath enabled Soul to consciously dwell in the spiritual and physical worlds while housed in a physical body. In this form, Soul had the potential to realize Its highest spiritual identity while still learning the lessons of the lowest Physical Plane.

This potential for dual consciousness first emerged in the Causal Plane. Soon Astral Plane dwellers became more aware of their spiritual identities. They realized there were realities beyond their world. Soul sought out the divine messages hidden within every manifestation and learned about the current of Sound and Light that sustains all life.

Individuals on the Astral and Causal Planes eventually learned of the importance of consciously connecting with the return current of Sound and Light. For only then would they discover their true nature and their spiritual destiny.

Certain human beings discovered that the return flow of Sound and Light began in the Physical World. They realized that their primal desire to enter increasingly lower vibratory rates was actually a divine gift. God was leading them to the only realm which would allow them to be fully initiated into this flow and indelibly linked with it.

Ironically, by moving away from the Golden Kingdom, toward the Physical Plane, they would attain their spiritual goals. Only by connecting with the return current in the Physical Plane could they be freed from the primal desire which compelled them to explore the lowest vibratory rates.

The consciousness of animals already inhabiting the Physical Plane began to rapidly expand. Their evolution was encouraged by higher Souls who wanted to incarnate for their turn on the Physical Plane. Consequently, physical forms quickly evolved toward what you know as the homo sapiens.

All the floors in the glass building were now occupied with innumerable living forms, including man and woman. Interestingly, many of the once-amorphous forms in the higher

41

Mental and Subconscious Worlds began to also resemble the human body.

Sat Nam responded to my observation. After a while, individuals in the Causal, Astral, and Physical Worlds tend to adopt the human form in their subconscious and mental bodies as well, *he explained.* Soon you will learn more about how these lower bodies exchange information.

For now, let us explore reproduction on the lowest planes. You will recall that on the Causal Plane, the positive and negative forces within the Sound current converged to manifest the neutral force. This force is present but un-manifested in the Mental and Subconscious Planes.

Manifestation of the neutral force makes reproduction possible. Although both positive and negative aspects of Spirit are embodied within every individual, the positive, active, progressive principle is predominantly expressed in the male parent. The passive, negative, or receptive force is dominant in the mother. I use the terms positive and negative in their electrical sense only. During the course of reproduction, these two forces converge to manifest the neutral force, which is symbolized by the embryo. This manifestation occurs through blueprints contributed by both parents.

Now, observe the Souls who are stepping into the Causal, Astral, and Physical Planes and the forms they enter.

Once again, I studied the glass building carefully. "In all cases, the blueprint manifests a complete form before a Soul enters it," I said.

Very good, *Sat Nam replied.* We discussed the reason for this earlier: a Soul cannot enter the Subconscious, Mental, Causal, Astral, or Physical Plane unless it is protected by a fully-formed sheath. Otherwise, both the Soul and the plane itself would suffer severely. This is true regardless of the complexity of the form.

"Does that mean that a fetus cannot house Soul until its biological functions and organs are matured?" I asked.

42

Yes. If Soul tried to enter a fetus before its matrixes were developed and ready—before it could survive without its mother—the fetus would cease to function. It is not ready to protect the Physical Plane from the high vibration rate of the astral body.

On the other hand, a fetus may be mature enough to house the mental and astral bodies of Soul, but for some other reason is not able to accept Soul Itself. It too cannot survive, for Soul is the animator of all the lower bodies. The blueprints that formed the fetus's unsuccessful sheath will be destroyed.

If Soul enters the form, and the sheath continues to function, its blueprints become established. Eventually the sheath may have the opportunity to propagate. It will seek its opposite and join with it to fulfill the pattern of the neutral force.

Sat Nam paused for a few moments, as if to allow these words to register within me. Then he continued.

Within the Sound, the Creator planted seeds or messages for Soul. These divine instructions can be found within every form and manifestation. They remind Soul of the Golden Kingdom, and of the Sound Current which can lead it home. You must learn how to become more aware of these messages all around you.

Sri Peddar will now share an exercise with you called 'The Hidden Message Technique'. It will expand your awareness of the divine communication within all things.

Once more, Sat Nam waved his hand across the scene in front of us. The glass building vanished and the panoramic view of the lake and waterfall reappeared. He nodded toward Peddar and stood, bowing to us both. May the blessings be, *he concluded. I watched momentarily as Sat Nam walked toward the waterfall.*

The Hidden Message Technique: Finding Hidden Messages from Spirit in Daily Life

Peddar continued the discourse. This exercise will help you recognize Spirit's guidance everywhere. All things can relay a spiritual message to Soul, which can be heard by the human consciousness. This communication can be as simple or as complex as Soul requires it to be at the time the message is recognized.

The message can produce a simple awakening, provide information about your present state of consciousness, indicate a major turnabout in your affairs, or guide you to a greater viewpoint of life.

The Hidden Message Technique is an active one. Soul will never rediscover the Golden Kingdom by idly sitting by—nor by passively meditating with stilled mind and emotions. The individual must learn to be active and creative in all aspects of his being.

The key to creativity and self-awareness is the imagination. Most of the techniques in these discourses have their basis in imagination. It is sad that society today views the imaginative dream-spinner as unrealistic and foolhardy.

On the contrary, that which is imagined is real somewhere in the lower worlds. If you can see it in your imagination, it exists. In fact, nothing is created or manifested unless it is first imagined. Nothing can be set into motion nor materialized in the outer worlds unless you first contact it in the inner worlds.

You do this by seeing it in your inner vision, or in other words, by imagining it. The more attention you give to something imagined, the more 'real' and manifested it becomes. This kind of imagining refines Soul's creativity—which in turn leads to greater self-mastery.

This technique can be done anywhere, at any time. Begin by nurturing an attitude of joyful expectation. Then look for something to catch your attention. It could be anything: a person, a thing, an incident, or even a sound.

Put your attention on this stimuli, and say, 'I hear you God. What message do you have for me today?'

Then listen for a message. It may come from an outer source, such as a comment overheard on the street or someone speaking directly to you. Or a phrase may light up for you in a song on the radio or a passing conversation.

On the other hand, the message may also come from within. This might manifest as an inner picture, a voice, written words, a feeling, or just a sense of knowingness.

When you become adept at this technique, you will accept the message as coming from God. You will not fool yourself into thinking it is just your mind speaking to you.

If you do not receive a message, use your imagination! Imagine what a message from Spirit *might* hold for you. In other words, dream up your wisdom from within! You can do this—for you are a spark of God Itself.

Here is an example of how this exercise might work. Let's say you are in the bedroom and want to perceive a message. Simply walk out of the room, and with joyful expectation wait for something to catch your attention.

Perhaps at that moment, your husband will call you to the kitchen. You might have expected something else to catch your attention, but this happened first, so you go to the kitchen. Say to yourself, 'I hear you God. What message do you have for me today?'

Your husband might then say, 'Honey, we ran out of ice cream'.

Now, although these words may seem mundane, record them in your memory. As soon as you can, contemplate on the message, 'Honey, we ran out of ice cream'.

What does ice cream mean to you? Is it something you enjoy? Then 'Honey, we ran out of ice cream' might mean

Spirit is telling you through your husband: 'Honey, we ran out of things to enjoy'. Maybe God is trying to tell you that you are placing too much attention on work, and not enough on play and enjoyment.

Here is another example of how to practice this technique. Next time you get into your car, say to yourself, 'I hear you God, what message do you have for me today?' Then turn on the car radio. Listen for the first words that catch your attention. What spiritual message do they have for you?

Perhaps none of the songs or announcements on the radio seem noteworthy. In fact, nothing may catch your attention until after you have driven down the street and reached five red lights in a row.

Then, suddenly it dawns on you that the five red lights are communicating your personal message. God could be telling you to stop, or to slow down at an important intersection.

Contemplate on what this means for you. Perhaps the intersection represents a crossroads in your life, or an important decision. Maybe God is telling you to stop and wait before making the decision, even if it's just for a few minutes.

Perhaps you need to let the 'cars' in the other lanes go by. In other words, the other people involved in the situation may need to play their hand, or express their thoughts and feelings before you proceed down the road you have chosen.

When you practice this technique, if an object, plant, or animal catches your eye, try talking to it, or asking it what its message is to you. You can do this in your imagination without attracting the attention of others.

It is not necessary to take time out from your day and sit down for this exercise. Instead, actively incorporate it into your activities. All it takes is your decision to listen to the divine within all. You need not skip a heartbeat in your usual routine, except to listen and contemplate on the divine messages you are receiving.

As Peddar finished speaking, I gazed in silence at the distant mountains beyond the lake. Soul was soaking in his words and reveling in the beauty of the scenery.

Gradually, the scene faded and I became aware of the sounds in my house. They were like a lullaby, comforting and familiar. I felt the soft cushions of the sofa beneath me and curled up into them. In moments I was asleep.

Chapter 5

Finding Your Spiritual Tools

Wake up! *whispered Peddar insistently.*

It had been a hectic day, and I was indulging in a nap. I gently resisted my teacher's prodding and continued my enjoyable dream. With split attention, I telepathically reminded Peddar, "All our inner world experiences have occurred at the same time of night. I'm not expecting to meet you again for several hours."

Spirit doesn't wait for those who truly wish to be Its vehicles, *Peddar replied softly.*

I knew he could sense how tired I was. But I also knew the disappointing price one pays for not listening to Spirit. I stored quick mental notes of my dream and roused my physical body to prepare the tape recorder for an inner discourse.

Since I hadn't fully awakened, my consciousness was already somewhat separated from my body. As soon as I got the tape going, I stepped almost instantly into the Golden Kingdom with Peddar.

This time the setting was a beautiful garden a short distance from Sat Nam's palace. A hundred or more Souls were gathered beside us. Like me, I sensed they had travelled here from the Physical Plane. Peddar spoke to a few of them, and we learned that the great Sat Nam would soon address the gathering.

A spring gurgled happily from a small hillock nearby. It caught my attention, and I followed it a short distance down the golden hillside until it trickled into a stream. Scanning the horizon, I spied its destination in a river and then a far ocean. I was fascinated by the nature of the water, which sparkled like liquid diamonds.

While Peddar conversed with some fellow Souls, I studied the dazzling waters. Most of the sparkle was pure white, but it also threw off flashes of each of the seven color rays. As I watched, fascinated, it radiated brilliant beams of red, orange, yellow, green, blue, indigo, and violet light.

I recognized the life-giving energy of this spring. It closely resembled the healing flow I experienced as I worked with certain Therapeutic Diamonds. These diamonds, located on the Physical Plane, also expressed all seven color rays.

Gemstones and diamonds have a special place in my life. I find them beautiful and their very existence on Earth remarkable. I've also learned that some of them have powerful healing qualities.

For years I have been attending nightly classes at a cultural center called Asklesposis on the Astral Plane. There I study Therapeutic Diamonds and gemstones and their gifts. Part of my present life's work is to share the healing secrets of Diamond and Gemstone Therapy with others. This study has lead me to discourse with the spiritual guardians of many different gems. In turn, I record what I learn from them not only for physicians and therapists, but also for other interested Souls who are looking for tools to catalyze spiritual unfoldment.*

I always knew I would one day receive information about the subtle bodies, which would help others to better appreciate and understand the uses of Therapeutic Diamonds and gemstones. The information I was currently receiving from Peddar and Sat Nam fulfilled this dream.

---

* This information is available from Golden Age Publishing. See back pages of this book.

Suddenly, the hum of conversation died down. Several individuals stepped aside to form a path as Sat Nam strode to the center of the group. The circle enclosed him again in a cluster several Souls deep.

Sat Nam scanned the group in attendance. I am here to talk about spiritual tools. Please be seated. Make yourselves comfortable.

He spread his hands and invited us to settle on the grass around him. The spiritual forces, the Sound and Light, *he began,* provide tools to guide and assist your return to the Golden Kingdom. They are planted within every vibratory rate of every plane, for your availability.

These tools come in many different forms. A few examples might be certain books, spiritual exercises, herbs, gemstones, and musical instruments. Spirit has also provided spiritual masters, guides, and teachers to show you how to use these tools of the divine Light and Sound.

Also know that one person's tools may not suit another.

Often, the most vital tools for your return journey to the Golden Kingdom appear outwardly insignificant. Likewise, true spiritual teachers do not flaunt their mastership. They fit into society in unobtrusive ways. There are no barriers—but neither are there any obvious clues—as to their mastery or the powerful truths of their teachings. The individual Soul must earn the discernment necessary to locate their help and wisdom.

Spiritual tools are disguised this way as well. They appear commonplace. Only Souls who have gained certain spiritual abilities can see their gifts. Humility is one of the virtues which allows the heart to recognize, know, and accept a spiritual tool. For instance, it takes humility to know that a divine message can be received anywhere, from anyone, and anything. Information can come to Soul even when, from a human viewpoint, the person or object sharing it appears negative.

51

Individuals may stumble across spiritual tools, or consciously seek them out. You have put aside your earthly duties to spend time in contemplation, which is a way of consciously locating the tools best for you.

The knowledge I am giving you now will help you recognize your tools both consciously and unconsciously on the Physical Plane. When you find a tool worthy of your attention, it will awaken memories of your divine nature. It will make you feel more alive. This is one of the purposes and gifts of a spiritual tool.

When you accept a tool into your life, your spiritual unfoldment will accelerate. As you master it, your return journey to the Golden Kingdom becomes more swift and smooth.

Spiritual tools stir and awaken memories within you: the knowledge that you are not your physical form; that you are greater than any of your sheaths; that you are Soul. The awakening of these memories is the secret to your successful return to the Golden Kingdom.

Pressing the palms of his hands together, Sat Nam concluded his talk and bowed to the attentive Souls grouped around him.

I watched as many of the Souls thanked Sat Nam for his gifts of wisdom and advice. The glow of each being brightened considerably as it expressed simple, heartfelt gratitude. Soon all but a handful of Souls departed. The remaining few lingered as if someone unseen had asked them to stay on for another purpose. I recognized almost all of these individuals from the Diamond Therapy classes at the Astral Plane cultural center.

Sat Nam motioned for those of us left to again sit in a circle around him. In this lifetime, *he commented,* your curiosity has alighted upon gemstones as therapeutic and scientific tools. Perhaps I can expand your awareness of their spiritual value.

We nodded, eager to hear more. From your vantage point here in the Golden Kingdom, you can see that gemstones are vortexes of concentrated spiritual force. To others in the lower worlds, they are instinctively valued, but their energies and healing properties are cloaked in a shroud of matter.

All agree, however, that gemstones are rare and precious, *Sat Nam continued.* If you study their true reasons for being, their properties, and how to access their energies, they can become powerful tools for your spiritual unfoldment.

Certain gemstones can serve both physically and spiritually. As physical tools, they can heal, re-balance, and smooth disharmonies in the human body. As spiritual gifts, they can open and clear pathways for Spirit to flow through the lower bodies. This flow helps the individual connect with higher truths and operate more consciously as Soul.

Gemstones can be employed for spiritual purposes, just as any object or activity can be of spiritual value. The application depends on the individual's intention. Gemstones, of course, are not the path to spiritual unfoldment. However, they are a means, perhaps more powerful than one might expect, for clearing obstacles from Soul's path home to the God Worlds.

When you look at and appreciate a gemstone, there is a part of you that feels, knows, and recognizes the concentrated Light and Sound within it. Your attention on the gemstone forms a connection between you and certain rays of the Light and Sound. Via this connection, a channel opens through all of your sheaths. This pathway can allow Soul's energy and wisdom to enliven even the physical consciousness. In this way, gemstones can help to stir and awaken the memory that you are Soul.

The Gem Within

Gemstones are special gifts Spirit has given to the planet and its people. Regardless of their natural or man-made shape, gems possess qualities worthy of any spiritual being. They express the Light and Sound which manifested them— and continually channel these divine forces through their matrixes.

Gemstone qualities can be contemplated and then incorporated into one's being. I will share with you a technique for doing so, called 'The Gem Within'.

Examine a gemstone that you admire for its beauty and for the harmony that rings between it and your heart. You may choose a physically manifested gem, ask to receive a stone in your inner vision, or create one in your imagination. The shape may be spherical, faceted, or crystalline.

Take time to contemplate this beloved gemstone and its many characteristics. These might include clarity, uniqueness, brilliance, beauty, strength, and perfection. Now, turn your attention to a single characteristic of the gem. It is important to choose just one.

Consider how you can incorporate this property into your own being. For example, perhaps you are intrigued by the brilliance of a faceted gemstone. A gemstone's brilliance flashes as light reflects off its surface and dances within its crystalline matrix. How might you shine the Light of Spirit and Soul through your sheaths, so you transmit its brilliance like a sparkling gem?

This technique can strengthen Soul's influence in all of the bodies It wears in the lower worlds. It can lead one to the realization that he is truly Soul. Why don't you try the exercise for a few minutes, to experience its effects for yourself.

Sat Nam relaxed on the grass while we all closed our eyes.

In the contemplation period that followed, I chose to study the colorful brilliance of a therapeutic, color-ray-bearing diamond. I wanted to emulate its sparkling quality which was so much like the effervescent water bubbling from the golden ground nearby.

As I contemplated, I felt a colorful, sparkling light enter my bloodstream. I felt the life-giving color rays surge through my veins and nourish my entire body. Just as the spring would eventually meet the sea, I imagined the diamond water reaching outward beyond all my cells to touch everything and everyone who was ready for the gentle blessings of Spirit.

As I traced the flow of diamond light, I slipped out of the Golden Kingdom and back into my physical body. I was tingling all over as if an electrical current was coursing through my veins. The flow of Spirit had increased manyfold.

The physical tingling diminished after a few minutes, but the effects of the diamond water remained in my consciousness as I made dinner and put the children to bed. It was still with me at ten o'clock, when I sat down for my usual appointment with Peddar in the inner worlds.

There he was, right on time.

Chapter 6

The Healing Diamond Light

*P*eddar and I returned to the spring of liquid diamonds, where only a few hours before we had received a discourse from Sat Nam. The handful of Souls who shared the second part of his discourse still lingered, talking casually among themselves and with Sat Nam. It seemed as if I had been gone no more than a few minutes.

Soon Sat Nam invited the group to his palace. He led us the short distance up the steps and across the golden threshold. Peddar and I trailed the group as it entered the enormous room with the sparkling, translucent throne. As Sat Nam walked purposefully toward the back wall, I noticed for the first time a mysterious set of doors. The ruler opened one near the center of the wall, and we filed into what was obviously a sacred sanctuary.

On the walls of the small room hung full-length pictures of various spiritual masters. The portraits were so lifelike I wondered for a split second if these adepts were looking in on our group. A circle of chairs provided ample seating for all.

As I sat down, I noted a feeling of special closeness among us, which was due to more than shared proximity. We enjoyed a unique harmony that had been formed during the Diamond Therapy classes at Askleposis.

As I watched Sat Nam find a place within our circle, I glimpsed just a fraction of the meaning of co-workership with God. A co-worker, I noted, does not place others above nor below him in any thought, action, or deed.

He looked briefly and warmly at each of us. I have gathered you here because you are each working with diamonds therapeutically. You have noticed their direct, positive, and uplifting influence in your spiritual life. I can see within your hearts the need to know why this is so, and why only certain diamonds have healing properties.

The answers to these questions must ring clearly within you. The presence of nagging questions takes up space within one's heart. *Sat Nam looked squarely into my eyes.* In your case, the space is needed for further information in this discourse series.

Sat Nam paused before addressing the group again. First, I want to impress upon you the importance of knowingness. Your mental body thinks, your astral body feels, and your physical body performs actions, but Soul alone knows.

When one has knowingness, life in the lower worlds is no longer something to complain about, take for granted, or scorn. It is recognized for what it truly is—a divine blessing. Knowingness allows you to see Spirit within all people, things, and events which had once seemed mundane. The stranger you brush on the street is recognized as a potential spiritual master.

The gemstones worn as baubles of fashion are appreciated as potential spiritual tools. The trip you take to the supermarket becomes a spiritual journey: Can you find the messages Spirit has hidden within the experience, to help you in your life? The secret is in the knowing.

As Soul unfolds in awareness, it grows into more conscious knowingness. It perceives more of the information God imparted in the original Sound impulse that created the lower worlds. Spiritual students today are learning to incorporate this divine current into their daily lives.

Sat Nam leaned toward the center of the circle as his expression became more serious. His voice quieted. But something else was planted in the Sound. Its value could not be revealed until many cycles of humanity had been completed in the Physical Plane. The time is now right.

The explosion which manifested the neutral force and marked the beginning of the Causal World, unleashed three energy streams: positive, negative, and neutral. These streams contain the patterns—divine combinations of Sound and Light—needed to manifest all living and non-living forms in the Causal, Astral, and Physical Worlds.

These patterns consist of blueprints and matrixes. Blueprints manifest living forms and consist exclusively of life-giving, color-ray frequencies. Matrixes help create non-living objects and are made up of non-color-ray frequencies or combinations of color-ray and non-color-ray frequencies. Note that the word 'matrix' is also used as a general term for all the Sound-patterns of Spirit.

Soul's bodies are therefore made of color-ray frequencies, and live in an environment of both color- and non-color rays. Color-ray frequencies nourish and maintain the health and well-being of the lower bodies. Non-color-ray frequencies may benefit or harm Soul's sheaths. Their precise effects are determined by the individual's causal-body blueprints. These blueprints determine how non-color-ray frequencies affect an individual's bodies—and to what degree.

Causal-Plane blueprints not only dictate how the positive, negative, and neutral forces will manifest atoms in the Physical World, they also prescribe how these atoms will interplay with all frequencies. This information is encoded in the interplay of the atom's neutral and negative forces which you know as neutrons and electrons. Their relationship dictates if and how the atom will react to each frequency it meets.

Blueprints do not contain information for physical body immortality. These details are missing from them. This planned obsolescence is intentional, ensuring that all physical forms eventually die. Only Soul is eternal.

The blueprints can be adjusted to prolong the life of the body. In addition, man can learn how to remove many common obstacles in his daily life, which will boost his health for the full life span of his blueprints.

The blueprints' missing information, however, does indeed exist. It is implanted in the Sound in the form of supplemental matrixes. If contacted, these matrixes can facilitate longevity in the human blueprints. They can free the lower and subtle bodies of many of the burdens of illness and aging.

Aging results from the accumulation of non-color-ray frequencies, which prevent cells from accessing their own original, healthy blueprints. If these matrixes were contacted and stimulated, they could drive away the disharmony that clouds the blueprints, Soul could then enjoy a prolonged and unobstructed path toward greater states of consciousness.

When the Causal World was created, a special non-living matrix was set aside to carry complete blueprint information—with nothing missing—into the Physical Plane. In fact, the neutron-electron relationship of the chosen matrix stipulated that only complete blueprint spectrums could flow through it.

This atomic matrix was extremely durable, for it was designed to carry and protect the blueprint information through time. The information it carried would remain true and intact. This matrix, which houses the healing information in a crystalline form of carbon, is known to you as the diamond.

Spiritual guardians were assigned to the carbon crystals. It was the duty of these guardians to ensure that Souls could eventually find the diamonds and learn to use them. They would hold the secret of the diamonds' powerful effects for health and well-being. These secrets could change life in the lower worlds if enough people were aware of them. Souls would become ready for their return journey home sooner than expected, and in full clarity. Those already established on their path home could accelerate their movement.

When it was observed that diamonds were forming on Earth, the guardians did all within their power to hide the diamonds' whereabouts and properties from the negative forces. Unfortunately, manifestations of such importance could not be concealed.

Although they tried, the negative forces could not stop the manifestation of diamonds. So instead, they interfered with the Sound as it manifested the character, substance, rhythm, and magnetism of many diamond crystals. The Light frequencies of these tampered-with diamonds were no longer pure. The altered gems no longer carried blueprint information.

This mutation of a portion of the diamond population was more dangerous than if the negative forces had successfully stopped all of them from manifesting on Earth. People would now be unable to discern between the life-giving stones and those which carried destructive, non-color-ray frequencies. If used for therapy, the altered diamonds could be just as harmful as the original, therapeutic-quality diamonds are healing.

Only recently has man learned to carve and facet diamonds into a particular shape which allows their frequencies access to the fundamental energies of living beings. This shape allows the diamond's character, rhythm, substance, and magnetism to interact with those of humans.

The frequencies carried by such diamonds can affect the life of the human body and its subtle sheaths. Whether this effect is positive or negative depends on the frequencies carried by the diamond. If they are blueprint, color-ray frequencies, they can be healing. If not, they can be unspeakably destructive.

In the future, other ways to fashion diamonds will be found and even greater benefits discovered.

In an attempt to prevent acknowledgement of their therapeutic use, the negative forces have continued their attack on diamonds. They spread rigid ideas, circumstances, attitudes, and emotions about diamonds. Yet at the same time, forces on the positive side are already preparing the way for their increased availability and recognition as healing tools.

Be aware that because of this conflict over their creation and uses, Therapeutic Diamonds are extraordinary and rare. You will find them hidden in remote areas throughout many planets, as tools to help Souls everywhere on their journey home.

Now I will return to my throne. I must continue my contemplation of the awakening of Soul to Its true self, and the myriad ways by which each Soul can make Its way homeward.

May the blessings be with each of you, on your spiritual journey. *Sat Nam raised his right hand in farewell, then left the room.*

The group remained silent for a few minutes, in contemplation of Sat Nam's words. Then we rose and dispersed in companionable groups of two's and three's.

Peddar and I sat down on the palace steps to talk for a moment. My heart felt clearer, freer and more open, now that I knew more about the Therapeutic Diamonds I worked with. Perhaps I'd made room for more learning now, as Sat Nam promised.

I realized how careful I had to be in the future, not to let questions, doubts, and uncertainties overcome my thoughts and emotions. They filled my consciousness with clutter and sapped Soul's learning energy.

Improving Inner Sight

I would like to share an exercise with you now, *said Peddar.* Coincidentally, it involves a diamond. This exercise will strengthen your imagination, as well as your ability to see non-physical realities.

Part 1

First, cup your hands together as if you were using them to completely cover a small ball.

Slowly lift up a thumb and look into the darkness created by your hands. Now, in the center of this darkness, visualize a faceted Round, Modern, Brilliant-cut Therapeutic Diamond of perfect color and clarity, free of flaws. Do this with eyes open or closed, whichever works best for you.

He gave me an image of a Round, Modern, Brilliant-cut diamond. I remembered its shape and properties from my classes at Askleposis. I noticed that this one carried a full spectrum of color rays, properly proportioned, and was therefore therapeutic.

If your inner vision is not your strong suit, try to feel the diamond's shape—its smooth facets, broad, flat table at the top, and sharp point at the bottom. Or simply *know* and sense its special presence in your hand.

Look into this diamond and imagine a rainbow of colors beneath its facets: red, orange, yellow, green, blue, indigo, and violet. You do not have to see all of these colors at the same time, but look for each individually.

Turn the diamond over and examine it from different directions. As you look at it, contemplate on what it means to have balance in your life and alignment throughout all your sheaths. Be aware of yourself as Soul, in charge of your sheaths instead of an unconscious slave to their whims and spontaneous reactions to stimuli.

Part 2

The second part of this exercise is particularly helpful for clearing and opening your spiritual sight. Visualization of any object can improve your inner focus. But imagining a color-ray-bearing diamond is particularly helpful for clearing blockages and accumulations which may specifically be impairing it.

To perform this part of the exercise, simply look into your cupped hands. Practice seeing the imagined diamond inside them with your eyes open, and then with your eyes closed. Some people will see it more easily one way or the other. If you lose the image with your eyes open, close them again and reestablish it, or vice versa.

Do not be disappointed if you are unable to see the diamond equally well with your eyes open and closed the first time you try this exercise. It may take practice.

When you have finished the exercise, imagine the diamond dissolving back into the ethers. Know that you can re-manifest it in your imagination whenever you need it.

Also, do not become engrossed in the development of clairvoyance. The ability to see into the inner worlds is only a step on the path to God. Furthermore, inner vision is not the only way to prove the existence of the inner worlds.

Peddar stood up. I look forward to starting a new phase in this series of discourses. We will be examining each of the lower bodies, one at a time. To round out your understanding of their spiritual purpose, I want to introduce them by discussing spiritual achievements. These achievements document one's degree of connection to the returning current of Light and Sound. The Soul responsible for maintaining this homeward flow is the most important being in your spiritual life. He is called the Wayshower.

The golden mist of the Golden Kingdom slowly faded. The grayness of our dimly lit bedroom greeted me once again, and I wondered about the being Peddar called the Wayshower.

Chapter 7

The Wayshower

I joined Peddar on the Astral beach we had strolled a few nights before. Across the bay, the city of tall spires and golden domes glistened under a clear sky, lit by unusual pink and yellow clouds.

We walked companionably by the bay for awhile before crossing to the base of the cliffs. There we found some smooth rocks to sit on as we talked. The salty breeze combed my hair as we listened to the sea and the calling gulls. Soon Peddar began his discourse.

You have witnessed the creation of the lower worlds, and Soul entering into them. You have been introduced to the etheric, mental, causal, astral, and physical sheaths which protect both Soul and the worlds It enters.

Most people are not aware of the relationship between the inner sheaths and the physical self. If conscious attention is never placed on them, the inner bodies resemble deflated balloons which do not hold awareness or conscious life.

With practice of spiritual exercises such as the ones I'm sharing with you, these balloon-like sheaths gradually fill with spiritual life. They take on form and substance. Those who successfully travel out of the body have inflated their inner body forms through loving practice, until they are alive and awake enough for inner-world journeying.

It takes much devoted preparation and practice to consciously travel the other planes. Those who can do it on their first try have been getting ready—perhaps unconsciously—for many lifetimes. It is a skill that is earned over a long series of incarnations.

The inner sheaths must be developed at each level for conscious use. Of course, this is true for the lower bodies only. Soul is always aware of Itself in Its own dimension.

In the lower worlds you are faced with the influences of matter, energy, time, and space. Soul's goal is to channel Its energy and wisdom through not just a physical body, but through the subconscious, mental, causal, and astral bodies as well. Each of these is needed to help It function as a co-worker with God in the Physical World.

As I mentioned, most people cannot distinguish among their lower bodies. They are aware of the astral body only in so far as they either express their emotions or feel a painful build-up of emotional suppression.

Likewise, the causal body usually comes into play only when a memory is awakened. Memories are simply Soul's catalogued experiences in the time and space continuum. They are recorded in organized patterns and matrixes on the Causal Plane for later access. When one of these patterns is awakened by Soul's attention, an experience is reflected from the matrix. This is what you call remembering.

An individual can tap his causal body more directly once he understands the laws of cause and effect. When he realizes that every action has a reaction, he can trace the outcome of his deeds and thoughts, commonly known as karmic patterns. In the causal body, he becomes aware that he is ultimately responsible for all his creations in the lower worlds.

As for the mental body, most people access it solely through simple thought. Thoughts can take many forms. There are many areas of the mind, just as there are many ways of thinking and expressing creativity. The greatest artistic expressions and scientific discoveries both spring from the mental body. To produce either, Soul has simply placed

Its attention on developing different areas and qualities of the mental machine.

When the individual awakens to the reality of Soul—that he is more than his mind, emotions, or physical body—it marks his first great spiritual achievement. Until this self-recognition occurs, Soul lives unconsciously in the lower worlds, moving as if in a deep sleep.

Every great spiritual teaching was originally designed to help the individual awaken and recognize himself as Soul. Some religious founders knew this goal, while others simply followed their instincts and destiny.

Unfortunately, most religions have forgotten their prime objective: to rouse Soul. At best, they provide a place for interaction and support among members; at worst, they are little more than social clubs, moral reformers, or dictators of what they themselves consider to be acceptable and proper.

Yet even in the absence of helpful teachings, Soul eventually recognizes Itself.

Now I would like to speak directly to those who will later read your account of these discourses. You are Soul. You are using your physical eyes to read this page and your earthly hands to hold the book. Your mental body is processing the information printed on it. The feelings in your emotional body enhance the experience and make this story come alive.

But you are a spiritual being apart from all these influences. Can you imagine this reality? It is the first step homeward. But recognition of Self is not enough to complete your journey. You must be ready for the Key.

I was so excited, I interrupted Peddar. "What is this key? Sat Nam referred to it once, and now you are mentioning it again. Where can I find it?"

Peddar fell into silence, and I studied his face as he gazed thoughtfully across the water. He appeared to be searching for just the right answer to my question.

Even in that moment of still preoccupation, his light blue eyes sparkled with inner light. How would I ever convey the essence of this man? I had never met him physically, yet he was my dearest friend—my writing tutor, teacher, and spiritual guide to the inner realms.

As I pondered his gifts, a door seemed to open between the adept's thoughts and mine. I knew exactly what Peddar was thinking. I have often used telepathy in the inner worlds, but this was different. Instead of receiving fully-formed ideas, I was aware of the vast stream of all his thoughts—even as they came to him. My mental body ached as it stretched to encompass worlds and realms totally foreign to my awareness.

Then mercifully, the flow ceased. Peddar turned to look at me with a piercing stare. Close the eyes of your astral body—the body you now occupy—and connect with your true Self, *he commanded.* From this viewpoint beyond the mind, you will be able to sort out what I have just conveyed to you.

The thoughts may seem jumbled and overwhelming at first. But try this technique and then, as an exercise in communication, tell me what you have learned.

I closed my astral eyes. It wasn't easy finding my spiritual center. My mental body was so full of new and exciting thoughts! I had to plow through worlds of them just to touch the simplicity of Soul. Finally, I just let my mind go.

Instantly, I stood in the Golden Kingdom. I was Soul, looking down into the mind. I could sort any number of complex thoughts, like a child reaching into a chest to rearrange her toys.

Here is some of what I learned:

Soon after the lower worlds were completed, the Divine One observed there was no pathway for the flow of Sound and Light to return to its source. In fact, the further the Sound and Light tumbled into the lower worlds, the stronger became the lower worlds' negative pull. The Sound was increasingly bottlenecked, unable to flow upward again. Eventually, a negative polarity built up in the lower worlds, designed to prevent the Sound and Light from ever escaping.

To recirculate the Sound and Light, the Creator decided to establish a positive pole in the lower worlds. This pole would emit the substance, character, rhythm, and magnetism of the return flow to God. With this positive generator, Souls in the lower worlds would have a hope of returning to the Golden Kingdom, for they would have a returning current of Light and Sound to lead them there.

Now one might wonder, is the Golden Kingdom, in all its purity, the positive pole? The answer is no. Only the lower worlds are capable of duality, or opposing forces. Therefore, both the positive and negative poles exist solely in the lower worlds.

Remember, in the Golden Kingdom, Spirit is not divided into Sound and Light. It does not contain even the merest breath of duality. However, visitors to the Golden Kingdom often perceive the divine current as Light and Sound. Soul is bathing in undivided Spirit, but the mind can only grasp it in terms of lower-plane duality.

To introduce a positive pole into the lower worlds, the Divine One encased it in a durable, bubble-like space. The very existence of this bubble was an exception to the laws of lower-world reality. It was as if a piece of the Divine Itself was encapsulated and released into the lower worlds.

To maintain the sphere, a Soul was required to occupy it at all times. Furthermore, the chosen Soul had to be manifest in each of the lower worlds, including the physical. This allowed the positive pole to influence all the lower planes, and to take its root in the physical realm.

The Soul within the sphere could not be a puppet of the lower worlds. He would have the power to access higher states of consciousness at will, and even bring them into the physical consciousness if necessary.

Today this sphere acts as a passageway between the Physical Plane and the Heart of the Divine Itself. It is like a rod of power, through which the Divine can speak directly to the Soul that inhabits it.

The bubble, or sphere, is an added sheath that only one Soul can occupy at a time. Intense training is required to be the bubble-tender. Only those who are spiritually strong in all aspects can maintain this extra sheath, as well as all the other bodies of Soul.

A sacred lineage of Souls is trained to serve within the sphere. They belong to the Order of the Bourchakoun. These beings pass the most severe tests of all the inner and outer worlds, before assuming the awesome responsibility of upholding the positive pole.

The Soul chosen by the Divine One is Its pure vehicle. He must serve all of life and all Souls, regardless of their religion, beliefs, or experience in the Physical World. This is the creed of the Order of the Bourchakoun, or Wayshowers.

Currently, as always, a Wayshower maintains the positive pole of the lower worlds. Without it, Souls would be unable to return to the Golden Kingdom. The mere presence of the Wayshower is a divine prod which awakens Soul to its true identity.

The Wayshower works at all levels. Therefore, he must have a physical body to carry the light-giving bubble or rod of power into the lowest of worlds. The Wayshower uplifts all the bodies of Soul. He can work with an individual on the outer as well as the inner planes.

Wrapped in the bubble of God, the Wayshower shares the attributes of God. He is the only one who can manifest divine qualities in the limited worlds—without dilution or distortion.

The Wayshower's primary duty is to awaken Souls to their spirituality. This marks an individual's First Spiritual Achievement. It brings the desire to return to the Golden

Kingdom, and the yearning to know more about himself as Soul.

The first task of the one who has earned the First Spiritual Achievement is to gain control over his lower bodies. He must master each of these sheaths so they help him home to God, instead of clouding Soul's perception and hypnotizing It to sleep.

When viewed from the awakened Soul perspective, life takes on great clarity. Man begins to understand his reason for being. He grasps who and why he is, his motivations, and where he is at all times. As Soul, he can glimpse his destiny.

Above all, Soul expresses a great joy, which goes far beyond astral emotion. This inborn joy is a profound and incomparable experience in the lower worlds. It embodies a love for all life, natural to the residents of the Golden Kingdom.

As Soul awareness grows, the individual desires to be in this expanded state for more than just fleeting moments. This yearning draws Soul to the positive pole of the universe, to the Wayshower.

At first, one might feel this magnetic pull in one of the inner sheaths. This could result in a meeting with the Wayshower in a dream or on one of the inner planes. In fact, Soul usually meets the Wayshower for the first time in the dream state. Later, one may be blessed to meet the Wayshower physically, though this is not always necessary. One can connect with him through one of his agents.

The Wayshower's agents are found in every country, at every economic and social level, and in every religious teaching. Their duty is to support the Wayshower's mission by promoting true spirituality for all.

After waking Soul up, it is the duty of the Wayshower to link It to the Sound and Light. This accelerates and eases Soul's homeward trek. This linking is called the Second Spiritual Achievement. It is Soul's return ticket to the Golden

Kingdom. Without this connection to the Light and Sound currents, Soul remains in the lower worlds.

The Wayshower links those who are ready, to the return flow. This is the Key to the journey home!

This, as I said, was just some of what I learned. I looked at Peddar.

Yes, the Wayshower is the Key, *he replied softly. He let the realization sink into my being.*

"How can one find the Wayshower?" *I asked eagerly.*

Tuning In to the Wayshower

When you are ready, nothing can keep you from the positive pole of the universe. However, there are steps you can take to prepare yourself.

First, recall the images you received about the description of the positive pole of the universe. Perhaps you imagined it as a huge bubble surrounding a special Soul. Or you might have envisioned an individual encased in a great rod or column of Light. Others have glimpsed a thread connecting the Wayshower's heart to the heart of God, allowing a continual stream of insights and divine direction to flow into the world.

Hold your own picture of the Wayshower in your mind. Then say to aloud or to yourself, 'Wayshower, I am ready to meet thee'. Repeat this invitation several times.

Then allow yourself to daydream. Begin by seeing yourself at a favorite place, or engaged in some enjoyable activity. Then allow the daydream to take on a life of its own. Or simply let your mind drift until it picks up images that you feel are in tune with the idea of the Wayshower.

When your daydream is over, write it down, even if it seems unrelated to your goal. Remember this: You must write down your daydream! It is an important part of the exercise.

Later, contemplate on the meaning of what you have written. Ask what Spirit or the Wayshower is telling you. Unravel the message in each image; what did the dream symbols represent?

Then take some action based on what you understand from your daydream. Do this even if you only grasp one small part of its overall meaning. For example, if the dream symbols point to a particular place or acquaintance, go to that place or contact the person. It's important to initiate some physical action based on what your daydream is telling you.

This daydream may not lead to direct contact with the Wayshower. But it may take you a step closer to finding him, or one of his agents, in the physical or inner worlds. It may help release attitudes that are delaying this encounter. Or it may attract experiences which strengthen your spiritual love, placing you in a better position to align yourself with the positive pole of the universe!

Peddar stopped speaking as a flock of nearby sea gulls abruptly took flight. We watched them circle and soar upward toward the high cliffs, a thousand-fold flutter of wild wings and shrill cries. My eyes were blinded as the sun struck the whiteness of their beating feathers.

As I struggled to adjust my vision, the vibrations of the Physical World gently swirled into focus. I felt the familiar embrace of the sofa and the soft glow of the bedroom lamp. I remained seated for several more minutes before rising, deeply grateful for the existence of the Wayshower.

Chapter 8

Spiritual Achievements

I returned to the beach near the cliffs, expecting to meet Peddar at any moment. I was alone except for the sea gulls and a few sand crabs which scuttled back and forth between the gentle waves lapping the pale yellow sand.

Looking up, I noticed two distant figures walking along the water's edge. I immediately knew one of them as Peddar and went to meet him.

As we grew closer, I also recognized Peddar's tall companion. It was Gaelil Kibran Jhonès, my Diamond Therapy Class professor. He was wearing his customary brown and tan trousers and knee-length robes. His dark brown hair was short and thick, and his beard was streaked with gray.

I have admired Gaelil for as long as I have known him. He seems to have complete command over his mind. I have often been amazed and inspired by his self-discipline. He can scientifically analyze an object or idea with strict objectivity, then instantly sensitize himself to its subtle energies.

His magnificent intuition and inner guidance allow this quick interplay between subjective and analytical perception. Although he comprehends so much, thankfully he is able to distill his knowledge into simple discourses. I am honored to be among his students.

We exchanged greetings. Then Peddar said, Today I would like to explore the spiritual achievements further.

Gaelil will help me in this. We will be looking at how each spiritual achievement affects the spiritual biophysics of the physical and subtle bodies. He has studied this extensively and is considered an authority.

Gaelil smiled humbly and suggested we stroll along the beach. I walked between the two masters. Peddar, who was on my right, continued to speak: As you know, the First Spiritual Achievement occurs after one realizes he is more than just a physical being, but a spiritual identity we call 'Soul', and commits himself to learning more about his own divinity. In the Second Achievement, the Wayshower links Soul with the homeward current of the Light and Sound.

The individual prepares for this connection from the day he attains his First Spiritual Achievement. When he is ready, the Wayshower lifts him to the Golden Kingdom, to make the link with Spirit. During this experience, the other sheaths remain safely under guard in the lower worlds.

Here Soul rediscovers the gift of divine love imparted at the beginning of Its journey. This love is now fused into Soul's heart and made available to each of the lower bodies. The more aware the individual becomes of this gift, the more the love grows and becomes of daily, earthly use. This gift can transform not only the physical reality, but Soul's astral, causal, mental, and subconscious realms as well.

This link with the gift of divine love will glow in Soul's heart regardless of how many more physical or non-physical sheaths It embodies. It prepares Soul to leave the physical consciousness and proceed on Its way home to the Golden Kingdom.

Gaelil and I had been listening attentively to Peddar. At this point, Gaelil interjected enthusiastically, I like to think of Divine Love as a magnetic force. It draws Soul, with the help of the Wayshower, into higher states of consciousness. It establishes a connection that can be likened to an elastic band. At one end of the elastic band lies the Golden Kingdom;

76

the other end is anchored in the individual's physical consciousness. However, unlike common elastic bands, this one does not stretch out over time. Instead, it gradually retracts, accelerating Soul's movement into the God Worlds.

What activates this retraction? Specifically, Soul's connection to the return flow of Light and Sound. This link acts like an electrical switch inside the sheaths of Soul. Formerly, the subatomic particles in Soul's lower bodies were aligned with the downward flow of Sound and Light. They pointed away from the Golden Kingdom. With each spiritual achievement, more become polarized toward the positive, and align with the returning spiritual current. Soul is literally magnetized to move toward home and God.

This does not mean, however, that until one attains the Second Spiritual Achievement he is heading in a negative direction. On the contrary, the link with God only occurs after a lengthy purification process. Soul must discover Its Selfhood and ride the upward spiral of life for a time. Nevertheless, the atomic direction of Soul's sheaths remain aligned with the negative pole until the Second Achievement is attained.

With this achievement, the switch is activated and half the subatomic particles in the physical sheath realign with the Golden Kingdom, where the Sound current originates. The remaining particles still point toward the negative pole. As consciousness unfolds, an increasingly greater percentage of these particles will make the switch.

At the Third Spiritual Achievement, half the subatomic particles in the astral body realign themselves. This expands the return flow into the Causal Plane.

At the Fourth Achievement, half the particles in the causal body make the switch, extending the return flow into the mental arena.

The Fifth Spiritual Achievement allows the return flow to pass through the mental and subconscious bodies, and reach its destination in the Golden Kingdom. Thus the circuit is completed.

By the way, there is no outward sign by which one can determine the orientation of an individual's subatomic particles.

"Do spiritual achievements change the atoms?" I asked.

Gaelil replied, The change occurs at the most fundamental levels of the lower bodies: the subatomic levels. This is where one's physical, astral, causal, and mental beingness expresses itself as pure Light and Sound.

To understand the nature of subatomic particles, one must look at the atom differently than most scientists. Just as the physical body represents just a fraction of the vibratory continuum of your entire being, the physical atom is only one part of the true atom.

In other words, a study of your physical body reveals only a fragment of who you really are. Likewise, examining only the physical parts of an atom discloses just a tiny slice of its true atomic structure.

The circuit manifested by the Second Spiritual Achievement neither adds nor takes anything away from one's atoms. Rather, it envelopes them in a new electrical and spiritual field of energy. Within this envelope, the one-way flow of Light and Sound is now able to make a U-turn and return upward. This return flow is the first step toward building a circuit between Soul and all of Its lower bodies. As I said, a circuit which is completed at the Fifth Spiritual Achievement.

The masters gave me time to contemplate what I had just learned. Then a question occurred to me. "I know that everyone generates a field of thoughts, emotions, and memories. People even express a physical energy. I notice it most in myself right after I exercise. But even when a person is resting, you can feel heat coming off their body. Aren't these manifestations of a return flow?" I asked.

No, they are not, *Gaelil answered.* All the expressions and emanations you just described are confined to the lower-world vibratory rate at which they originated. Physical vibrations can only be felt in the Physical World. Emotions from the astral body flow out in a lateral motion which can drift downward but not up. None of the sheath's natural emanations contribute to a complete spiritual circuit within the individual. Your inner body expressions are confined to their corresponding Mental, Causal, Astral, and Physical Plane vibratory rates.

Your lower bodies swim in a sea of Light and Sound. These currents nourish each body at its own vibratory level, and carry their expressions outward, not necessarily upward or inward.

But when Soul is linked with the Sound and Light during the Second Spiritual Achievement, It is able to receive and circulate the Light and Sound upward—back to God. But the feedback stops at the astral level. The astral consciousness is given direct access to information about the physical body.

At the Second Spiritual Achievement, a feedback loop is set up between the astral, or emotional body, and the physical body. At the Third Spiritual Achievement, the causal body exchanges awarenesses with the astral and physical vehicles. The mental and subconscious bodies receive valuable data from all the lower sheaths at the Fourth Achievement. And finally, at the Fifth Spiritual Achievement, Soul gains the direct and complete information necessary to act with clear knowingness in all Its lower aspects.

This feedback has many benefits. It unites and compares the blueprints of one sheath with those of others. It links the mind, heart, and body into a harmonious unit, and establishes resonance among all aspects of the individual.

With each spiritual achievement, alignment is activated for the next higher body. Its atoms become charged with spiritual current. They awaken and orient themselves to the return current of Light and Sound. The body begins to drop needless burdens of accumulation, untangle blockages, and resolve the karma associated with them.

Thus the individual's mental, emotional, and physical expressions are uplifted to match his growing awareness. These adjustments are facilitated by the feedback loops created among all his bodies.

The lower bodies thrive on this feedback. Without direct input, they can only guess how to respond to life situations based on past experience and their observations of the bodies lower than themselves. They must rely on roundabout inter-body communications, societal patterns, and the unconscious circulation of information through the bodies' life systems.* Adjustments are made in the dark, so to speak, without absolute assurance that they are truly in one's best interest.

The Second Spiritual Achievement touches off a much-needed karmic burn-off in the astral and physical bodies. This burn-off is fueled by the increase of Light and Sound now available to the astral body. The Light and Sound of the Astral Plane can energize the emotional body to a much higher degree, because Soul now has a circuit working between the astral and physical bodies.

Let's say the individual has some karma to resolve with dogs. In the burn-off process, he might get bitten. If the bite happened before the spiritual achievement was earned, the individual's astral body would probably respond with fear and anger, thus furthering the karmic relationship with dogs.

However, through its new, direct link to the physical body and the Light and Sound, the astral body can now become aware of a higher purpose at work behind the dog bite. This added element uplifts the emotional response just a bit, to a more holistic view.

---

* Life systems will be described in later chapters.

80

Although the bite may be just as painful, and the victim just as traumatized, he might also instinctively realize the bite as a gift—a re-balancing of an old cycle. This insight is the key to resolving karma, instead of deepening it. Now he can bless the situation and release it.

Or he might have an insight that if he had respected the space the dog was protecting, he would not have been bitten. This attitude of understanding, in which responsibility is taken and blame is not placed on another, also resolves the karma.

As Soul moves on to higher spiritual achievements, It has access to feedback at more refined levels. The Third Achievement awakens the causal body, and the fourth enlivens and cleanses the mind. At the Fifth Spiritual Achievement, all aspects of the individual can directly access and benefit from the lower bodies' returning energies. The circuit of inflowing and outflowing spiritual energies is complete.

Light and Sound pour directly into Soul from the Golden Kingdom. In turn, Soul can now circulate them through each lower body in service to all life, before returning them directly to their source in the God Worlds. Thus at the Fifth Achievement, Soul can emulate some of the gifts of the Wayshower, albeit within the much smaller scope of his own being.

The ability to receive complete spiritual nourishment at increasingly higher vibratory rates is indeed a blessing. It brings certain nutrients that strengthen Soul. But this does not guarantee the individual will have awareness on these lofty planes. Though the path and the means to walk that path are provided, the individual must work if he wishes to become consciously awake in each sheath.

Initiating a return flow opens the door for more Light and Sound to then enter into a person. As a result, more current flows into the lower worlds as well. The goal of each individual is to become a an open channel for as much inflow and outflow of Spirit as possible.

It is vital for the awakened Soul to give or outflow at every level possible for It. Without this reciprocal flow, the bodies cannot accept additional inflow. The atoms, cells, and organs may even develop energetic blocks that continue even when the outflow is reestablished.

Inflow must equal outflow in order to remain spiritually healthy. This is why a person's atoms can be burned if a too high a concentration of spiritual energy is directed into him. They may become singed as if scorched by fire.

But if one gives out the Light and Sound in a balanced way, he can accept an increasingly greater inflow. This influx in turn carries much useful information through Soul's lower bodies.

Before entering the Second Spiritual Achievement, Soul must be strong enough to accept the nourishing inflow and outflow of vibratory rates higher than those of the Physical Plane. It must also overcome the lower worlds' natural resistance toward achievements.

At each spiritual achievement, more of the lower bodies' subatomic particles are aligned with the Golden Kingdom. As a result, the negative pole receives even less Light and Sound. This sets up a resistance, which can make one's earthly path more difficult. This of course, is one way the negative force fulfills its duty. It must help the individual grow by placing obstacles in his path. However these tests serve the individual by helping him develop spiritual strength and stamina.

"What if the individual fails these tests, and renounces his spiritual path?" I asked. "Do his subatomic particles switch back toward the negative pole?"

If the negative forces are successful, *Gaelil explained,* the individual might give up or forget his quest to return home. As his awareness and attitude weaken, his atomic particles begin to reorient themselves to the negative pole. But once Soul has gained the Second Spiritual Achievement, there will always be some—or at least one—subatomic particle pointing toward the divine kingdom. This holds true regardless of how many lifetimes follow his achievement, or his submission to the negative forces.

There are various techniques to build strength and diminish the negative effects of the Physical Plane forces. One way is to chant or sing the holy word 'HU'. This is the same word you use to move your consciousness to the inner worlds.

Singing HU imparts a spiritual vitality unmatched by any other mantra or heavenly word. HU lights up every atom of the body by establishing a clear connection to Soul. The purpose of singing HU is to reach into the heart of God, to connect with the highest state of consciousness—the God-state—and from there be uplifted.

Sound is a powerful force—one that lies at the very heart of creation. The vibration of HU can connect one directly to this source. By singing HU daily, you can expand your awareness further and further into the inner worlds, giving Soul access to spiritual knowingness. This state brings help and answers to the daily struggles and questions of life, as well as upliftment and well-being for all aspects of the self.

Gaelil added, The HU can also attune you to your blueprints—the optimal beingness that exists within each sheath.

Blueprints are made of Sound and Light. More specifically, they consist of Sound matrixes organized to form the fabric of one's being. These matrixes are completed by a unique spectrum of the seven color rays of Light. These color rays are drawn to the Sound to fulfill the manifestation.

As long as a cell is alive, it is nourished by a range of colors. If it is healthy, the spectrum of light that nourishes the cell matches that of its blueprint.

However, negative influences can cloud the blueprint. The sound matrix is no longer able to draw the proper spectrum of color to itself. Soon a different ratio of color rays begins to feed the cell. As a result, the cell's health degenerates from the ideal.

When you sing the word HU, the sound waves stimulate, awaken, and recharge the magnetism of your blueprint spectrums. As a result, color rays that match the body's original blueprints flow in. This influx of color rays, at the ideal ratio, helps the body adjust any distorted spectrums that are feeding it.

"How do the effects of singing HU differ from those of a spiritual achievement?" I asked.

Gaelil thought for a moment then answered. A spiritual achievement reorients subatomic particles. It leaves a permanent mark on the individual's atoms and blueprints.

Of course, as you have learned, this mark will diminish if the individual does not inhabit and maintain the heightened state of awareness the spiritual achievement allows. But the mark will never disappear.

The HU enlivens one's blueprints, increases the in-flows and out-flows of Light and Sound through the atoms, and heightens one's state of awareness. This higher state diminishes as quickly as the individual's attention returns to mundane thoughts and activities, although its benefits do linger in the consciousness. HU should be sung for a period of time, approximately ten to twenty minutes, at least once every twenty-four hours for best results.

"I have learned that Therapeutic Diamonds can also enliven blueprints," I commented. "How do their effects differ from those of singing HU?"

Diamonds are tools, the HU is an ancient name for God. The HU enlivens one's blueprints in order to help the lower bodies adjust to the higher state of consciousness this sacred word provides.

Therapeutic Diamonds are tools whose primary purpose is to awaken blueprints. They facilitate spiritual unfoldment only by clearing accumulation and releasing blockages in the physical and subtle bodies. Spiritual unfoldment is often inhibited by this energetic accumulation and impaired by physical, emotional, causal, and mental blockages.

As a Therapeutic Diamond imparts its own spectrum to the body, the cells' blueprints recognize a harmony between their substance, character, rhythm and magnetism, and that of the diamond. As a result, the blueprints are stimulated, awakened, recharged, and able to attract more of their own color rays.

Energetic blockages and accumulation, which prevent harmony between the body's blueprints and the diamond's spectrum, also prevent ideal color ray spectrums from reaching the body and used color rays and unwanted energies from moving away from it. The Therapeutic Diamond can release, resolve, or diminish these blocks with proper application. As a result, the body's ability to heal and nourish itself is enhanced.

You may ask, what does this have to do with spiritual achievements? These levels of unfoldment occur according to a natural timetable. However, the First Spiritual Achievement can be hastened if disharmonies are cleared from one's physical blueprints.

Cleansed blueprints nourish the individual better. They also carry crucial information about the lower bodies' ideal state of being. Their influence can open a window in the physical consciousness. Through this window, an individual may catch a first glimpse of himself as Soul, existing quite apart from his sheaths.

The same is true with general health and well-being. If an individual eats lighter, more nourishing foods, his mind grows less clouded. He can then perceive his life and his habits more accurately.

Therapeutic Diamonds can prepare the individual for awakening and the next stage of unfoldment. If applied to a healthy cell, the diamond boosts the cell's strength and ability to deflect negativity. Unhealthy cells are reconnected with their blueprints and placed on an upward spiral toward health. Consequently, the sheaths become more vital.

Diamond Therapy can help one withstand any negative resistance or reaction to subatomic realignment. It helps the particles move within the atom to accept a new direction.

After a spiritual awakening, a Therapeutic Diamond can help to clarify feedback among the lower bodies. As a result, specific adjustments can be made in one's thoughts and feelings, which are more appropriate and beneficial for unfoldment. However, the diamond will not automatically make the adjustments indicated by this heightened feedback. That is the responsibility of the individual. The diamond merely helps one see and understand his lower bodies more clearly.

Adjustments based on lower-body feedback take conscious effort. You cannot grow spiritually unless you re-evaluate what you have been doing in life so far and then make appropriate changes. A Therapeutic Diamond, of course, is not necessary to do this, but it helps.

With clearer feedback, one can move more swiftly toward the state of Soul awareness, while still retaining balance. The ideal is to operate from the viewpoint of Soul, rather than from a jumble of the physical, emotional, or mental viewpoints.

Right, *said Peddar.* From the lower-sheath vantage points, one cannot grasp the whole of Soul's movement and unfoldment. Each lower body typically only works for the benefit of itself.

Peddar continued, From the Soul viewpoint, on the other hand, your efforts are for the benefit of the entire system of bodies, as well as for the good of all life.

We reached the far end of the beach, a point of land where the untamed waters of the open sea hit the reef. To our right, gentle waves lapped the narrow crescent of yellow sand. The bay stretched beyond for miles toward the city of spires. To our left, thundering ocean breakers tumbled over the jagged rocks of the cliffs, sending spray sparkling high into the sunlight. I watched the waves as they rolled in and back out to sea. Their sound soothed my mind after such a detailed discourse.

After awhile, we drifted back along the beach and Peddar resumed the lesson. I wish to add to our discussion of subatomic particles, and their realignment during the Second Spiritual Achievement, *he began.*

The flow of Light and Sound through these particles can be thought of as a river. Every so often the river rises, and once in a while it floods. As increased spiritual energy courses through an individual, it whittles away at his riverbanks.

Eventually, these riverbanks relax and give way. As they do, the river widens and a greater flow of Light and Sound nourishes the individual. The occasional flood occurs just before the individual enters the next level of unfoldment or spiritual achievement.

After each new achievement, the pressure of a much stronger current gradually subsides. The individual becomes accustomed to the new rate and volume of flow. When it is time to prepare for the next level of unfoldment or spiritual achievement, the feeling of flow increases again.

Each increase of flow brings with it a barrage of tests, designed to purify the lower bodies. The increase in spiritual energy magnetizes new experiences for learning. These situations challenge the sheaths' ability to maintain harmony within themselves and with each other.

Even the atoms, molecules, and cells must learn to maintain balance and harmony, both within themselves and with all life. This principle of harmony applies to human beings, animals, plants, and even minerals. Each must learn to express balance with its fellow beings, as well as with those of both higher and lower states of consciousness.

If Soul does not pass the tests of harmony, it is because some part of the individual is out of tune with the life current.

This is often due to his or her attitudes, concepts, or emotions. Such disharmony can result in disease or malfunction. Of course, illness provides lessons to help the individual release blockages and achieve harmony with all other states of consciousness. Poor health may humble him in exactly the way needed to adjust the misaligned attitudes and emotions.

Disharmony causes a change and distortion of the color ratios drawn to the physical and subtle bodies' blueprints. These changes depend on the unique physiology of the sheath and the lessons needed in order to reassert harmony. The more distorted the spectrums that feed the body, the less they match the body's original blueprints. This deviation makes the body even more susceptible to disharmony and illness.

How can attitudes move an individual out of harmony with life? Let's say he learns that gemstones can serve as therapeutic tools. He scoffs at the idea, for he only sees them as symbols of power and wealth. This attitude reflects an imbalance in his relationship to lower states of consciousness, namely, the mineral kingdom. On the other hand, he could remain neutral, having no strong feelings for or against the idea. In this way, he demonstrates a balanced relationship with lower states. He remains free of disharmony on that subject.

Negative attitudes deflect the spectrums of color that feed the body. The light moves away from its ideal ratios. As a result, non-blueprint spectrums enter and cause disharmony to manifest somewhere in the lower bodies.

One day, perhaps lifetimes later, the individual will find a way to clear this disharmony from his blueprints. Perhaps he may interact with a Therapeutic Diamond or gemstone to return the spectrums to their original specifications. Or, his negative ideas about gems may be resolved after giving or receiving jewelry, such as a diamond ring, as a gift of love.

He may also reestablish harmony with the mineral kingdom through an interest in collecting rocks and gems.

These are examples of ways balance can be re-established, and a lesson about Soul's relationships with lower states of consciousness learned.

Whenever a lesson is learned, one's relationships with all life—within, around, above, and below—is brought into greater harmony. This increased harmony corrects distorted spectrums, which allows clearer blueprint information to feed the body. As a result, the individual becomes healthier.

However, even when the need for a health condition no longer exists, the body often remains in old cycles, resisting changes toward health. It avoids letting go of the conditions which once provided important learning experiences.

One can sing HU, *Peddar reminded us,* to lift the consciousness out of these old patterns and conditions. With the elevation of awareness that HU brings, the individual experiences greater spiritual flow. And when attention is placed on Soul, he is lifted from the disharmonious conditions.

Singing HU and centering oneself in the Soul awareness dissolves old patterns. They are no longer enlivened by spiritual energy. The energy is redirected to a higher ideal. This reallocation occurs every time one sings the HU-song.

Gaelil added, Of course, if one needs additional help in stepping out of old states of consciousness, one can see a physician, perform self-therapies, or select from a variety of spiritual tools available.

A Therapeutic Diamond is one of these tools. It can hasten the release of old patterns and conditions. In their place, the body is presented with an optimal ratio of colors. This spectrum guides the sheath toward its original blueprints. If your blueprints' spectrums are freely expressed, you are in harmony with all around you, above you, and below you. Then the manifested condition is resolved more quickly.

Peddar added, One can also practice spiritual exercises, such as those learned in our discourses, *he said.*

The technique I want to share with you now will help you recognize yourself as Soul.

Mapping Your Inner Being

Part 1

Stand in front of a full-length mirror, or look at a full picture of yourself. Examine what you look like from head to toe. Close your eyes, but continue to see your image in the inner screen of your mind. If you lose the image, look at your reflection or picture again. Practice this until you can see your image clearly in your inner vision.

Then sit down and get comfortable. Close your eyes and again visualize the image of yourself. Imagine yourself moving around the room.

As if watching a movie, see yourself lie down on the bed, get up, sit at a desk, stand up, or brush your hair. If you wish, you can watch yourself walk into another room. You might even go into the kitchen and do something like drink a glass of water.

If you lose the image of yourself, go back to the beginning. Look at yourself again in the mirror with your eyes open and then practice seeing yourself with your eyes closed.

Part 2

While sitting comfortably with eyes closed, once again visualize an image of your physical body in the screen of your mind. Watch this image lie down on the bed.

Examine the image of your body on the bed from different angles. Gradually move your viewpoint to a position above the bed where you can look down at this sheath. This is your supra-physical body which you will learn about later.

Notice that it is encased in a cocoon made of golden light. This light casing is an extension of your supra-physical form lying on the bed. It completely surrounds your physical body as well, and varies in depth from about two to six inches. Examine this golden cocoon carefully.

Do you see any dark patches in it? Dark patches or spots indicate areas where your body might be weak, susceptible to disease, in pain, or out of balance. Take note of them if you wish to pursue therapy later, but do not attempt to do anything about these dark patches now, except to observe their location.

Now, move your viewpoint a step back. See the golden cocoon surrounded by a sheath of light. This form may extend from one to two feet out from the previous one. It may be a lighter or darker shade of gold, or its color may be different.

Step back again and notice a third sheath surrounding the other two. This one may also shine out one to two feet from the borders of the second form.

Take another step back and notice a fourth form surrounding the other three. This one is much bigger than the others, reaching from three to four feet beyond the previous body.

Step back again to examine this fourth sheath from a greater viewpoint. Notice that its border is different from the others. It is a band about two to six inches thick, with a much darker overall appearance than any of the other sheaths.

Now, look at all of the sheaths together.

Part 3

Turn around and find yourself in a land of pure golden Light. A haunting, sweet flute plays an unending melody. The song brings the most indescribably profound joy into your heart.

You may not have been aware of it, but when you stepped back to examine the thin, dark border of the last sheath, you stepped out of the lower worlds and through a gateway into the Golden Kingdom.

91

Perhaps you will be greeted by someone who will give you a tour of the Golden Kingdom. You might also receive a discourse from Sat Nam.

When you wish to leave the Golden Kingdom, place your attention inside your image lying on the bed. Then, get up off the bed and walk over to your physical body sitting on the chair.

To reenter your physical body, sit down on your own lap—and you will snap into physical consciousness. Or, simply think about your physical body sitting on the chair, and you will be there.

If something interrupts you during the exercise and you suddenly return to physical consciousness, spend a few moments re-centering yourself before getting up. Singing HU will help you regain your balance. That is all.

"I like this exercise, Peddar!" I exclaimed. "By following the steps in my imagination as you said them, I entered the Golden Kingdom before any thoughts of unworthiness or inability stopped me. The transition was easy and effortless."

As it should be, *Peddar replied.*

You may be amazed, *Gaelil added,* once you realize how much your own thoughts and feelings get in the way of spiritual awareness and unfoldment.

"I realize that somewhat already," I said.

We walked in silence until we arrived back at the place on the beach where the discourse had begun. As much as I wanted to stay with these masters, I knew it was time to go.

Take time to practice the exercise given, *advised Peddar.* We will meet again when you have gained some proficiency with it.

May the blessings be, *he said, holding his palm up to me in farewell.*

Gaelil also bid me goodbye and they walked away. For a moment, I watched the two masters stroll the beach together.

Then I opened my eyes to physical consciousness. I felt exhilarated by the memories of this experience. As I took a deep, relaxing breath, I detected a delicious aroma of the sea lingering in the air of my room.

Chapter 9

The Subconscious Body

*I*t *took several days of careful practice before I felt I'd mastered Peddar's light-sheath visualization. Finally I was ready for the next discourse.*

Upon stepping into the inner worlds, I found my teacher sitting on a large, flat rock amidst a grassy plain. After some moments of disorientation, I saw the sparkling sea far beneath us. We were atop the huge white cliffs fronting the beach. The bay shimmered quietly below, stretching toward the golden city and the luminescent mountains beyond.

Peddar seemed preoccupied. We sat quietly for a while until his voice broke the silence. I'm pondering whether we should discuss the deeper aspects of each subtle body, or ways to harmonize oneself with all vibratory rates, *he explained.*

Silence returned as he knotted his brows in contemplation. Suddenly he looked up with a bright expression of knowingness. No matter how well one may claim to know the ways of Spirit, *he proclaimed,* one can still be surprised by It. Spirit cannot be second-guessed.

I had planned to offer a different perspective on the information you have already learned. But the flow behind the concepts and words isn't there. Therefore, we'll tackle an alternate topic. Perhaps it is time we begin a study of each subtle body.

As if to collect his thoughts, Peddar again paused before continuing. We will begin with the subconscious body. The 'subconscious' is a word man commonly uses to describe what I call the etheric body. Indeed, the name is appropriate to how this sheath functions in relation to the physical body.

For most people, the subconscious body does indeed act like something 'sub' or 'under' the consciousness. Even most spiritually aware individuals don't fully understand this aspect of the Self.

Souls living in the Subconscious Plane are blessed in a special way. They are aware of the Golden Kingdom which lies just beyond the border of their world. And, unlike most material-plane residents, they have an awareness and an objective view of the worlds below them and the borders that separate them.

Once again, the lower worlds are made up of a continuum of vibratory rates. The division between one world and the next is definite, yet there is no actual break in the spectrum of vibrations. This might be compared to the colors of a rainbow which, while distinct, also blend harmoniously into each other.

The division between adjacent planes actually takes place over a narrow transition area. This is a sort of 'no man's land' where the laws of each plane can apply. It shares the properties of both the world above and below it, yet belongs to neither. Souls may explore this transition zone without changing sheaths. Only if they wish to step beyond the transition zone must they release their current body for an appropriately-tuned vessel.

Movement into the inner planes beyond the physical realm, while retaining a physical body, may be done in many ways. One is a method called astral projection. Another is through a transition of consciousness directed by Soul. The first method is much more tedious, demanding, and limiting than the second.

Let's say an individual living in a physical body wants to explore the inner planes. Using astral projection, it is possible for him to raise the vibratory rate of his physical consciousness into the physical-astral transition area. This requires effort and concentration. When he has reached the farthest boundary of the astral-physical zone, he may shed the physical body awareness for some minutes.

He then finds himself in the astral sheath or body. After much more effort, he may explore a few of the more than one hundred levels of astral existence. Many consider this area heaven. But it is no more than the Astral Plane.

Only the rare human being will then be able to perform a similar, conscious trek into the Causal World. This technique could be called 'causal projection'. Either projection technique cannot provide access into the pure spiritual planes of God. They only allow for movement among the Physical, Astral, and Causal Planes.

Using the second method, however, a spiritual traveler can easily and effortlessly shift from one sheath to another at will, moving faster than the speed of light. Rather than 'projecting' to another plane, he learns to switch his viewpoint from the lower bodies to that of Soul. From this limitless vantage point, it is much easier to consciously operate from any of the material bodies—or beyond.

This technique can be called 'inner world exploration'. It can provide great understanding—through direct experience— of all of one's sheaths and the worlds in which they exist.

The purpose of inner world exploration is to gain the information, strength, and stamina necessary to maintain Soul awareness, while still living in the lower worlds. In this Self-Realized state, one consciously experiences the Self as pure Spirit.

Inner Travel also prepares Soul for its greater mission. After Self-Realization, Soul must strive for God Consciousness and realize Its destiny as a co-worker with God. This grand purpose is sometimes glimpsed at the Second Spiritual Achievement.

However, Soul can only know It's God-mission fully when It has released all attachments to lower forms. This doesn't mean that one must die to know his spiritual mission. Soul may still occupy material sheaths, but It will no longer identify with and become bound by them.

Peddar stopped abruptly, remarking, I believe I'm getting ahead of myself. *He closed his eyes in thought. As I waited, I reflected on the discourse so far. His words held special significance for me. Instinctively, I'd always known that Soul's return to the Golden Kingdom was not It's ultimate achievement. There was a greater spiritual focus—to enter into and serve the divine Heart of God Itself.*

Peddar reopened his eyes. I want to continue exploring the subconscious body, *he said,* so you will know what to expect in this Etheric World.

The Subconscious World represents a delicate transition area between Soul's reality and the realm of the mind. It is so vast that Soul must use a specific sheath to function in this transition zone.

The subconscious sheath is the first to surround Soul when It enters the lower worlds. It remains in place until Soul drops all lower body forms. This may occur when It enters the higher worlds for good, or takes a sabbatical from lower world existence.

Compared to the Golden Kingdom, the Subconscious World is dark. But looking up from the physical realm, it seems inconceivably brilliant. It is the first world to host Spirit in its divided form of Light and Sound. The Light further splits into color rays here, while the four qualities of Sound—substance, character, rhythm, and magnetism—find definition.

The Subconscious World is perhaps the most difficult of the lower worlds to describe. It shares many qualities of the Golden Kingdom, which are beyond the conscious mind's understanding.

Interestingly, its visitors offer no consistent description of this world. Upon arrival, it is seemingly empty. But soon its forces mock up a particular setting expressly for that individual. This is because Soul determines its own experiences here.

The Etheric World can look entirely different at various times and to separate beings. Individuals encounter familiar settings to match their understanding of life. Therefore, descriptions of this world reveal more about the describer than the unique properties of the plane itself.

A single color ray dominates the subconscious body and the spectrum that feeds it. This ray corresponds to the particular gateway Soul originally traversed from the Golden Kingdom. Although all seven colors of the spectrum are present in this world, the individual's main color ray comprises and nurtures more of the subconscious sheath than any other.

From the viewpoint of the Physical World, this etheric body serves as the 'subconscious'. Other sheaths often encounter experiences they aren't ready to deal with or don't need or want to be conscious of. The job of the subconscious body is to take this data and store it.

Thus, the etheric body acts as a repository for all of the lower bodies' odds and ends. This includes habitual tasks we perform almost unconsciously. Suppressed experiences are dealt with here too, so we do not have to face and resolve overwhelming emotions or thoughts. The subconscious also stores messages from Soul or spiritual truths for eventual integration.

The mind stores ingrained attitudes and habits in this sheath, as well as many automatic reactions to experiences and stimuli. This relieves us from having to formulate new reactions to everyday tasks like driving to work or brushing the teeth. Without it, the mind would have to rediscover how to do these tasks each morning!

On the other hand, the subconscious can be a stumbling block. Let's say a child is deeply hurt by a strange man in a red shirt. The child's fear, pain, and confusion is stored in the subconscious body.

Later in life, other people in red shirts might innocently evoke these same painful feelings. The subconscious may even generate an inexplicable aversion to the color red. Until this stored pattern is released from the subconscious body through some type of healing therapy, it forms protective knots of seemingly inappropriate behavior and attitudes. These blockages prevent Spirit from flowing freely through all parts of the lower sheaths.

As mentioned, the subconscious body is a two-way street. It can also receive messages and information from above, from Soul. It stores these spiritual truths until the lower bodies are ready to accept them. Let's say the aforementioned individual received therapy to heal his experience with the red-shirted man. Soul may then provide a corresponding inflow of data on the real reasons for the experience, as the energy channels become unblocked in the lower bodies. These insights are parceled out by the subconscious body to the other sheaths as they can accept them.

As the individual passes the Second Spiritual Achievement, difficult tests may arise in the Subconscious World. First, the individual must begin to face all the information and garbage he has stored here over many incarnations. Gradually every habit and attitude is brought to conscious awareness for examination, resolution, and release. This process can bring hardship.

At the same time, the Subconscious World is a springboard to greater freedom. As each stored reaction is released and the test of the experience passed, the lower bodies become more conscious of Soul and the Golden Kingdom. As trapped knots of energy disappear, pure Light and Sound pours in to fill the vacuum.

This allows more love into the individual's life. Light and Sound are just twin expressions of the one divine spiritual current of Love. This divine love enlivens and strengthens Soul, urging it to complete its sojourn in the lower worlds.

Soul releases its most precious attachments in the subconscious realm, as well as influences from all the lower bodies. Here It must face Its last test, before moving permanently into the Golden Kingdom. It must overcome the fear of death in the lower states of consciousness. This might more aptly be called a test to release the fear of life, for when passed one enters true life!

Attachment to physical form, emotions, and thoughts: all must be released to dwell as Soul in the worlds of pure Spirit. This does not require physical death, however. Nor does the individual have to leave his family and sell all that he owns. That would be trying to let go of the Physical World while still being attached to it!

In fact, one must bless the objects of his attachment—be they people, things, or experiences, for they will teach him detachment, or divine neutrality. I'm speaking in a much broader sense than being non-attached to mere material wealth or beingness. The ultimate test of detachment is to live in the Physical World while separating oneself as Soul from all the lower senses.

So you see, one must live in the Mental World in order to become detached from the mind, and in the Astral World to master emotions. Thus, physical life is a golden opportunity to release physical as well as all lower-world attachments.

Attachment is an attitude, and attitudes are of the mind. Therefore, the release of attachments signifies the release of the mind over Soul's movements in the lower worlds.

When a person becomes aware of himself apart from the mind and lower bodies, he can enter the Golden Kingdom while still in a physical body. It is, in fact, necessary that one do so before leaving the lower worlds forever.

Everything must be examined and released in a state of balance. Only Soul Itself can pass through the highest boundaries of the Subconscious World and into the Golden Kingdom. The entrance to the God Worlds is like the eye of a needle. There is no room for the thoughts, feelings, and objects which provided lower-world experiences. There is not even room for the experiences themselves.

Do you understand this?

"Yes Sire," I replied. "The physical body is one of Soul's greatest gifts, for it is the only body that can teach one how to release all possessions."

Exactly. When an individual faces what he has stored in the subconscious body, he loosens his ties to the lower worlds. This prepares him to enter the Golden Kingdom. This time of preparation may be one of great inner and outer hardship. It is sometimes described as the Dark Night of Soul. Everything may seem to go wrong at home, at work, and in every aspect of life. The mind can become confused and the emotions overwhelming.

During this Dark Night, the subconscious body is cleaning house, so to speak. Even though the sheaths experience a natural elevation of consciousness, there may be a negative reaction. The subconscious body may be releasing no-longer-needed data at a faster rate than the lower bodies can process it.

Also, as the bodies become more positive, the negative current surrounds them even more tightly. This is because in the lower worlds, the positive and negative forces continually seek to balance each other. This can cause hardship even as the sheaths are attaining their own higher states. Eventually, however, the individual will balance himself holistically at a new, higher vibratory rate. But during the transition process, his life may be in a turmoil.

If the individual can realize these negative patches as just one half of the growth cycle—and release them—he will move rapidly through the Dark Night. As soon as he lets go of problems, Spirit will flow in to heal and uplift him.

This marks the positive half of growth. After a Dark Night of Soul, the negativity which obscures vision is released, and the seeker sees the Golden Kingdom shining in his inner vision. This experience may come during a contemplation or in a dream.

It is not necessary to wait for a Dark Night of Soul to clean house in the subconscious. Indeed, a periodic tidying up, metaphorically speaking, is beneficial. It averts the necessity of going through an intense Dark Night of Soul. It also allows you to grow in a more rhythmic way. A Dark Night releases huge chunks of negativity all at once, causing hardship. Therefore, instead of being at the mercy of the subconscious body, it is better to establish gradual control over this sheath and all it contains.

A Subconscious Body Clearing Technique

Tonight's exercise encourages and regulates subconscious-body housecleaning. Most individuals avoid certain experiences or lessons because they are uncomfortable, and store them in the subconscious body. However, these assignments cannot be avoided forever. The best strategy is to regulate their entrance into your life. Orderly lessons, learned one at a time, are digested more completely and deeply at all levels.

This technique exercises your imagination in combination with a word of special vibration. Singing this word, with its specific consonants and vowel sounds, will help you consciously enter the Etheric or Subconscious World. Because of the nature of this plane, it is difficult to access it via the Light alone. The word, which lets you use the Sound element, is an essential tool or key.

First, close your physical eyes. Gently place your attention on the spiritual eye, which can be thought of as a screen behind your forehead. It is located between and behind the eyebrows, and correlates with the pineal gland in the physical body.

Although images usually race across this screen like the scenes of a movie, keep it empty for this exercise. Replace any scenes with the image of a blank screen in your imagination.

Those who have difficulty seeing with their spiritual eye will probably enjoy this exercise, because it doesn't requires you to see anything! Look only for blackness.

Now begin singing the word or sound, 'Ah-Noon'. Repeat it slowly in the exhalation of one breath. Draw the vowels out so the song sounds like this: ahhhh-nooonn-ahhhh-noonn-ahhhh-noonn...

At the end of the breath, inhale very slowly through the nose. Then resume singing the sound in a string again. Let the singing of the 'Ah-Noon' fill your head and entire being.

Keep focusing on the screen behind your forehead. Sing into it as if leaning on a window sill and singing through the window into the black night. Soon you may see stars in the night. Otherwise, let the sky remain black.

You can practice this exercise daily, for about fifteen minutes at a time.

When you are ready—perhaps the first time you practice this technique or on the third or fourth try—look for something on your inner screen.

To do this, continue singing the 'Ah-Noon' sound while looking deeper and deeper into the blackness. Allow your attention to move past the window sill and into the night. The singing of the word will keep you grounded in the Physical World, so you need not be afraid.

You can move as quickly as you wish into the darkness. The chanting will comfort you, while at the same time empowering your movements. It opens the window into the night and helps you move through it.

If you see a star in the blackness, feel its magnetic draw pulling you forward. Accept its help. Often stars seen in the inner vision—especially blue ones—are symbols of the Wayshower coming to help and protect you. Continue gazing into the night.

After you have reached deeply into the night—and this depth will vary with the individual—you will see the image of one or more boxes. The appearance of the boxes will vary, again, according to the individual. To some they may be as simple and plain as a cardboard box, while to others they may be covered with jewels.

If you see many boxes, look for one that particularly catches your eye. Or ask inwardly for Spirit to guide you to the right one.

Continue chanting while you slowly open the lid a few inches. Try to perceive what is in the box. Get a sense of it.

If its contents seems too overwhelming, or if you feel fear, call for help. There are Souls in this world available to assist you. If you have a spiritual guide or master, call upon him or her for help. Remember also that the Wayshower is always available to protect and guide you anywhere in the lower worlds, as well as in the God Worlds.

When you are ready, open the lid completely and look inside the box. Perhaps you will see an image, an object, or nothing at all. If you find an image, study it. If your gift is an object, lift it out of the box and examine it. Ask what lesson or insight it holds for you. Learn from it and then release the lesson.

If you see nothing, simply gaze into the nothingness with love for a minute or two before closing the box. Do not be disheartened. The absence of images suggests you may not be ready to consciously face its contents.

However, the very fact that you opened the lid and looked in, shows tremendous willingness to confront and resolve issues. You have taken a big step toward the resolution of the contents of this box. Some part of you has become more aware and will begin resolving its issues.

After closing the lid, continue singing the 'Ah-Noon' word. Do not go to another box at this time. It is best to work on only one issue per session. Now see the box recede in the distance, growing smaller and smaller. You might envision this as if watching the box from the rear of a departing car. Feel yourself approaching your original position at the windowsill.

I suggest you wait a few days before doing this exercise again, although you may perform other spiritual techniques. During this time, be especially aware of the situations and experiences that enter your life. You may notice changes.

Some people become aware of a lesson or truth they have been avoiding for lifetimes. Others may simply notice a new-found freedom and clarity or an increase in life energy.

The next time you practice this exercise you might open the same box—perhaps to learn more about its issues—or another one.

Peddar grew silent. I wondered what new feelings, thoughts, or experiences I should anticipate from performing this exercise. Whatever they would be, I decided to greet them with love and understanding, for I myself would invite them into my life.

Let's take a break, and then we will examine the mental body, *Peddar suddenly announced.*

As soon as I wondered what he meant by a 'break', my consciousness slipped back into the physical body. I slowly opened my eyes, stretched, and walked downstairs for some apple juice. I felt wonderful—full of enjoyment for the blessings of this material world. Living here and now could bring complete spiritual unfoldment in this lifetime!

Chapter 10

The Mental Body

*A*fter a short rest, I returned to my favorite chair to *practice Peddar's technique for clearing the subconscious body.*

Following his instructions, I examined and disposed of the contents of a container. As I left it behind, it felt like a burden had lifted. A healing of the seed issue had already begun. I thought about why I had chosen to store this issue in my subconscious rather than resolve it when it first occurred. The issue which had seemed so overwhelming when I had stored it, now seemed trivial. Then I promised myself I would look for and resolve any outer lessons this exercise released.

Suddenly, I was keenly aware of Peddar's presence. Although I couldn't see him, his voice came through. Now, stop and remember, *he commanded.* When you were doing the exercise just now, you used your mind to contemplate the released issue and to decide to face and resolve any associated lessons. What did you do to leave the Subconscious World and enter the Mental Plane?

Peddar's form was now visible to my inner eyes. He was seated on the same rock as last time, overlooking the green grass and the bay. I took a seat nearby and thought over his question. I couldn't find anything noteworthy about my transition to the Mental World. My transition to the Astral Plane where we were now seated was also uneventful.

107

"I just began to think," I replied, wondering what special experience I had missed.

Exactly, *replied Peddar.*

I was astonished. Peddar smiled, realizing that I didn't quite understand.

Your movement from the Subconscious to the Mental Plane occurred just by thinking, *he explained.* Similarly, when Soul first wanted to enter the Mental Plane—where Its subconscious sheath could not provide protection—It merely placed its attention there.

As you have learned, the Sound combines with the Light to manifest a sheath out of the fabric of the Mental Plane. Of course, only certain frequencies of this fabric are used. At this point, the mental body is little more than an empty shell which houses Soul and Its subconscious body.

When Soul enters a new sheath in the Mental World, the colors of the subconscious body's blueprint creates spectrums which fill the new mental body. This process is dictated by instructions inherent within the Sound. It is designed to formulate the mechanical machinery of the mind, so that it will directly reflect the uniquenesses of the individual Soul and Its subconscious body.

Each of the color rays in the subconscious body's blueprint—except the main color-ray—forms one new spectrum. Each of these six colors predominates in its new spectrum. At the same time, the main color-ray manifests two separate spectrums. One of these spectrums does not have a predominate color. All the hues glow with a special intensity. Its twin spectrum, however, expresses the main color-ray with an intensity that is greater than in any of the other spectrums.

These spectrums total eight. In seven of them, one color ray predominates over the other six; in the eighth, all colors are present in relatively equal amounts. In turn, these eight spectrums replicate themselves. Their offspring separate into groups of like kind then merge together to form the intricate interworkings of the new mental body.

This process begins just at the borders where the Subconscious Plane blends into the Mental Plane. Here the mental body's spectrums are simple and uncomplicated. When the process ends at the borders of the Causal Plane, one finds that the mind has become a complex mass of blueprint spectrums working together to perform all mental functions.

The body manifested by these spectrums has no particular shape. From a lower viewpoint, our mental bodies appear human simply by reflection. Out of habit, they may even continue to adopt a particular form after its physical, emotional, and causal counterparts are dropped. The mental body can appear to be of any age, sex, or race—depending on the viewer's perspective. This is one of the ways the laws in the Mental World are unique.

I thought about this for a moment. "So time is more fluid here. Perhaps it explains an experience I once had. I met a spiritual master in my dreams and contemplations years before he actually attained mastership. Did I see him on the Mental Plane?"

Perhaps, *Peddar replied.* Masters of Spirit can overcome limitations of time and space to serve a purpose. Therefore your experience could have occurred on any inner plane.

But let's get back to the makeup of the mental body. The eight spectrums which lie at the apex of the new sheath form a 'newborn' mind. When Soul first takes on a mental body, It is ignorant of the ways of this world. It is just like a baby who is unschooled in the ways of the Physical World until it gains experience.

As the eight color-ray spectrums take on increasingly more mental substance—just as a child's growing body gets bigger—the sheath matures. However, the mental body gets 'bigger' only in the sense that its eight spectrums clone themselves and the resulting structures become organized.

Just below the apex of the Mental World, the new mental body's spectrums briefly join to communicate. Then they divide into three main channels. The first two channels have their greatest impact on the first, uppermost level of the mind. These channels collect their spectrums into what might be described as separate pools. These two channels and their corresponding pools represent opposite schools of thought: analytical and creative.

There are few purely creative or analytical thinkers in the realms of God. Generally we use a mixture of these two approaches. But most people have more spiritual energy flowing through one channel than the other. As a result, they favor one type of outlook over the other.

Those adept at mental mastery can shift the Light and Sound flowing through either channel. The greater your awareness, the greater your flexibility will be in this skill.

There is only one rule: you must not direct the mental flow of Light and Sound outside yourself. This is the beginning of the end for your mental body! Do not direct your mental current toward others, or use your mental powers to control them. This sets a very common negative cycle in motion. Soon, you will begin to suffer from all the negative effects caused. Misuse causes the mind to become debilitated, siphoning off energies that would otherwise nourish its growth.

The true goal of the mind is to control the flow of spiritual energy within itself and one's lower bodies. Mastery includes redirecting the attention from one way of thinking to another, to address previously unfathomable nuances. For example, a great artist might learn to effortlessly switch from creative to analytical mode to correct his brush strokes in a beautiful painting.

At the same time, an analytical scientist or inventor might make a quantum leap forward by tapping into his imagination while solving mathematical equations. Einstein always maintained that imagination was far more important than information. In both of these examples, balanced detachment is the crucial factor. It allows one to regulate and harness the Light and Sound as it flows through either channel of the mind.

One must be gentle when shifting mental modes. If you divert the entire flow of Sound and Light from the creative channel to the analytical one, it will feel like a train jumping from one track to another.

If an artist arbitrarily threw such a switch without practice, he could lose his creative flow. Authors call this writer's block. Likewise, an analytical thinker would lose his trail of proven, solid truths, if he abandoned them for creative imagination.

Make no mistake, mental body mastery can be consciously developed. However, merely moving between analytical and creative thought does little good by itself. The switch is too fundamental to one's self-identity. Many other mental processes rest upon the choice of left- or right-brain thought. It is best to adjust these processes first.

A thought stream is formed when a mixture of analytical and creative thought is drawn from each of its corresponding pools. Once they mix, many secondary channels can branch off. Each of them governs a particular mental process.

These mental processes require different amounts or degrees of analytical and creative expressions. To help you understand, imagine a faucet which dispenses hot and cold running water. Pure cold water represents the analytical expression, while the purely creative expression can be thought of as steaming hot.

Because the faucet is connected to both the analytical and creative pools, you can adjust the temperature and flow of the thought stream you bring to any mental process.

Let's take, for example, the function of the mind that perceives beauty. It can run hot or cold—with either creative or analytical thought. An individual who perceives beauty in an analytical way might wish to see life more creatively. He could consciously move his thoughts from ice cold to burning hot. If he is wise, however, he will strive for a temperate, balanced view.

Even if he warms his perceptions of beauty, the rest of his mental functions may retain their analytical emphasis. By making one change at a time, it's easy for the mind to keep its balance.

The mind has many other functions besides the perception of beauty. Each process has its own metaphorical faucet. By adjusting only one mental function at a time, the individual can decide if he likes the change or if another setting would be better. He may even find the original temperature best for him.

Let me list some other mind processes. One relates to the causal body. It helps the individual see repeating patterns in life. Other functions gather feedback from the emotions and physical body. The process of discrimination is another process which can be performed with varying degrees of analytical or creative emphasis.

The mind also has the ability to organize data and solve problems. Furthermore, there is the function of the mind to perceive what is seen with the physical eyes. Another relates to the perception of the physically unseen. Similarly, the mind registers what is heard with the physical ears as well as the inner ears.

Intuition is also heeded in a range from analytical to creative. This sixth sense is one of Soul's unique channels to communicate directly with the lower bodies. When you get a 'hunch' or a 'gut feeling' about something, it is often Soul speaking. It's up to you to interpret it creatively or analytically before acting.

The ability to recognize truth is yet another function of the mind. When elusive information of a spiritual or religious nature is presented, the mind asks, "Is this truth? Is it something that I can accept now?"

As I mentioned before, after Spirit flows into the main channel of the mental body, it splits off into three currents. We've already talked about two of these currents: analytical thought and creative thought.

The third channel becomes active in the second level of the mind, though it also influences third-level mental function. The second level has five mental expressions. These also flow warm or cool. However, unlike the other mental functions which co-exist side by side, these follow one after another along a singular channel.

The importance of these functions depends on the amount of spiritual force coming through the individual. The first expression is the 'I', or the ego. To continue the hot and cold analogy, if this process is overheated, the individual will express vanity and egoism. On the other hand, if the setting is cold, false humility will be expressed. Balance lies near the midpoint. Here the individual finds true self-recognition as Soul.

The more Light and Sound flowing through a person, the stronger these mental expressions will be, regardless of their hot or cold settings. This flow of Light and Sound is increased in two ways: self-discipline, and the attainment of spiritual achievements. These also bring more balance to the mind, gradually moving each mental function closer to the midpoint.

Individuals who have earned a greater flow of Light and Sound must take careful responsibility for their expressions, in order to remain on the middle path. A temporary swing will not immediately lower the spiritual flow. But if they do not return the setting to midpoint, their inner flow of Light and Sound will decrease.

The second mind function in this string of five is one's attachment to or detachment from the lower worlds. It measures how easily one forgets his true identity as Soul. Soul can get lost and identify with one of the lower bodies. But eventually It realizes these bodies are only tools to accomplish Its divine mission.

On the hot end of this function, the individual has a strong attachment to material things and attitudes. At the cold extreme, he thinks he is achieving spirituality by denying everything he has. If taken to its logical end, the seeker may give up all his belongings or even his life.

Once again, the desirable state is one of balanced neutrality. This represents both enjoyment of and sufficient detachment from life to let Spirit have Its way. Other pitfalls of attachment are perfectionism or procrastination. This occurs when one grows so attached to being right that he impedes his own actions or those of others.

The ability to discriminate relates to the third function. What is good and necessary for unfoldment? At the hot end of the dial, there is an excessive inflow toward the self. Greed and vanity set in, and the individual expects the world to revolve around him.

At the cold setting, the individual pushes gifts on others—but with strings attached. This is 'silent greed', the desire for control of others through guilt and false selflessness. At the center point, again, is balance—right discrimination.

The fourth dial represents the ability to be content. Can you be at peace with your mind, surroundings, and yourself? The individual who burns hot on this issue lusts for power and control over himself, his mind, and his environment. One who is too cold will be passive and powerless. He lets the world trample him, perhaps with the false idea that this behavior is spiritual.

It is interesting to note how leaders and followers are often at opposite ends of this function. Misguided leaders often use power to suppress others, keeping them in ig-

114

norance and submission. Weak, listless followers, on the other hand, allow themselves to be led like uncaring sheep to the slaughter.

The ability to tolerate and forgive is the fifth mind process. How well do you dismiss negative thoughts, actions, and emotions in yourself and others? When this function is set at midpoint, it is easy to dismiss off-target actions with understanding and compassion. Extremes include on-going, corrosive anger and subtle irritation at one end. At the other is false forgiveness and self-negation, which allows others to siphon off valuable mental energies.

If one can maintain balance in all these functions, the flow of thought energy moves effortlessly from the apex of the mental body to the borders of the Causal Plane.

The mental realm is a vast area comprised of more vibratory rates than all the other lower planes put together. Instead of describing all the subdivisions, I have tried to combine them into one explanation. When people become more aware of this sheath—for it is more than just a conveyer of thoughts—more information will be brought out.

For now, it is enough to know that if any of the settings are too hot, thought energy and Soul impulses are curtailed. Often they build up and cause the mind to act like a monster. Blocked mental energy can manifest as angry, malicious, or negative acts. These imbalanced expressions may include slander, evil gossip, profanity, fault-finding, jealousy, resentment, mockery, and destructive self-criticism.

If the flow is too cool, spiritual energy is diverted by outside influences. Other times it recycles within the mind, moving through the same pathway over and over again. Consequently, the mind becomes passively lost in itself. The individual may think there is simply no way out. There is no room for new ways of thinking, new ideas, or new input, because the same record plays over and over again. Inactivity sets in, causing Soul to become restless and bored.

But at whatever rate it is allowed to flow, the Light and Sound of the third pipeline passes through the first and second levels of the mind to enter a third arena. Here the pipeline splits into many branches, which represent more functions of the mind. Each branch passes through a regulatory faucet or dial, returns to the main pipeline, and then feeds into the causal body.

Again, the amount of Light and Sound moving through each of these branches determines the strength and balance of its corresponding mental function. Zero on the dial which measures one's organization, for example, would represent total chaos, while one hundred would indicate an excess of rigid rule-making.

Other mental functions are influenced by these particular extremes. One who is totally unorganized might also be undisciplined, whereas one who is totally organized might ignore the free-flowing aspects of life. Here again, the balance mark is usually around midpoint, though other factors can be involved. If the type of work you do requires strong organizational skills, your organization dial would be set somewhere between the midpoint and one hundred. If, on the other hand, organization was inessential for your lifestyle, it would be fine to have this dial set closer to thirty.

Although there are many dials in the third level of the mind, I will only mention a few here: There is one for self-discipline, as well as perception and management of time. Attitudes and opinions about others are formed here, plus self-opinion. The ability to initiate new pathways of thinking governs yet another dial, as does forming conclusions. This latter function is somewhat different than making decisions. There is also a dial that gathers data for these two previous functions.

Peddar paused for breath. My mind was reeling with the flood of information. But the lesson continued after only a moment's respite. I felt like I was in a mental-body marathon.

When an individual attains the Fourth Spiritual Achievement—initiating the return flow of Spirit through the mind—all of the mental pipelines expand to accommodate the flow. This returning energy moves up one side of the channel, while the outward flow travels down the other side.

Balance in all the mental-body functions becomes even more crucial. If a setting is too extreme, certain energies flowing toward the lower bodies or Soul are severely curtailed. Other problems include functions that start swinging back and forth from one extreme to another.

In any case, the return flow brings the individual greater awareness of his mind. But if he has not worked toward balance in the first three achievements, he will have a serious struggle on his hands to control the many inflows and outflows of the mind.

As an individual attains higher spiritual achievements, the parameters for balance become narrower. In other words, hot and cold—one hundred to zero—no longer represent the extremes. Instead, forty and sixty might mark the acceptable boundaries. Eventually, the gap from forty-nine to fifty-one may represent one's entire functional arena. Impulsive reactions, fixed thoughts, and pre-formed attitudes do not fit in this slim zone.

The mental body is just a machine. As it becomes more finely tuned, the individual realizes the mind does not even really think. Soul is the only source of creativity. Soul gives out impulses which can then be directed by the mind's myriad spectrums. As they flow downward, they are formed into what people perceive as thoughts.

Tangled mental energies can slow this flow, but 'mental blocks' are usually the product of several combined problems in the causal, emotional, and physical bodies as well as the mind.

Resetting the Dials of the Mind

For now, I am going to share an exercise to help individuals gain control over the mind. It involves adjusting the dials or faucet settings that correspond to mental function and expression.

Most people use their physical body and earthly surroundings as points of reference. In this exercise, a well-known combination of consonant and vowel sounds will help the real you, Soul, to use the mental body and the environment of the Mental Plane as reference points instead.

Begin by sitting quietly and comfortably with your eyes closed. Inhale deeply. On the exhale, sing the vowel 'Ahhhh', followed by 'Ohhh', and finally the consonant 'Mmmmm'. Extend the 'Mmmmm' sound until you run out of breath.

Inhale once again, and repeat the three sounds.

Do this at least five times, and as many as nine.

Next, think about an aspect of your thoughts you want to change. Visualize the corresponding dial or faucet for it in the mental body. See the label for that aspect written above the dial.

Observe what the current dial setting is. Then imagine turning it to the desired setting. If you cannot visualize the dial, just think about what this more balanced setting would be. In the Mind World, you can make changes without imagination or inner sight. All you need do is 'think' about the current setting a dial might be on, and then 'think' it to a more beneficial position.

Let's say you want to adjust your self-image with regard to vanity. You might picture a meter or dial labeled 'Vanity'. Watch as it moves a few degrees closer to the middle. The vanity meter is now registering sixty on the dial instead of seventy, or forty instead of thirty. Remember to move toward the midpoint slowly.

The breeze ruffled Peddar's clothing as he leaned back on the rock. The grass was a vivid green that soothed my mind and eyes. Eventually I turned my thoughts back to his discourse and asked, "What is the significance of the vowels sung in this exercise?"

Peddar smiled and replied, The 'Ahhhh' sound opens the mind and the consciousness. It gives a feeling of expansion.

'Ohhh' connects the physical consciousness with Soul. Ultimately, it is the physical body that feels the final effects of any adjustments in the mind area. Therefore, this sound helps one decide, from a Soul viewpoint, which mental body changes are best with respect to the physical body.

The 'Mmmmm' opens and awakens the mental area. It helps clear Soul's communication with the mind.

I nodded and Peddar concluded, That will be all for today. Tomorrow we will continue our discussion of the mental body.

We sat in silence for several minutes while I let Peddar's discourse settle into my consciousness.

The cool breeze swept across the fields again, carrying with it the fresh, salty smell of the ocean far below. Sea gulls glided over the grass, eyeing our quiet camaraderie with bright black glances. I closed my eyes and listened to their soft cries, and gently returned to physical consciousness.

Chapter 11

Another Look at the Mental Body

I *was busy typing when Peddar's luminescent form ap-*
peared in my peripheral vision. At first I doubted his presence
and tried to ignore it. Then a wave of love engulfed me and I
knew he was really there. I thanked him for the reassurance.

Now let's get down to business, *he said briskly. I found*
my tape recorder and turned it on. As I did so, Peddar's
glowing form played hide and seek with my physical vision.
Every time I tried to look directly at him, it faded. When I gave
up the struggle and looked away, his form reappeared at my
side.

Peddar noted my trouble with a delighted laugh. Meet
me on the Astral Plane, *he suggested. I immediately followed*
him inwardly to the grassy field where we had met before.

There is another aspect of the mind I would like to talk
about, *Peddar began. I gave a sigh of dismay at the thought of*
another technical discourse. My teacher smiled. I know this
discussion of the mind is long and involved, but it will help
you in your spiritual unfoldment.

I want to talk about the reflective aspect of the mind.
This mental function is devoted to receiving impulses from
Soul, interpreting these messages, and then passing them
along to the causal, astral, and physical bodies.

The mind is like a mediator between Soul and the lower
bodies. When this aspect is working in its best and highest
capacity, the mind is a clear channel for a continual flow of

Soul impulses. It is free of limiting attitudes and concepts. Thoughts simply relay information between Soul and the lower bodies.

I say 'simply', and yet, as the previous discourse illustrated, the mind is not a simple matter. Having all of one's 'dials' set at midpoint with the mind completely free of limitations is only an ideal.

In addition to communicating Soul's intentions, the reflective aspect also acts as a mirror. It reflects all emanations it encounters. This includes an individual's own thoughts as well as his actions and emotions. By mirroring one's own activities in the lower worlds, introspection and self-evaluation are possible. We are able to learn from our experiences.

The reflective aspect also mirrors the thoughts, emotions, and actions of others. Hence, people see in others what is also within themselves. This applies no matter what a person's state of consciousness.

If you see a good quality in someone else, what you are really noting is one of your own qualities, mirrored in the person's mental body. If you think a negative thought, it will unconsciously and automatically be sent back to you.

However, the mind does not necessarily remain unaffected by what it reflects. The positive and negative emanations your mind reflects can have an impact on you. This is because the mind does more than just reflect—it also collects. An imbalanced mental body collects the images of all that it reflects. On the other hand, an optimally healthy mind is not permanently affected by the emanations it reflects, nor is it obliged to collect them.

Of course, some reflections are useful. If you mirror a positive thought or impulse back to a person, you will also be affected by that good. Your mind accepts this quality as being within you, and begins to magnify it. Can you see why it is so important to look for the God-qualities in others?

Unfortunately, most people don't hold positive thoughts, feelings, or actions. Typical impulses include: 'She's fat', 'He's sloppy', 'How ridiculous he acts', 'What a terrible job she did', and on and on. These thoughts are reflected back to the person who sent them, and collected in his mind. But they may also be imprinted in the recipient's mental body.

You can protect yourself from collecting these negative emanations of others. One method is to sing HU. This charged word envelopes you in pure spiritual current. You can also call on the Wayshower for protection.

Later in this discourse I will give you a technique for clearing the mind of rubbish. Clutter attracts clutter, so you must prevent unhealthy accumulations. It is a good idea to visually clean the mind and jettison all unwanted reflections at the end of each day.

The more the mind is burdened by garbage, the more it acts like a piece of film in a camera. All that is directed toward the individual is imprinted within. The mind becomes little more than an endless storehouse of these imprints.

The mental sheath can get so cluttered it no longer accepts impulses from Soul. Then it starts to run its own introverted game, sending out thoughts from within the over-burdened storehouse. It tries to be the master instead of Soul's communicator. Soul sadly becomes unable to affect the lower sheaths.

When this happens, the mind is even more convinced its stored pictures are the only reality. A negative, downward spiral begins, and the mind's discrimination is further weakened. Soon it is unable to recognize truth in any situation. This blindness further closes the mind to Soul. The dial of the ego, the first of the five dials in the second level of the mind, swings to an extreme. Soon other dials are unhinged. It is interesting to note that, although these extremes seem to inflate the mind's role at first, they will eventually close off the inflow of Light and Sound and cause the mind's downfall.

On the other hand, a mind that consistently listens to Soul can easily separate Its impulses from mere lower-world reflections. Soul helps the mind weed out thought-energies that do not nurture the whole of life and the individual.

I tried to picture this healthy state. "Do positive or negative thoughts about oneself also become imprinted in the mind?" I asked.

Yes.

When someone has a good thought about herself, it becomes a part of her being. The same is true for a negative thought. Eventually, the individual outwardly expresses this positive or negative quality in some way.

The mind also reflects one's emotions and physical health. Ideally, Soul has control of the mind which allows Sound and Light to circulate freely through the lower bodies. The more Soul is in control, the less the mind collects. Soul directs the mind to be a true mirror—to reflect images instead of collecting them.

It is vital to listen to Soul, because the mind cannot see the Golden Kingdom. The mind is passively programmed to receive information. If Soul is not providing this information, where does the mind get its direction? Usually from below. Most minds are focused on collecting reflective, second-hand input from the lower worlds outside themselves.

The mind is so sophisticated, however, that it often thinks that it can produce its own ideas. It is very much like a computer. I suppose one could make a computer that could outdo its user. There are many science fiction stories built around this theme.

But without Soul, the computer of the mind cannot receive primary, first-hand information about life. At the same time, Soul cannot be liberated from identifying with the mind until the mental sheath is firmly placed in the category of a useful servant. It is a very poor master, one which will eventually run the individual to despair.

So the reflective aspect of the mind gathers information from the emanations of others. This is how the social norm arises. Because most people today are unable to receive original impulses from Soul, they cannot get an objective overview of their inner and outer lives. They accept the mental reflections of their neighbors as truth. This locks them into the spoken and unspoken rules of society that dictate acceptable social behavior. The undiscriminating mind accepts these instructions on how to act and direct the lower bodies.

The term 'closed minded' fits very well here—because the mind is closed to Soul. An individual only heeds thoughts which comfortably fit the social norm he has adopted. Therefore, his actions become limited to a narrow spectrum of expression.

I was astounded by the scope of this everyday illusion. How would it feel to be truly free in one's mind? I turned to Peddar and inquired, "How did all this begin? How does the mind become closed off from Soul?"

Well, when Soul first took on lower bodies, It was surprised by the incessant stream of lower-world stimuli that tested them. The lower bodies strived for balance, but they lacked the required knowledge and experience. To compensate, the mind thought it could help by controlling the other sheaths. Unfortunately, the mind discovered it liked this new role, and Soul lost Its rule.

All interaction with life and the environment reflects the bodies' imbalances back to the mind in an attempt to show the mind its failed efforts. These reflections are collected by the mind as clutter.

Now, this clutter is comprised mostly of non-color-ray frequencies. These are waves of Light and Sound that are not life-giving to Soul's sheaths. But they still serve a divine purpose. These frequencies are necessary to run the lower planes—indeed they make up the very fabric of these worlds.

125

Only the sheaths of Soul exist apart from them. As you recall, Soul's unique sheaths are made up of color-ray frequencies.

Of all the bodies of Soul, the mind is the most sensitive to these interfering frequencies. Non-color-ray vibrations are all around us, but their concentration is greater in space—outside the Earth's protective atmosphere. When the Earth's atmosphere is punctured or its integrity violated in some way, these frequencies shower the planet. The mental body is affected more than any other sheath.

When an individual experiences optimal health, the fabric of his being—which is made of Sound—attracts only pure color-ray Light. However, when one's 'dials' register anything but balance, other frequencies are caught in the Sound matrix.

When non-color-ray frequencies infiltrate the mind, it reacts to more reflections and collects more clutter. The flow of Light and Sound slows and the mind is less able to recognize and respond to Soul's input.

As the mind fills with clutter, pure Soul instructions and images are unable to flow unchanged to the lower bodies. So the mental body acts on inferior reflections from its own and others' storehouses. The mind develops these impressions, like photographic paper, into thoughts.

Thoughts move through the mind in the same way current moves through a wire. The wire itself doesn't move, and one can't see the electricity running through it. Nothing in the mind changes, yet the image is transported from one part to the next, until eventually it reaches the lower bodies.

Unfortunately, Soul's impressions can become distorted by the mind's stored reflections. By the time Soul's impulse reaches the lower bodies, it is often fundamentally different than the original message. This can wreak havoc on the lower sheaths—especially the physical, which seems to bear the brunt of our mental inefficiencies.

Now, Soul does have Its ways of reclaiming control of the mind even when the channels are clogged. It does this by flashing a strong, distinct image or message. The image acts like a mental debugging device. It is a mechanism that the mind does not recognize until the fuse has already been set aflame, so to speak. As the message is distorted by the mind, it works to rid it of the very debris that causes the distortions.

These flashing impulses clean the mind and ultimately put Soul back into the driver's seat. But Soul can only send these mental debugging devices when the machine is unconscious. Otherwise, the mind would block it.

A Mental-Body Clearing Technique

The more you place your attention on cleaning the mental body, the more Soul is encouraged to send debugging signals through the mind. One simple technique to aid mental-body housecleaning is to sing the vowels and consonants described in the last exercise I gave you. 'Ahhh, Ohhh, Mmmm'.

Then, instead of imagining a hand adjusting mental dials, sing HU in long, drawn out breaths for several minutes.

To increase the effectiveness of this technique, hold the image of a spiritual master on your mental screen with your eyes closed. That's all there is to it.

As you know, there are many things the mind can do. It can be used to adjust each of the lower bodies, or even to heal a physical disease. But if the mind is in control of your identity instead of Soul, attempts at healing and balance will not be very effective.

When Soul is in control, It sees the lower bodies' conditions from a much greater vantage point. It can then direct the mind's affirmations and positive thoughts to heal all the lower bodies.

If you allow It, Soul will clarify the mind's image of the lower bodies. This ideal image is held until it manifests. Soul can further impart direct knowingness of unwanted conditions and what they were intended to teach. Then you can release them with no further repercussions.

The mind can't heal without Soul's guidance, for it lacks crucial information on the entire individual's well-being. Intellectual changes from within are usually only salves, not transformations.

"Why would one's own mind work against oneself?" I asked. "Is it because it is clouded by clutter?"

Yes, *Peddar replied.* This clutter prevents even the most healing influences from successfully reaching the physical body.

Now, let's identify which part of the mind collects clutter. When you dream, one part of your mind rests, another part works, and a third part awakens. The part at rest is the collector of reflections. The working part maintains bodily functions. And the awakened portion funnels Light and Sound directly through the lower bodies.

In some, this last part may not awaken fully, but it is less impeded by the conscious aspects of the mind at night. This is one reason why sleep is nourishing to all the lower bodies.

If Soul is in control of the mind, your dreams will be filled with useful instructions for enhancing the lower bodies' well-being and improving the quality of life. Often these instructions are converted to symbols, and the meaning of the dream is missed. The individual may not become consciously aware of Soul's impulses until he decodes his own dream symbols.

A Daydreaming Technique to Awaken the Mind

I will give you another technique to help Soul take greater charge of the mind. It will also help you conduct Spirit into the lower bodies without mind's reflections getting in the way. The technique I'd like to share involves daydreaming while awake. This means allowing unstructured thought to amble through the mind at a leisurely pace. The goal is to become aware of yourself daydreaming—and to continue the dream under your conscious control.

Trying to catch and change your thoughts is hard. During a daydream, however, the mind is in a relaxed state similar to sleep. When you become conscious of yourself during a daydream, you open a window between the mind and Soul. That's the first step.

This is not as hard as it may sound. People commonly catch themselves daydreaming, and admonish themselves for allowing their minds to wander. Why? All through our school days we're told, 'Stop daydreaming!' This is reinforced by employers and loved ones throughout our lives. Just giving yourself permission to daydream is constructive.

The second step is to gently take control of the daydream. This lets Soul in through the back door of the mind, so to speak.

But to strengthen your control, you not only must catch yourself in a daydream, but continue it. If you are not used to daydreaming, you might want to sit down and consciously create one.

For example, daydream about taking a vacation. Allow your thoughts to wander. Think about a place you would like to go and what you would like to do there. Once these images come to mind, you are daydreaming!

Now keep it going, even if it takes a lot of imaginative effort. For example, you might imagine you are at the beach, playing in the waves and building sandcastles with the kids.

129

After that, you might lay in the sun for awhile or enjoy a picnic lunch with your family.

After doing this consciously a few times, you will become more comfortable with daydreaming and will probably do it more. Again, when you find yourself in a dream, continue it. Just keep the experience going, as if you were a movie director or a screenplay writer. What do you want to happen next?

When you catch yourself daydreaming, and Soul develops the ability to control the dream, allow your mind to listen to Soul. What might Soul be trying to tell you that your mind otherwise shuts out?

Eventually you will be able to consciously daydream, and receive messages from Soul, even while performing complex functions. And no one need ever know that you are exercising control over your mind!

I suggest varying the content of your daydreams. For instance, if your daydreams are always about being by the ocean, the mind will eventually catch on. It will try various evasive maneuvers to prevent Soul from taking over.

There are many mind control techniques. Unfortunately, most of them use the mind to control itself. In other words, they only exercise the mind's own power. Repetitive mental exercises don't reestablish Soul's control. Trying to release mental habits is also self-defeating, for the mind can be like a spoiled child. If you try to take something away from it, the mind is convinced of its need and may have a temper tantrum.

This daydream technique does not strengthen the will nor exercise the mind. It lets you, as Soul, reclaim rightful control of your mind through imagination. This is Soul's ultimate skill in all the lower worlds. When you consciously exercise your imagination, the mind is relaxed and less resistant.

Go ahead—try this exercise now. Then meet me here again tomorrow and we will discuss the causal body.

Peddar waved goodbye and walked toward the buildings of Askleposis, about a half mile to the east.

I closed my eyes and let my thoughts wander. For awhile I was lost in a wonderful daydream. Then a sudden loud noise jolted me back into the physical body. A gust of wind had slammed a door shut in another part of the house.

Even though the noise was loud and disruptive, I recognized it to be a gift of Spirit. It awoke me just enough to become aware that I was dreaming.

Chapter 12

The Causal Body

*P*eddar arrived before me. I found him standing near the
rocks on the same grassy field where we'd met before. His gaze
was fixed on the city across the bay. He turned and greeted me,
then suggested we walk the footpath along the cliff's edge.

As you know, there is a great difference between the
Golden Kingdom and the lower worlds, *he began.* There is an
equally great difference between the mental realm and the
worlds below it: the Causal, Astral and Physical Worlds.

Although the neutral force is inherent in all the lower
worlds, it does not materialize until we reach the Causal
Plane. Its manifestation unlocks new information embedded
within it. This third Spirit force combines with the positive
and negative streams to form packages which you call atoms.

These bundles of positive, negative, and neutral energies
combine into many different kinds of atoms. Each package
expresses its own version of substance, character, rhythm,
and magnetism. Hence all chemical elements have their birth
on the third or Causal Plane. Since substances here are
charged with positive, negative, and neutral qualities, they
can form manifestations not possible in the Mental Worlds.

In order for atoms to interact, their character has to be
expressed. The Sound's magnetism and rhythm allows this
expression. The magnetism attracts Light to the atomic
matrix. This in turn reflects an image to other atoms for
interaction.

The rhythm of the Sound sets the cyclical pulse or frequency at which the Light interacts with the Sound. Consequently, atoms that are attracted to each other are able to bond when their rhythms are compatible.

In this way, the positive and negative forces are inextricably woven into the fabric of the three lowest worlds. The paradox is that positive and negative act as dual, opposing forces here. That is why the neutral stream is necessary. It acts as a balancing force between the other two.

Male and female are opposite energies which attract each other. The masculine principle is electrically positive, active, and progressive, while the female force is receptive, creatively life-giving, and electrically negative. These two energies naturally come together to conceive an embryo—a manifestation of the balancing neutral force.

Hence, men and women are attracted to each other in the quest to find and manifest the neutral force within. There is certainly pleasure and reward in being united, but the search for the neutral force is still the unconscious motivation.

When Soul wants to take on a causal body, It focuses Its attention, via the subconscious and mental bodies, on the Causal Plane. The causal Sound responds by building up positive and negative charges. This increased magnetism is attracted by men and women in love and draws them together. Some couples may conceive a causal embryo. Soul then chooses which family It should join. Often this choice is made with the help of Spirit or a spiritual guide.

When the fetus is born, Soul, along with its mental and subconscious bodies, enters the causal sheath. A similar process occurs in the Astral and Physical Planes.

"You've just answered many of the questions that I never dared to ask," I said.

Even unspoken questions are answered in time, *Peddar replied softly.*

The causal body is very much like the physical body, just as the Causal World is very much like the Physical. However, there are some differences. All the frequencies present on the Physical Plane exist at a higher vibratory rate on the Causal Plane. The opposite is not true: all causal frequencies are not necessarily manifested physically. In addition, the Physical World is a three-dimensional world, while the Causal Plane is governed by laws that include the fourth dimension.

Within three dimensions, space, time, and matter are difficult to change; they tend to be fixed and set. In the fourth dimension, however, they are more fluid. Therefore, the Causal World's laws, such as the law of gravity, differ considerably from Physical World axioms.

These differences allow changes to be made in the causal body much more quickly than in the physical body.

A question occurred to me, and instead of waiting for an answer to be presented in time, I decided to ask for it now. "Is causal life any different if one also has a physical body?"

Peddar answered readily. When one dwells solely on the Causal and higher planes, life is perceived in much the same way as earthlings see the Physical World. To the unenlightened, the Causal Plane is thought to be the only reality.

However, when one also lives in the Physical World, the causal body has more perspective and mass. It stores information from the emotional and physical sheaths. Similarly, when Soul enters a new causal body, the mental body takes on an added role as a conduit. It accepts still more complex tasks when Soul enters astral and physical bodies.

The causal realm is a world of patterns. These patterns actually have more significance for the astral and physical bodies than for the causal body itself.

Peddar paused, and stroked his chin in thought. Let's travel to a higher perspective. There we can learn more about the patterns of the causal body.

I wondered about the 'we' in Peddar's suggestion. "You mean, you don't know?" I asked.

Peddar chuckled. No. *You* don't know—at least, not at this level. Why don't we sit down here in the grass, and journey to the Golden Kingdom. Direct experience is the best teacher.

I closed the eyes of my astral body and put attention on the highest part of myself. With Peddar at my side, I entered the Golden Kingdom to observe my causal body.

I immediately noticed thin lines running through it of various lengths. Most of the lines neatly followed the contours of my body. But some were grouped together, and in a very few places, the lines jumbled into a confused and disorderly clump.

These lines represent the genetic material or DNA in your causal body cells, *Peddar explained.* They are part of the fabric of information Spirit used to form your causal body.

Individuals who can see the physical aura might perceive these lines of the causal body as long, thin needles, giving it a porcupine-like appearance. However, when the causal body is the primary point of reference, these lines do not appear.

Causal lines are invisible to causal eyes, just as your earthly DNA is invisible to your physical eyes. The difference is that physical DNA are not arranged into lines as they are in the causal and astral bodies.

By the way, the reason physical DNA is not linear, is that the return flow of Spirit starts in the Physical Plane. The somewhat coiled shape of DNA encourages a U-turn, to initiate and facilitate this return flow in each individual.

The lines in your causal body represent patterns of experiences collected throughout your lives. These are earned according to divine laws of karma, or cause and effect. Look at them closely and tell me what you see.

I focused my attention on a single line, examining it as if through a magnifying glass. It looked like a string of separate blocks. The blocks were divided into adjoining pairs. Although each unit was different, half of the first pair matched half of the second, in an unending chain. It was as if the first unit sent out a call, and the second answered it.

These blocks contain holograms of experiences, according to the laws of cause and effect, *explained Peddar.* In any one pattern line, the encoded cause-and-effect blocks resemble each other, because they revolve around the same issue. Effect follows cause until a lesson is learned, and the chain of experiences is complete.

Now, examine one of the blocks closer still.

I selected a single block and increased the magnification of my focus until it seemed as if I were looking at it through a microscope, rather than a magnifying glass. The block reminded me of a tiny television set. It was playing the scenes of an event that I remembered from my past!

I heightened the magnification of my vision again and observed that the scene was made up of thousands upon thousands of color-ray spectrums. These were similar to the myriad dots or pixils that form a picture on a television screen.

All causal bodies conform to the same basic structure, *said Peddar.* The number and location of Soul's original pattern lines is predetermined, just as there is a general symmetry of nose, eyes, mouth, and limbs in physical bodies.

The essential nature of the lessons each line teaches is also pre-set. However, each causal body has its own uniqueness, just as on Earth each physical body is different. This reflects the singular nature of Soul. The spectrums in each set of original 'causation blocks' in the causal body reflects the individual's needs. In this way, each Soul gains the exact experiences required for Its spiritual unfoldment. Everyone learns a particular lesson in a slightly different way.

I amplified the focus of my vision still more. "The color rays that form the scenes in the cause blocks are made of pure Light and Sound," I reported.

All is Light and Sound, *commented Peddar.* It builds upon itself to form a myriad of arenas for Souls' learning.

Now, move your attention away from the causal body and observe the mental body.

As the mental body came into focus, a new layer of lines appeared, extending four to six inches from the causal body. These denser, random lines were woven more tightly in some areas than others. As I traced a few of the threads, it seemed they carried an electrical current. Others remained dormant.

This is a sub-layer of the mental body, adjacent to the causal body, *Peddar explained.* Within it are all the reflected and stored patterns used to form the causal sheath. However, only lines currently being experienced by the individual carry an electrical charge. These lines can be seen by some clairvoyants when observing the physical aura.

I mused aloud, "So pattern lines alighted in the aura might relate to experiences currently manifesting in one's life."

Yes, that is basically correct.

Now let's return to the physical consciousness.

Instantly and effortlessly I returned to Earth—or so I thought. Actually, certain energy streams from the Astral Plane had carried over into my room. Part of me was fully aware of my physical surroundings, while another was still sitting with Peddar on the Astral Plane.

This feeling of duality was disorienting—yet somehow familiar. Perhaps I had become comfortable with splitting my attention over the many years of practicing inner world exploration.

As I sat quietly in both places, I felt like I was patting my head and rubbing my stomach at the same time. I laughed aloud at the thought.

You feel somewhat comfortable in this state? *Peddar asked.*

"Yes," *I proudly replied.*

Well then, here is a test for you. Try moving all your attention to the physical body—except for your astral hearing. Then you can try a physical technique while listening to me here.

I guess Peddar was offering me a lesson in humility. I struggled to follow his instructions, teetering back and forth between losing all connection with the next world and both seeing and hearing with my astral senses.

Peddar continued calmly with the exercise. Gradually I gave up my struggle, and decided to sit in the physical body while latching my attention on the sound of his voice.

Karmic Pattern Identification, Evaluation, and Management Technique

This technique increases your causal-body awareness by helping you evaluate and manage your pattern lines.

Find a comfortable position and keep your eyes closed. Take a few deep breaths.

Now say aloud or to yourself, 'One, Two, Three, Mahh-Nahh'. Repeat it several times.

The word 'One' represents the physical consciousness. 'Two' awakens the emotional awareness, and 'Three' taps the causal consciousness. By saying 'One, Two, Three' you are recognizing each of these lower bodies and moving through them with your attention.

Singing the word 'Mahh-Nahh' focuses Soul's attention on the Causal Plane. The 'Mmmm' sound awakens the mind, especially when it is combined with the 'Ahhh' sound. Because this word follows your singing of 'Three', the awareness is directed downward from the mind to the causal body. The sound, 'Nahh', reinforces this movement.

"I've always wondered about the apparent science of singing vowels in sacred patterns," I said. "It seems every one of them has a precise purpose. By changing just one syllable, the effect is often entirely different."

That's right. For example, if one sang 'Mahh-Nuu' instead of 'Mahh-Nahh', this technique wouldn't open the causal awareness. The vowel 'u' focuses attention beyond the mind. Here we want it to go just beneath the mind, to the causal body.

After you have sung 'One, Two, Three, Mahh-Nahh', as many times as you wish, the next step is to visualize what your pattern lines look like as a whole. To do this, imagine opening a box containing thousands of straws. Pour out the straws so they cover your entire causal body.

In the Physical World, the straws would land directly on your body or next to it. But remember, the laws of gravity don't necessarily apply in the Causal Plane. Most of the straws will be suspended in space, within a layer about a foot or two wide. This layer corresponds to your causal form. They will also land in specific places and orientations: each will correspond to a causation line.

Visualizing the straws will give you an idea of your pattern lines' locations and your causal body's overall state of health. Are the straws jumbled in one heap over a congested area? A 'traffic jam' of pattern lines may indicate a knot in this part of your causal body.

Do many of the straws point in one direction? If so, toward which organ are they pointing? This area may soon be involved in a process of karmic resolution. Pattern lines often point to an area before collecting over it. The energy they direct prompts an individual to learn certain lessons. If these lessons are learned, there might be no need for a jumble of pattern lines to collect directly over the area.

Are the straws scattered regularly over the body with relatively even spaces between them? This may indicate that one's resolution of karma is occurring in a steady, rhythmic way. There is no unnecessary burden on one area of the body.

If there are many tangled pattern lines, the straws will be intermixed and scattered unevenly throughout the body. Such patterns typically correspond to times of intense learning. Many different lessons and experiences have been activated at once in the individual's life.

Learning is inefficient in such situations. The idea is to gain knowledge and wisdom from your experiences. Evenly-spaced lines offer the best learning while preventing undue stress on the physical body.

Now, separate and untangle your pattern lines. Ideally, none of the straws should be touching each other. Lines that have fallen in big bunches should be carefully parted, one straw at a time. This part of the technique will give you greater command of your causal body. This in turn gives you more control over your life experiences.

I practiced the visualization as Peddar described it. Selecting a small bunch of tangled lines behind my shoulder blade, I carefully moved a line on top of the tangle to one side. The surface lines were easily separated, but those closer to the center of the tangle seemed stuck. I was unable to lift them and asked Peddar for help.

They are caught in an accumulation of unnecessary energies, *he explained.* These energies are the result of the entanglement of karmic pattern lines. Sometimes resolving a single karmic situation can release a pattern line that keeps many other stuck.

I decided to apply a Therapeutic Diamond over the area as soon as our meeting was over. This would clear the accumulation, thus loosening the pattern lines and facilitating their resolution. Then I wondered if there was a technique for untangling pattern lines that would expedite the process, and

141

that could be used by those who didn't necessarily have access to Diamond Therapy. I asked Peddar if he knew.

Pattern Awareness Technique for Resolving Old Habits and Karmic Influences.

Yes, *Peddar answered.* The technique I have in mind identifies and untangles pattern lines associated with a known condition. However, one cannot force a stuck pattern line free without conscious awareness of the lesson it is designed to teach. Simple awareness of a pattern's nature is often enough to accelerate its resolution. The pattern line slips free of the entanglement. Though it may still require resolution, its negative influence on the condition should diminish.

Start once again by singing 'One, Two, Three, Mahh-Nahh'. Imagine yourself pouring a box of straws over your causal body.

But before you look at the straws, think of the condition you want to change. Say, 'Will the pattern associated with (name the condition) please light up'.

Now, look at the pattern lines outlined by the straws. A single line or a group of several will catch your attention in some way. If a group of lines light up, separate them as you did in the previous exercise. Find one that is stuck.

Focus on this line. Get so close that the cause and response blocks in the line look like big television sets lined up in a row, just like in a store display room.

Notice the television sets are turned on at one end of the line. They are not displaying any pictures, only lighted blue screens. These correspond to cause-and-response blocks of the past. Next to them are two or three televisions with images on their screens. These feature recent or current experiences. Next to them, and extending to the opposite end

142

of the pattern line, are turned-off sets. These correspond to cause-and-response blocks yet to be manifested.

Now, look at the screens that are reflecting active images. One of the televisions are showing the most recent causes in this pattern. These are events that made you react to this pattern. The TV next to it is featuring images of your latest responses to this karmic maze.

If the third television is active, it will be showing events still forming in your life. They may not have manifested yet, but will soon cause you to respond in some way. When they do, the next television set in the line will turn on and record your responses. At the same time, the previous pair of television sets will lose their pictures and become lighted blue screens.

If you are unable to see the scenes on a television, find its controls and turn the knobs. This will adjust the picture. You might also turn up the volume, so you can hear the sounds of the experience as well.

To see what lessons might be available on these television sets, refer to the program guide resting atop the first blue-screened TV. Open it and read whatever catches your eye. It will outline the lessons you need to learn.

If you are not able to read the program guide, try to *simply know* its contents. Or just pretend you're reading it, knowing that at some level you will soon become conscious of the core lessons involved in this pattern-line.

When you become more adept at this visualization, you can spend more time watching these TVs to preview and smooth your spiritual unfoldment.

If you like, you can also go back and turn on the blue-screened sets that feature situations in the far past. Again, adjust the dials until you can see the pictures. They may reveal situations in past lives. When you are finished, return the dials to where they were and push the power button off, so the screens again show blue.

143

There are two rules you must observe in this exercise. First, don't try to move the television sets. Second, do not unplug the sets. If you try either, you will receive an electrical shock. Though you might not feel immediate physical pain, the shock's effects will certainly manifest in your life.

Peddar smiled and concluded the exercise. To return to physical consciousness, sing the following syllables in this order: 'Mahh-Nahh, Three, Two, One'.

When returning from such a detailed and absorbing exercise, it often helps to say aloud, or to yourself, 'Here I am!' or 'Welcome back to the Physical World!' Do this as you open your eyes, to reaffirm your presence in the Physical Plane. It will help to ensure all your consciousness is focused in the earthly world.

I followed Peddar's instructions. As I opened my eyes, I felt my home welcoming a whole, undivided 'me' back into its arms. "Here I am!" I said aloud. This helped re-center my hearing back in the physical body.

Sitting on the couch, I mused that it was probably not healthy to keep the conscious attention divided among the lower bodies for long. Dual consciousness made me feel 'spaced-out', tired, and unfocused.

Peddar's voice startled me as he chimed in. The consciousness you have been practicing is different, of course, from holding one's awareness on Soul. Soul awareness is life-giving, it aligns all your lower bodies for maximum well-being.

Peddar must have been listening to my thoughts. "Yes, thank you," I replied, surprised that he still maintained our connection. I strongly felt Peddar's presence but I couldn't see him.

Ginny, *he continued,* the technique isn't over yet.

I quickly tuned my hearing back into the Astral plane. I was getting plenty of practice in flexibility today!

144

Whether or not you were able to read the program guide, *Peddar continued,* go to your bookshelf and find a book that inspires your spirituality. Choose one you feel particularly drawn to.

Open it at random and read a paragraph or two. The sentences you read will tell you more about the karmic lesson you need to tackle first in your outer life.

For example, if the paragraphs speak of self-discipline, you can put more attention on this quality in all aspects of your day. The awareness gained from this book technique and the TV visualization—combined with diligent work—can help resolve old patterns.

Tomorrow we will begin a discussion of the astral or emotional body. I will leave you to do your homework which is practicing these exercises.

Thank you for choosing to meet with me tonight.

"Thank you for everything," I replied.

Chapter 13

The Emotional/Astral Body

I arrived earlier than usual on the Astral Plane. I wanted to study this World and my emotional body for a while before Peddar began his discourse.

What were some of the differences between here and Earth? Surveying my surroundings, I noted the grass at my feet seemed typical of any healthy lawn. The breeze swept clean, fresh air into my lungs—just as one would expect in such a natural setting.

The shimmering ocean to the south reminded me of several seas in the Physical World. But watching it from these unusually tall cliffs reminded me of looking out at the tiny waves from an airplane.

The city to the west was an entirely different matter. Its transparent dome-and-spire architecture, smog-free skies, and golden aura certainly differed from anything on Earth.

The mountains behind it would dwarf the Himalayas, I whispered to myself. I could not conceive of their distance or altitude. The snow-capped shapes reminded me of the Rocky Mountains, which I had often admired from afar.

Across the hilly landscape to the east lay Askleposis, a major cultural learning center of this Plane. Its classical Grecian buildings included towering classrooms, libraries, offices, a spiritual temple, and a healing center. The brilliant white masonry was encircled by elaborate gardens for students to enjoy. The grassy green field I stood in swept around the commons and rolled on for miles.

I turned my attention to my astral body. At first, it felt no different than my physical sheath. But on closer examination, I realized how light and free I felt. Stiffness and aches seemed an impossibility here, as did the discomforts of hunger, tiredness, heat, or cold.

Amazement swept through me as I examined the astral form. During the many sojourns in this body, I had never studied it closely. Although it resembled my physical body, it was made up of millions of tiny light particles. Each atom seemed to sparkle as it sped in tiny circles.

Peddar caught me examining how the light particles responded when I moved my fingers.

The astral body is as natural and normal to the individual in the Astral World, *he said,* as the physical body is to someone on Earth. The only reason you find the astral flesh so fascinating is because you are noticing the differences between it and your physical skin.

I looked up at Peddar and saw that his body sparkled in the same way mine did, though with a much greater intensity. "I remember noticing this glittering effect the first few times I traveled in the Astral World," I replied, "but I haven't thought about it since."

That's because it has become natural and ordinary. Tell me, have you ever eaten here?

I had to think for a few moments before the question even made sense. "No," I replied.

That's because the astral sheath is fueled differently from the physical body. Many people here have no need of food. They take in sustenance as they breathe.

As you know, the physical body digests and metabolizes food, then organizes the molecules of nourishment and distributes them to various parts of the body. Similarly, the astral body digests breath-energy or prana. It breaks it down and then organizes and distributes the metabolized energy to various areas of itself.

The prana or breath-energy is produced by the Sound current as it flows into the Astral Plane. It stimulates the positive, negative, and neutral forces within the astral body. These interact with the forces of the astral universe to produce a special kind of energy. The astral sheath obtains nourishment from this energy just as the physical body does from food.

People here rarely eat. Of course, there are exceptions for Souls in the lower zones, who may still desire the sensation. Some Souls are still simulating life in the Physical Plane, with its lessons of detachment regarding emotional cravings for food.

The causal body, on the other hand, takes in nourishment even more directly. Its skin is semi-permeable, allowing this sheath to absorb energy directly from its environment. However, this works only to the degree that the causal body is healthy. At times it may require certain healing foods or preparations for nourishment and clearing.

Peddar motioned me over to the flat rocks and we sat down. Now let's consider the relationship between the astral and physical bodies, *he said.*

The Astral World is often referred to as the Emotional Plane, and the astral body as the emotional body. The astral body breaths in nourishing energies very naturally, but it has some difficulty returning them to the astral atmosphere. Instead, the astral body channels its outflow through the physical body. This outflow is experienced as emotions.

Both inflow and outflow of energies are required for maximum health. By expressing emotions through the physical body, the astral body maintains an energy equilibrium. Its outflowing energy returns to the atmosphere, albeit the physical one.

Those whose lowest sheath is the astral body, do not have a physical body through which to funnel this outflow. These individuals are predisposed to 'overeating' in the emotional sheath, because energy is so abundant. Without a lower body, the astral form is susceptible to poor circulation. Therefore, from one point of view, it can be unhealthy to remain in the Astral World without a physical existence.

This tendency for astral energy build-up acts as a cosmic safety mechanism. It ensures Soul will not linger here indefinitely without manifesting the physical body necessary for Its complete unfoldment.

Although millions of beings enjoy the astral form alone, there is an incompleteness to their lives. Soul eventually takes on a physical sheath, unless, of course, It is on the return trip back to the Golden Kingdom. Such experienced Souls are less susceptible to astral-energy build-up as they travel homeward on an upward spiritual spiral.

As in all the planes of existence, there are specially-trained Souls here whose duty it is to help others home. They have unfolded their consciousness beyond the lower worlds and are able to dwell in the Golden Kingdom or beyond. But they choose to serve out their spiritual assignments in the Astral World.

Their astral bodies are still prone to energy accumulations. But they stay in balance by directing the astral body with the same detachment a puppet master uses in operating a puppet. Eventually, all Souls learn this detachment, as well as how to purge the astral body of excess emotion.

The valves of outflow used to release astral energies correspond to the seven chakra centers. When Soul has a physical body, they are channels through which emotions are expressed.

An individual must occupy a causal, astral, and physical body in order for the chakras to be fully functional. They are of little use without a physical body. Their seeds or matrixes exist in the causal body, their roots are present in the astral body, and their energies manifest in the physical body.

So, the seeds of the chakra centers are born in the Causal Plane, grow in the astral body, and bloom in the physical sheath. The mental and subconscious bodies only contain reflections of the chakras.

The causal body influences the astral body with its many patterns. Especially significant are those patterns which determine how the astral body accepts and organizes energy, and which emotions get stored and which get expressed.

I interjected, "In one of my healing classes at Askleposis, I learned that the causal body determines the essential nature of an illness. The astral body influences where it will occur, and the physical body determines how it will manifest."

Yes. Physical illness occurs where excesses collect in the astral sheath. For example, if energies build up over the knee, the individual will eventually have a health problem there.

The chakras must be kept clear to express astral energies, or there could be a harmful backwash. When emotions cannot enter the physical body, they flow back on the astral sheath. This back-tide of energy can collide with the normal flow of expression, creating a disharmonious rift in the body-area where it occurs.

This rift compounds itself and prevents the life force from flowing freely. The health of the physical body is eventually affected.

"What about the mental body," I asked. "How does it influence the emotions?"

There are many misconceptions about the mind and emotions. A person cannot express emotion without thought. It's impossible. Think about it. Can you feel insecure, for example, without the thought of insecurity? And when you spark an emotion in someone else, it is always due to a mental attitude or intention.

Let's reverse the viewpoint. If someone raises an emotional response in you, what happens? You observe the person's actions, and your mind reflects their emotions and thoughts. It also reflects your own thoughts about the matter. The images recorded in your mind's photographic plate help you decide how you will react, and what emotions you will express.

The physical body gives the mental body direct feedback about a stimuli through a connection in the physical brain. This connection is at the crown chakra, on the top of the head. The mind is also directly linked with the pituitary and pineal glands, which are often associated with the chakra centers.

The final decision about how you will react is shaped by the many dials of the mind—some of which we looked at in the discourse about the mental body. The mind then transmits its decision to the causal, astral, and physical bodies.

Thoughts travel from the mind to the lower bodies along intricate systems of inter-body connections. Of course, the lower bodies exist as a continuum and there really are no divisions among sheaths. But these communication paths, called life systems, keep the bodies' vibratory rate continuum organized. They interconnect all the sheaths and arrange their energies according to function. You will learn more about these life systems in a later discourse.*

"In other words," I said, *"thoughts are transmitted downward from the mental body through the life systems. They do not ride the current of Light and Sound as it flows into the lower bodies?"*

Life systems *are* vehicles for Light and Sound, in the form of color rays, as they move through the lower bodies in order to sustain them, *Peddar explained.* Thoughts ride this spiritual current as it moves through the lower bodies.

*See Chapter 20.

152

"Now I understand," I replied.

When thoughts leave the mind, *Peddar continued,* they are first presented to the causal body, where patterns are housed. The causal body modifies them according to whichever pattern lines are currently activated. This plays a large role in defining one's reaction and its intensity.

For example, if a person is currently in a pattern in which he withdraws, overeats, or reacts with anger, that pattern shapes the mind's decision as to which emotions will finally be expressed.

This information then passes to the astral body. There it is stored, perhaps only momentarily, until nourishing Astral Plane energies flow in to replace them. The information released from the astral fabric pours into a chakra center. The emotional reaction is then expressed physically, where an action takes place.

Emotions can be expressed through any chakra. Anger and other strong negative emotions are usually expressed through the lower base or sacral chakras. Fear, doubt, and worry activate the stomach chakra. Love, kindness, and happiness flow from the heart chakra. Compassion, sincerity, and the desire to serve others is often expressed through the throat chakra.

The emotions expressed through the top two chakras, the brow and crown, are foreign to many people these days. These emotions are the lower bodies' understanding of divine love and joy. Although divine love and joy can be considered emotions, they are closer to spiritual expressions than emotional outpourings.

"I have often wondered why I felt such love and joy when traveling the planes above the astral," I said.

Divine love and joy are qualities naturally expressed by Soul in the Golden Kingdom, *Peddar confirmed.* They are experienced directly in the Worlds of God, whether one has a physical body awaiting his return or not. The physical body cannot feel them in their pure form, but it can resonate with stepped-down versions of these refined qualities.

Divine expressions flow into the body through the crown and brow chakras. Here they are translated into feelings the physical consciousness can respond to. The more open these chakra centers are, the greater their receptivity. Open chakras make it easier is to keep one's attention on the Golden Kingdom and experience its gifts.

Other emotions move from the astral circulatory system, of which the chakras are components, to the circulatory system of the physical body. There they actually alter the blood chemistry.

This causes your physical body to act out or express a feeling. The actions then return your blood chemistry to normal. If you suppress these actions, the blood still releases the chemicals which the emotion produced. Often these chemicals collect in the weakest or most congested area of the body. If actions are continually suppressed, the chemicals' effect on these areas can be devastating. The disharmony created is a direct effect of mismanaged emotions. It also brings the issue to one's conscious attention and urges the individual to master the lesson involved.

This is one way Divine Spirit highlights the issues you need to master for growth and awareness. Circumstances that provoke the emotion will continue, until you learn the lesson and move past it.

For example, let's say a woman feels hurt by her husband's lack of positive emotional expression. If she suppresses her tears, or refuses to talk to her husband about her needs and feelings, the chemicals in her blood will collect somewhere in the body, such as the female reproductive organs. These organs will eventually display any of a variety of conditions.

Her husband in turn might be suppressing the love he has for his wife by never expressing his feelings. He may one day discover a problem in his heart, as a result of damming up his heart-flow.

People often dam up their feelings before they reach the physical body. In this case, emotions are suppressed in the emotional body and stored there. They do not enter the chakra centers or the physical body, nor do they affect the blood chemistry. However, they build up in certain areas in the astral body, and eventually the corresponding areas in the physical body can become stressed and burdened.

Non-expression of feelings and suppression of emotions are both common. Often it is the mind that aborts expression. The physical body has little say in the matter. To it, emotions are simply energies that must be expressed, and the process of the expression is mechanical.

When the mind as well as all other aspects of the individual want expression but none occurs, it's usually due to a 'traffic jam' of energies somewhere in the lower bodies. This blockage could be anywhere and consist of mental, causal, and/or astral energies.

Often, mental instructions regarding appropriate emotions to express are caught in the obstruction. Events that stimulate emotion compound the jam. The more entangled the energies become, the more blocked the Light and Sound is from nourishing the physical body. Eventually, physical disease might manifest in the area corresponding to the inner blockage.

Now let's add an awakened Soul to the picture. You'll find the scenario changes. Soul can bypass the mind as well as the causal and astral bodies. It can also bypass any blockages that may be present in these bodies, and direct the astral and physical bodies to express emotions.

Most of the familiar emotions are major ones: love, happiness, hate, greed, and jealousy. There seem to be more negative emotions than positive ones, but that is only because they generally attract more attention.

There is something else I want to make clear. Emotions are fueled by a narrow range of Astral-Plane frequencies. Within this range are numerous vibratory rates. They span the astral realm like a tall column. Each emotion has a different vibratory rate, depending on where on this column it originates. The emotion of human love is of a higher vibratory rate than jealousy, because it springs from a higher location of the Emotional World. The frequency at which an emotion originates determines its quality. For example there can be many kinds of happiness or jealousy: strong, weak, burning, short-lived, intense, or drawn-out.

The chakra centers not only receive emotional energies from the astral body, they also give feedback from the physical body. This feedback usually does not collide with emotional energies flowing in the other direction. It extends past the astral body to the causal body. This is how the causal body stores information, which it then passes on to the mental body.

"Is this return flow of feedback different from that initiated at the Second Spiritual Achievement?" I asked.

Yes. You see, even if an individual has not yet attained the First or Second Spiritual Achievements, information moves back and forth between the bodies through the life systems. Chakra centers are important life-system components. This feedback is, of course, of a different quality than that available after a spiritual achievement is attained. It is feedback essential to the survival of the lower bodies.

The return flow initiated during a spiritual achievement allows a new kind of feedback to circulate among the bodies. This feedback opens the consciousness and awakens the individual to his inner beingness, to the action of cause and effect in his life, and to the guidance of Spirit. It also allows for a more direct connection among the bodies and with the Golden Kingdom.

A Chakra Center Clearing Technique

Now, I would like to share two techniques to help you take control of the emotional body. The first is a chakra center 'housecleaning'.

Astral energies should flow continually through each of the chakra centers. If any centers are closed, they will simply flow through another, perhaps overburdening it. This exercise will help open and redistribute the load on your chakras.

After awhile, you'll be able to perform this exercise any time during the day. But it's best to start out with complete concentration, by either sitting or lying down.

So, as a suggestion, *offered Peddar,* why don't you lie down on the grass and practice this exercise while I explain it. You can perform this technique equally well in the physical or astral bodies.

When I had made myself comfortable, he continued.

We are going to take deep breaths while diverting the inhaled prana to various areas of the body. First, imagine you are taking in breath in each chakra center—almost as if your lungs were located there. We'll take a minimum of two breaths into each chakra, and as many as five or six breaths in ones that seem reluctant to expand or contract with the air.

Begin by pretending your lungs are at the top of your head. Take two deep breaths into your crown chakra. Feel your head expand with the inhale and contract with the exhale. The key here is to 'feel'. You must feel—or imagine that you feel—your head expanding and contracting.

Next, pretend that your lungs are behind your forehead and take two deep breaths into your brow chakra.

Now, your lungs are inside your neck. If this image makes you feel like coughing, you probably have an energy blockage in your throat chakra. Inhale and exhale at least twice.

157

Continue by breathing into your chest, where, of course, your lungs actually are. First move your shoulders forward slightly and as you inhale, expand the back of your rib cage. Exhale. Return your shoulders to their normal position. Inhale while expanding the front of your rib cage and moving your shoulders slightly back. Exhale. Repeat the inhale into the back of your chest and then the front, moving the shoulders accordingly. You may want to inhale a few extra times here. The heart chakra can use the extra attention.

Next, breathe twice into your stomach chakra, as if your stomach were your lungs. Try not to move your chest as you do this.

Now, breathe twice into your lower abdomen between your belly button and pubic bone. Placing your hand over the area may help focus your breath there. Two breaths are sufficient for this area, which includes the sacral chakra.

Finally, direct your inhales toward the lowest tip of your spine. Here you are breathing into your base chakra. Feel your pelvis expand and contract.

Congratulations, you're done! Don't be surprised if this exercise increases your energy. Most people find it a vitalizing and exhilarating experience. However, the increased flow doesn't necessarily mean you will feel more emotion.

Many astral outpourings are too subtle to result in dramatic feelings. They bring quieter sensations of well-being, strength, contentment, and vitality.

Locating and Releasing Emotional Body Blockages

A second exercise will locate emotional 'traffic jams'. These are the areas of the emotional body that have the greatest collections of excess energy. You can then release and disperse these congestions. This technique will also stimulate circulation between your astral and physical bodies.

Begin by breathing into your chakra centers as described in the previous exercise.

Now, breath into your right leg. Pretend it is a long, thin lung. With the inhale, feel your breath reach down to your toes. As you exhale, feel a subtle tingly sensation. This is due to increased energies nourishing the area.

Keep breathing until you feel this tingly sensation throughout your leg. If you still don't feel anything after a minute or so, proceed to the left leg. It may take a few practice sessions before you are able to sense more energy in the various parts of your body.

Repeat the process with the right and left arms. We work on extremities first, because it's easier to isolate the tingling feeling in them.

Now, breathe into your back. If you wish, you can do just the upper part first, and then the lower part. Next, breathe into your abdomen, chest, shoulders and neck, then the back of your head and your face. Each of these areas can also be divided into right and left halves and treated separately.

Take note of which areas of your body resist the tingly sensation. They are the ones that harbor blockages.

I stopped my breathing for a moment and asked, "What if one doesn't feel the sensation anywhere in the body?"

Try relying on your knowingness. Perhaps the tingling sensation will not be felt in the various parts of the body but within the heart, as a feeling of openness.

When you are finished, go back to the areas where you felt blockages. There are several things you can do to help open these zones. Imagine the congestion as a pile of jumbled toothpicks. Straighten them out so they all lie in one direction, or move them so that they are not as concentrated.

This will encourage the needle-like fibers in the astral body to become less tangled. We will discuss these astral body fibers tomorrow.

159

Or give the area love. When you have positive input reflecting on the photographic plates of your mind, it rearranges the lower bodies.

Another method is to imagine a stream of water flowing through the area. Let it clear out all the obstructions in its path. Or, flood it with the seven healing colors of the rainbow, one color at a time.

You could also use a Therapeutic Diamond to help open these areas as well.

I lost all sense of time while I practiced this exercise. I was completely absorbed in tending to the areas that resisted my breath. The sensation was deeply relaxing even for my physical body. As it drifted off to sleep I heard Peddar whisper softly, Good night. May the blessings be!

Chapter 14

Another Look at the Astral Body

I love gardens, and those surrounding Askleposis are my favorites. When I walk in the grounds, I soak in the gardeners' heartfelt enthusiasm for their work, and the plants' selfless joy for living. The flower beds are enveloped by warm blankets of love.

The artistic plantings follow intricate geometrical designs and inter-twining, free-form shapes. Some beds sport brilliant flowers several feet in diameter. Others produce grapefruit-size clusters of tiny flowerettes. They radiate clean, distinct fragrances and rich, vibrant colors that delight and uplift the senses.

On this particular day, I was joined by an unmistakable presence as I ambled down a cobblestone path. Within moments Peddar materialized next to me.

We exchanged greetings and discussed my progress with the astral body exercises. Then we walked down to a small clearing encircled by tropical plants and large, moss covered rocks. We were alone but for the colorful songbirds flitting from leaf to leaf.

We reclined on finely-carved gray marble benches in the center of the clearing. I would like to devote today's discussion to the astral body's needle-like fibers, which I mentioned in our last meeting, *Peddar began.*

We will explore what they are, their function, and the impact they can have on one's health.

To understand these fibers, I must first remind you that every atom, cell, and organ in the physical body has a manifested counterpart in the astral and causal bodies. The mental and subconscious bodies, on the other hand, do not reflect each body component because they are at such a high vibratory level. However, the mental and subconscious bodies do echo some components of the lower three sheaths.

The astral fibers, which are also called flow needles, are counterpart to the physical strands of DNA—the body's genetic material, as well as the causal body's pattern lines. Two main differences between flow needles and DNA are their function and shape. Astral fibers do much more than relay genetic information. Furthermore, they are straight, like needles.

In the astral body, spiritual energy travels both toward the physical body and away from it. The straight astral fibers supports these flows. In the physical realm, however, the energy makes a crucial U-turn to flow back into the subtle worlds. The spiral-like curve in physical DNA facilitates this return.

To understand what astral fibers do, may I also remind you that man's five lower bodies are linked in a smooth vibratory continuum. When you look at your hand, for example, you are viewing just a fraction of its continuum. The physical eyes perceive only a section of Physical Plane vibrations which don't even include all the physical vibratory rates that exist in your hand!

Similarly, scientific instruments that measure atoms perceive only a narrow band of vibrations—usually the ones they were designed to recognize! They may measure an atom at a single vibratory rate, when it actually has thousands. Hence, earthly instruments offer an extremely limited view of reality.

Energy circulates continuously from the subconscious to the physical body. Astral fibers help direct this flow among the causal, astral, and physical bodies. If the circulation is

diminished, some areas will not receive nourishment. Nor will they be relieved of excess energies through a healthy outflow.

If the astral fibers corresponding to a knee, for example, are tangled, the flow of Light and Sound is restricted there. The joint is soon under-nourished by higher, healing vibrations or burdened by the accumulation of excess energies it is unable to pass off. The result is a weakened, injury-prone joint.

The spectrum of light reaching the knee may be deficient in a particular color ray, such as red. The body may try to borrow red rays from other stronger parts of itself, or where there is an excess of this color. Or it may respond with an injury or disease that limits the knee's function. The limited mobility reduces the need for more red rays.

Let's say the knee borrows red ray from a nearby muscle. The ray will not be as in tune with the knee. Still, the knee will be able to use this red ray, and in the short term, maintain relatively normal function.

If an astral fiber blockage is released in this knee, the area may then realize its excess of borrowed red rays. These red rays were drawn from other areas of the body, to try to shore up the weakness caused by the blockage. Before the joint can function at a greater plateau of health and receive its own red rays, it must return the borrowed rays to the muscles that loaned them. The once-helpful borrowed rays which provided makeshift nourishment for the knee must be removed.

Consider that this example accounts for only one color ray! Tangled astral fibers may cause a confusion of color rays to be redistributed to an injured area. Borrowed rays are more in tune with the part of the body they originally came from. So the target area's regulatory mechanisms may not even recognize their presence. Hence the knee may continue to indiscriminately call color rays to itself. These color rays

can jam the energy passageways over the afflicted spot. As a result, borrowed spectrums accumulate.

Such accumulations typically cause physical repercussions. Fluids can pool in the area causing it to swell. Fat and/or minerals deposits can compact the area. Eventually, the problem may affect the DNA, causing abnormal cell growth and tumors.

"Aren't such symptoms directly related to causal pattern lines?" I asked.

Yes, *Peddar replied.* Astral fibers correspond to, but are not exact replicas of these lines. The causal body contains thousands of pattern lines, but only certain ones are energized. These highlighted lines are associated with lessons currently being experienced by an individual. All other patterns remain dormant. Some are already resolved and others are yet to be experienced. In the astral body, all the fibers are ideally active. Specific areas do not become highlighted or excessively charged.

Each causal pattern line represents a different set of experiences and lessons. But astral fibers are all basically the same. Still, there is an affinity between the two. A highlighted pattern line can entangle the astral fibers and weaken parts of the physical body.

In conditions that affect the entire physical body, such as obesity, all the astral fibers are not necessarily tangled together. If a pattern line dictates that a person must experience certain lessons by being overweight, it might direct the astral fibers to restrict the cells' outflow. The cells then become glutted, or the body's metabolism decreases. If the fibers are directed to restrict inflow, the individual may develop an uncontrollable desire for food. There are many reasons why a person may be overweight. But each is directed by the orientation of the astral fibers.

Behind the scenes, the causal body determines which condition manifests. The causal pattern lines orient the

astral fibers, which direct emotional energies toward the physical body or block energy from leaving it.

Any disease may be altered if one can gain control over these astral fibers. However, if I were to give you an exercise to control these fibers, it wouldn't do much good. The causal body would continue to redirect them into their former orientations.

Complete physical healing requires more than just physical or emotional treatments. One must also heal the causal body so its pattern lines can be resolved. To accomplish this, the individual must become consciously aware of the lessons related to a causal pattern line, and take steps to master it. Otherwise, there will be no permanent change in the patterns.

At the same time, the mind must be flexible enough to adopt new attitudes and renew its perceptions of the lower bodies. Permanent healing calls for many adjustments to the mental dials. Outdated reflections must be erased and replaced by new pictures and settings which sustain health.

If physical, emotional, and causal changes are initiated but the mind is still operating from old programs, the healing will not last. Even if the lesson is learned, the experience could repeat until the mind lets go of its old ruts.

"Why wouldn't the new, healthier state be reflected in the mind?" I asked.

The mind runs like a machine. It does what it's programmed to do. Its program won't necessarily change based on new input from the lower bodies. Changes must be made within the mental body itself. This can only be effectively accomplished from a state beyond the mind: the subconscious or Soul points of view.

The subconscious body also affects physical health, especially if it is stuffed with lessons the individual is avoiding. Often a subconscious body housecleaning is required for healing.

The Astral Fiber Flexibility Technique

Today's exercise is called the Astral Fiber Flexibility Technique. It rearranges and helps you control your astral fibers, but its greatest effects are on the physical body. It will help your physical body redistribute its color rays, instead of having to cope with deficiencies and excesses through affliction or disease. At the same time, it will help areas to return no-longer-needed, borrowed color rays to their lenders.

Begin by lying down on your back. Close your eyes, and make yourself comfortable. Imagine that the area six to eighteen inches away from your physical body contains thousands of astral fibers. These fibers are flexible; they can change their positions much like iron filings in the presence of a magnet.

Now, imagine just such a magnet over your head. See the astral fibers as they begin to point toward the magnet. Gently coax any fibers that seem to resist their new orientation. If a few seem particularly stuck, let them be; concentrate on those that are flexible.

Slowly move the magnet down one side of your body. Imagine the fibers turning to point toward the magnet as it travels toward your feet.

Then see the imaginary magnet beneath your feet. Imagine all of the astral fibers now pointing downward.

Slowly move the magnet up the other side of your body toward your head. Again, imagine the fibers following the magnet.

Continue circling your body two to five more times with the magnet. Visualize your astral fibers moving with it.

Once they have gained some flexibility, swiftly alternate the position of the imaginary magnet from above your head to beneath your feet. Practice switching the fibers back and forth as fast as you can.

As with any exercise, one should begin slowly, with short sessions of about two minutes at first. Gradually work up to about ten minutes.

As you remove the imaginary magnet, you may notice fibers that were previously stuck now moving freely. This exercise helps to loosen their tangles. If practiced only five or ten minutes, energy tangles will be released at a rate the body can handle.

I tried the technique and commented "My astral flexibility and agility do seem to have increased."

All of your astral fibers have received a good workout, *replied Peddar.* As I mentioned, tangled fibers are loosened, and healthy fibers become more responsive. This helps them relay energies back and forth between the causal, astral, and physical bodies. In addition, the exercise helps Soul to become more aware of its astral body.

When Soul is aware of Its lower bodies, one has control of his or her entire being. Subtle body awareness is an important step to self-mastery.

This is one of the reasons why I feel the information you are learning in this discourse series is important. A 'map' of the lower worlds, along with descriptions of the lower bodies, can help Soul avoid lifetimes of trial and error.

Meet me here again tomorrow night for the last discussion you and I will have about the lower bodies.

May the blessings be, *Peddar said and stood up.*

I rose also and thanked him. I wanted to linger in the gardens a bit longer. I strolled to the other side of the clearing, toward the sound of rushing water. There I found a small, ten foot waterfall hidden behind a cluster of large leaves.

I climbed over the rocks and stood inches from the falls. Peddar joined me and together we watched the cascade of bubbles and water droplets as the stream tumbled down the rocks.

Now that my astral body was more open and free, the air seemed fresher. The beauty and the life of the water was exhilarating. The sound of HU whispered softly in my ears, gradually turning into a resounding HUM.

I could have stayed there for hours.

Come, it is time to go, *Peddar reminded me after a few minutes.*

I smiled and nodded in agreement. It had been a long day and my physical body needed rest. The astral reality melted away, but the experience of the sparkling waterfall lingered as I returned to physical consciousness. I was still aglow with the splendor of the scene as I snuggled into bed.

Chapter 15

Communicating Directly With Your Inner Bodies

*O*nce again, *I met Peddar on the grassy field near the cliff's edge. He wanted to walk, so we set out on a path leading toward Askleposis.*

Today, I wish to speak of Soul's relationship to Its lower bodies, *Peddar announced as we walked.*

The bodies of an unawakened Soul follow their own mechanical workings and run as any machine does. In fact, they often operate independently, instead of cooperating with each other or following Soul's direction.

As Soul awakens, It gradually takes control of Its lower bodies. At first, one of the lower bodies might open itself to Soul's direction for just a few fleeting moments.

Eventually, each of the other bodies also gains this awareness. Soon the duration of these periods increases, until all the lower bodies operate under Soul's direction at the same time. This is truly a blessed moment in one's spiritual life.

When Soul consciously places Its attention on one of the lower sheaths, a direct connection or circuit opens between It and the Golden Kingdom. I call this the 'Soul-Initiated Circuit'. This circuit is independent of and different from those awakened during spiritual achievements.

The Soul-Initiated Circuit bypasses all other bodies to allow Soul to directly influence a particular body. When Soul takes control of the physical body in this way, It bypasses the astral, causal, mental, and subconscious sheaths.

Such circuits are temporary. They only manifest during those moments when the particular lower body is awakened. This connection raises the vibratory rate of the sheath. When it can no longer adjust to the heightened vibratory rate, the circuit dissolves. The connection with Soul closes and the sheath is given time to adjust to the energy it has received. After these adjustments, the body is again ready to connect with Soul—perhaps for a longer period of time.

Spiritual exercises, such as those you have learned during our meetings, build the sheaths' strength and flexibility. These help one adjust to higher vibratory rates and maintain a circuit with Soul longer. If a sheath is weak or inflexible, it will not be able to respond as Soul wishes it to.

When a lower body does not respond to Soul's commands, the circuit shuts off. The individual again forgets he is Soul, and the mind reasserts itself. But, this isn't necessarily bad—it's simply a safety mechanism.

For example, if the astral body was not strong enough to connect with Soul but the Soul-Initiated Circuit was enforced, the current passing through the astral sheath could singe its atoms. Metaphorically speaking, the astral body's wires would be fried!

Certain aspects of the astral body would remain disabled until the vibratory rate returned to normal. Then, the emotional body would have to heal from the intensity of the Light and Sound.

"What happens when the vibratory rate rises in a more gradual, balanced way?" I asked.

There are various effects, depending on the sheath.

In the subconscious body, 'boxes' in which previously-avoided lessons and issues are stored become unlocked.

In the mental body, negative reflections fade or are erased. Dial settings for mental functions move closer toward the midpoint, or balance.

In the causal body, energy accumulations which block or entangle pattern lines are released. The lines may even change so certain lessons become clear. Lessons that have already been learned but whose pattern lines continue to influence the individual are finally resolved.

The fibers in the astral body become flexible and less tangled. They reflect changes in the causal patterns and the true desires of Soul for its lower sheaths.

We came to a fork in the path, and followed the more-traveled right-hand branch. Several hundred meters ahead shone the white buildings of Askleposis.

Throngs of people joined us on the broad footpath, travelling to or from the cultural center. As we walked, I noticed several passersby cradled books in their arms. I assumed they were either attending the university or had visited one of the libraries.

Others displayed a particular sparkle in their eyes, suggesting they had just come from a class or lecture by one of the many spiritual masters at Askleposis. Still other faces held an expression of peace and fulfillment, as if their stay had met some deep spiritual, medical, or emotional need.

Peddar resumed his discourse. It is easier to establish the Soul-Initiated Circuit in the inner bodies, as their vibratory rates are closer to that of Soul. Following this logic, the circuit between Soul and physical consciousness is the most difficult to achieve.

It is interesting to note that raising the rate of one lower body does not disconnect it from the others. On the contrary, it uplifts all in unison.

For example, when one performs the Astral Fiber Flexibility Technique, the astral vibrations are heightened. Soul's conscious attention is on the emotional body, manifesting a circuit between the two. As a result, all the bodies benefit from the energy exchange.

Unfortunately, the physical body doesn't feel this lift as easily as the other subtle bodies. Circulation between the astral and physical bodies is not as open as it is among the other inner bodies. This is one of the fundamental differences that sets the lowest two bodies apart.

Although establishing a circuit between Soul and the physical body is most difficult, it is essential. It helps the physical consciousness develop the strength and stamina to pass the tests of life and enter Sat Nam's realm.

Only then can Soul begin the second leg of It's divine journey, into the heart of God Itself. There It learns of Its spiritual mission as a co-worker with Its creator.

"Does a Soul-Initiated Circuit established in any one body affect that entire sheath equally well?" I asked.

One might think it would, since the lower bodies are a continuum of vibratory rates, but it doesn't. The Circuit only benefits that area of the continuum occupied by an individual's consciousness. Let me explain.

If the vibratory rates that comprise the physical body were placed on a scale of one to one hundred, the average unenlightened individual would be operating in a low band, ranging from, say, ten through thirty. If this consciousness expands (even if to a greater understanding of the Physical World), his span of operable vibration might widen from ten to sixty.

As Soul becomes more aware and in control of the physical body, the conscious vibratory rates don't just widen. They also drift upward on the scale. Over time, the lowest operable vibratory rate in the span might move from twenty to thirty, then fifty, and perhaps seventy. Likewise, the highest reading moves upward into the eighties or nineties.

We entered the courtyard of the University at Askleposis, and stopped at the white steps of its main building. Classes were changing and scores of students and faculty members scurried up and down the steps to their next lessons.

Moments later, the courtyard again lapsed into quiet. Peddar continued: The exercises in these discourses are teaching you about Soul's lower bodies and how to open them to a greater flow of Light and Sound. This current awakens the sheaths to Soul's influence so a connection can be established between them.

There is a big difference between gaining the mental concept that you are Soul and *knowing* yourself as Soul. Unless we experience something firsthand, it is not a reality. Therefore, the spiritual exercises offer direct experience of Soul awareness.

At some point during a spiritual exercise, or perhaps for the duration of it, a Soul-Initiated Current is established in the body that has your attention. It will continue for as long as you can retain the Soul viewpoint. As you return your attention to life's daily affairs the circuit gradually fades.

Of course, you can only keep the Soul viewpoint for as long as that body can handle the heightened vibratory rates. Hence the importance of regularly practicing spiritual exercises to increase one's strength and stamina.

Practicing the Soul-Initiated Circuit

Your next assignment is to practice any spiritual exercise of your choosing. Watch closely to see if you can observe the Soul-Initiated Circuit manifested by the exercise.

A handsome man approached us from the building and politely waited as Peddar finished speaking. His sparkling blue eyes and long blond hair were striking above his flowing white robes.

Peddar smiled at him and concluded: Later, during your daily activities, take time to put your attention on Spirit, God, the Wayshower, or your spiritual Self. Look for the Soul-Initiated Circuit that forms as a result of your attention.

Peddar turned toward the man and they greeted each other warmly.

This is Gopal Das, the Guardian of Askleposis, *he said, introducing us.* He was once one of my teachers. In a way, I'm still his student—and always shall be.

The two masters spoke together for a moment. Then Gopal Das raised his hand in a silent farewell and turned and walked back toward the building.

I had been thinking of Gopal Das, *Peddar reflected,* because I wanted to tell you that he would present the next discourse. I hadn't expected him to appear in person. Perhaps he did so to prove a point.

You see, whenever you think about or say the name of a spiritual master, either inwardly or outwardly, he or she is there. This is true in the Physical World as well as the inner planes, although many individuals may not perceive the master's presence.

In the inner worlds, the technique works faster and may seem more real, because perception is different there. Physical eyes are tools which can only perceive physical vibrations.

However, individuals who use their brow chakra (also known as the third eye, spiritual eye, or tisra til), may perceive the vibrations of the aura, the inner bodies, and the masters as well. Since the physical eyes really aren't involved, these inner realities can be perceived with the physical eyes opened or closed. Perceptions of the third eye are registered by the brain in language familiar to the physical eyes. They take on familiar aspects of color, shape, and form.

174

Sometimes this inner sight is heightened when the eyes are closed, shutting out visual interference from the physical eyes.

This ends our discussion for tonight.

Tomorrow you will be meeting with the Guardian of Askleposis. Come to this same location, sing his name, and he will appear.

May the blessings be!

Peddar held up his hand in the familiar palm-outward salutation of his order of masters. Then he turned and walked up the steps into the building.

I decided to walk through the university gardens. As I ambled along, I thought about calling masters into one's world just by thinking about them or singing their names. What if the master was busy doing something else? Would I ever be bothering a master by calling on him?

Perhaps thinking about masters or singing their names was a way of giving them attention, a form of love. Yes, I thought to myself, giving loving attention to a master must set up a channel of love. Spirit allows the presence of the master to manifest, through this channel, into your consciousness. Therefore, one cannot 'bother' a master by thinking about him or her.

On the contrary, loving thoughts enhance the flow of Spirit through oneself and the one to whom the attention is given.

Satisfied with my conclusion, I turned my thoughts to Gopal Das and invited his image into my third eye. As I returned to the Physical Plane, the light of his countenance illuminated my inner vision. I practiced keeping his image in focus as I prepared for bed and finally drifted off to sleep.

Chapter 16

Visiting the Spiritual Learning Center of Askleposis

After contemplating on Gopal Das the night before, I felt I had built a compatible vibration between us. I was eager to meet him again in the inner worlds and hear his discourse.

I closed my eyes and tried to imagine the courtyard where I was to meet the master, but it wouldn't come into focus. My consciousness couldn't quite make the leap to the Astral Plane. I switched techniques and sang the name 'Gopal Das' aloud, letting the sound fill my ears. Suddenly a faceted, light-yellow gemstone, several inches in diameter, appeared in my inner vision. Its radiant beauty astounded me.

The gemstone moved closer until it almost touched my face. I couldn't help but pour my attention into it. As I did, Light and Sound filled my entire being. I felt nourished, satisfied, and joyful. I was also filled with a curiosity to know more, a desire to expand my consciousness, and a yearning to go where I had never been before.

The gemstone gently moved away. I studied its form. Then I noticed a pair of hands cradled the precious gem. They belonged to Sri Gopal Das.

Are you finished observing? *asked the Guardian.*

"Yes," I replied.

Then look into my eyes.

I felt his warm love melting every cell of my being, as if I were made of butter. A wonderful, delicious, aroma enveloped me. It was fragrant like a flower, yet nourishing like the aroma of freshly-baked bread. I wanted more, yet it was already so rich and satisfying I could hardly bear it.

I believe you will be able to complete your mission, *said Sri Das, releasing his gaze.*

I wasn't sure which mission he was referring to. Was it my present assignment of recording discourses for this book— or some grander spiritual mission?

After a speechless moment, I chuckled, "Thanks for the vote of confidence." We both grinned and laughed.

When the waves of merriment subsided, the Master handed the gemstone to an assistant who appeared at his side. The man carefully enveloped it in his arms and went to place it back in safekeeping. Gopal Das put an arm around my shoulder.

Come, let me show you around Askleposis.

I hadn't noticed my transition to the inner. We were standing in the courtyard where Peddar had introduced us. I walked up the white marble steps with Gopal Das as he chatted.

As you know, Askleposis is a spiritual learning center. It is the group of buildings you have seen from the cliff. Recently, there has been a tremendous increase in students. Our rooms have been unable to a absorb the numbers, so we have been holding some classes outdoors on the lawn. I believe you have attended some gemstone classes in this fashion. Fortunately the weather is mild. Many of the faculty and students say they prefer the outdoor environment.

We reached the top of the steps and I turned to contemplate the breathtaking scenery. Acres of grassy fields separated Askleposis from the cliff edge. Several roads and footpaths were carved into these fields. They led to Askleposis from different points of the compass.

Beyond the cliffs, and to the left, the ocean stretched as far as the eye could see. Straight ahead was the bay and the city beyond, which sprawled for miles into the foothills. The far mountain range swept onward to the right.

With your visits here, have you ever wondered just where in the inner worlds Askleposis is? Did it ever occur to you that this ocean, city, and school exist on a planet?

"No, it never dawned on me," I replied, quite surprised at the realization.

Just as in the Physical World there are stars, planets, cities, and people, these also exist in the Astral World. Everything in the Physical World is a reflection of something in this Astral World, which is much bigger.

This planet, for example, is about as big as Earth's sun. All the inventions and thought-systems of Earth are well-known on this planet. But of course, the reverse is not true.

"I thought the spiritual law, 'as above, so below' meant that everything in the inner worlds would physically manifest in some way."

Not exactly. The saying 'as above, so below' does not mean what's 'above' is also found 'below'.

Come, let's go inside.

We passed between two large, white columns and beyond the tall, double doors. On the other side lay an expansive entry way that fed into two side-halls. Straight ahead stood another pair of tall doors.

This building is the main university. It houses hundreds of rooms, including administrative and faculty offices, reading and contemplation studies, private laboratories and studios, classrooms, a gathering hall, and other special areas for self-renewal. There are four floors in this main building. The top level is a sacred place, reserved for the contemplation and self-renewal practices of the faculty and spiritual masters. Events there must remain cloaked in secrecy.

Sri Das led me a short way down the left hall into a reading room. It had many comfortable chairs and small tables piled with books. Paintings of spiritual experiences hung on the two side walls. The front wall was made entirely of glass, which afforded a view of the campus.

The huge window overlooked several buildings standing in a large garden. They too were made of a white reflective material. On the far side atop a gentle slope, stood a small, circular temple. It glowed with an extraordinary golden light, which extended from its domed roof into the heavens above.

The master motioned me toward the window. That is a Temple of Golden Wisdom, *he explained, nodding toward the illuminated structure.* It houses one of the twelve volumes of the Book of Golden Wisdom.

Thousands and thousands of years ago, Askleposis was just this one building we are in now. The book was kept here too, along with classrooms, libraries, and administrative offices. As more people came to Askleposis, a separate temple was constructed to house the sacred book. It has remained there ever since.

As you can see, the temple was built on a hill directly behind the main hall, the first in a circle of newer buildings. It is easily visible from the central gardens and rooms on the garden-side of buildings such as this one.

Those who have an office facing the temple are indeed blessed. *The master grinned.* Or perhaps a view of the temple is needed to remind them to keep an open heart. The Book of Golden Wisdom records ways to live with an open heart while carrying out all duties in the spirit of love. In that way, all thoughts, words, and deeds are infused with the character, substance, rhythm, and magnetism of Spirit Itself.

Just to give you an idea of the surrounding area, beyond the temple to the north and east lie miles and miles of rolling countryside dotted with small towns. The area is otherwise uninhabited, except for a few self-sufficient families who live off the land—maybe one per hundred square miles. To the south, there are larger towns along the ocean.

Soon after the temple was built, a central library was constructed to accommodate the growing student body.

Sri Das leaned toward the window and pointed left to a white building larger than the one we occupied. My eyes widened at the thought of the millions of books it must house.

It was constructed with the future in mind, *he said, reading my expression.* For as long as the Astral World exists, this library should be sufficient to house all the spiritual works.

Next, the Library of Science and Technology was constructed—just there, to the right of the Golden Wisdom Temple. *Sri Das pointed to a building one-fifth the size of the main library.*

"But the main library is so huge," I exclaimed. *"Why do books about science and technology need their own building?"*

It was constructed not only to house books, but also to act as a vehicle for higher technologies to filter through to the Physical Plane. Technological gains offer so much more than a comfortable and convenient lifestyle. Science reflects the spiritual consciousness of the people. It enables Spirit to be manifested physically and reveals new ways for individuals to work with the Life Force.

Science and technology help man produce tools to employ, direct, modify, enhance, alter, amplify, reduce, or empower other manifestations of Spirit. Electricity, for example, is one direct manifestation of Spirit. The light bulb is a tool that employs electricity to create illumination. The light bulb alone has greatly expanded man's hours for learning, play, and spiritual evolution.

Technology brings the reality of Spirit into even the most hardened and ignorant minds. The very existence of flying machines, for example, offers proof of unseen realities and non-physical energies. Machines and physical devices will eventually allow people to recognize Spirit as the primary force of the universe. They will come to realize that electricity, microwaves, and many other frequencies that power machines are just different voices of Spirit.

The Hall of Science and Technology provides a vortex for Spirit to enter the hearts and minds of scientists and inventors.

These individuals are outwardly capable of manifesting physical devices. Inwardly, they are brave and adventurous— and consciously or not, they are striving for spiritual awareness.

Their desire for Soul consciousness manifests in an ability to visit this Hall of Technology in their dreams or contemplative states. These spiritual scientists bring back new ideas and information and try to build what they have seen. Eventually they manifest much-needed change.

In doing so, these individuals not only raise their own consciousness but the consciousness of all who use their inventions. Hence, new technologies provide spiritual opportunities for all.

You may be interested to know that the Hall of Technology has fallen fifteen times. The one that stands before you now is the sixteenth building.

"Why was it destroyed so many times?" I asked.

The negative forces did not want the Physical Plane to have technological inventions which proved the existence of Spirit. But each time the Hall was razed by fire, earthquakes, or other means, the positive forces, led by the Guardian of Askleposis of the time, restored it. And with each restoration, an additional basement level was constructed to strengthen the foundation. Today, the Hall consists of fifteen subterranean levels, with only two stories above ground. It is the only building with such a basement.

The other small buildings here at Askleposis are mostly classrooms. And some shallow caves nearby have also been transformed into meeting rooms.

"I once attended a class in a cave room," I said. "It was a lovely place. The walls and ceiling of half of the room consisted of rock covered with moss and ferns. The other half was in the open air, surrounded by gardens and protected by leafy trees."

The caretakers of Askleposis take extraordinary pride in their work, *said Gopal Das.* I believe the beauty of the buildings and surrounding gardens are proof of this.

We stood in silence for a few minutes, enjoying the beauty of the central garden. I felt the love that went into its design. Hillocks of thick green grass were offset by valleys of colorful flowers. Trees stood like gallant sentries along the garden paths, their graceful silhouettes lending shade and peace.

Running through the center of the garden was a small stream which sprang from directly beneath the Temple of Golden Wisdom. Near the center of the garden stood an arched footbridge where students could cross the stream. On the other side, the stream forked into rivulets which flowed to a construction site.

That site will be the new healing center, *Gopal Das explained.* It is a replica of the expansive center for healing on the Causal Plane. It will house a medical library, as well as a Museum of Medicine. The rivulets will feed into several rooms in the healing center. There they will be used for healing, cleansing, and nourishment.

A subterranean river also flows beneath Askleposis. Its source is a range of mountains far to the north. In these mountains lies a secret tunnel to the Causal Plane. This river flows alongside this tunnel before plunging underground. The river passes beneath the Golden Temple, and the stream that springs from it, toward the first basement of the Hall of Technology.

There it enters a large columnar opening in the center of the Hall's subterranean basements. It bursts forth as a mighty waterfall which flows down through the center of the hall's subterranean levels. At the bottom, it flows down through the Astral Plane into the Physical World.

"Where does it reach Earth?" I asked with great curiosity. It occurred to me that such a spring might be a fountain of health and youth.

Gopal Das smiled enigmatically. These sacred waters have extraordinary curative powers. However, to preserve its sanctity, the location of the spring is kept a secret.

"Do people live at Askleposis?"

Some students, caretakers, and teachers live here, but most visit in their dreams or contemplations.

The master stepped back from the window and sank into one of the overstuffed chairs. I took a seat facing him across a small table.

Years ago, the classes taught here were directly about Spirit. But our teachings have become more available and open to the masses. Now our classes span a broad range of topics—from electronics to dance; cooking to wild animal taming; writing to healing techniques, and spiritual exercises.

What has not changed, however, is the spiritual intent of the teachers. All the faculty members are either spiritual masters or masters' apprentices. They are well-versed in the ways of Spirit.

The beings who attend classes here may not know their teacher is of a high spiritual order. In fact, they may not have a conscious interest in spirituality. But each teacher delicately weaves the principles of Spirit into his or her words and sentences. Spirit is the underlying fabric of all learning. Every lesson of every class reflects the substance, character, rhythm, and magnetism of the Sound Current.

Classes are presented in cycles. These vary with each semester. Some last only one or two weeks, while others continue for as long as a year. Usually, however, they are six weeks to five months in length.

A few weeks before a semester starts, the Board of Directors determines how long the semester will be. Their finding is based on a thorough study of spiritual tides, or the ebbs and flows of energy currents.

Before an instructor offers a class, he or she consults with one of the directors. They review an outline of the course material, how often classes will be held, and how many classes will be offered per day. Then, upon approval, the director may offer advice and suggestions.

There are regular deadlines for class proposals so course catalogs can be created. These subject catalogs are similar to those of any university on Earth, except for one important difference. Although the pages of every catalog are filled with complete listings of Askleposis classes, they will appear sporadically blank to most individuals. This is because one only sees the listings of those classes that the individual is eligible to take!

Each catalog responds to the vibration of the reader. The frequency of the words adjusts so that some of the listings are clear, others barely legible, and many invisible.

Information about some classes seems to jump off the page. These are the ones you particularly need. However, whether you choose to take such a class or not doesn't really make any difference. Spirit will teach you what you need to know regardless. It might be in a class here at Askleposis, or during some other life-experience.

Since individuals can't sign up for classes they don't know about, class attendees are pre-qualified. A teacher doesn't have to wonder about the background of his students or if they have met the prerequisites. He or she can be assured the students are ready to learn the information presented.

This readiness is an important ingredient of growth and understanding.

The classes are attended by beings throughout the lower worlds. Many travel here during spiritual exercises or sleep. Some are brought by their spiritual guides, unbeknownst to them. Other times Spirit Itself guides a wandering dreamer to an Askleposis library, introductory talk, or even an ongoing class. Anyone aware of these classes may attend; there is no entrance fee or examination.

If you share this in your book, your readers will know of us. Therefore, they are ready to learn a technique for visiting Askleposis and signing up for a class.

Enrolling in an Inner-World University

This technique will show you how to take classes in the dream state.

Before you drift off to sleep at night, lie in bed and think about something you would really like to learn about. Continue thinking about this subject as you fall asleep. Continue to focus on the topic for several nights.

Then one night, when you feel ready to register for a class, refer to the information I am about to give you regarding registration. Read and reread the information about how to register for classes. Then think about the process and imagine you are following these steps to register.

First, you are given a catalog. Imagine holding it in your hands and flipping through its pages. Subjects are arranged alphabetically. Turn to the topic you are interested in.

Let's say you want to learn about dream travel. Look under the letter 'D', where you will find all the dream classes described. To the left you will find the times when each class is presented. Remember, only classes in harmony with you are visible. Therefore, you will only find times that fit with your current schedule. If you decide to change your lifestyle or bedtime, other classes may become visible!

Classes may last anywhere from thirty minutes to one hour. A description of a Dream Travel class might read:

D

4:00am **Dream Travel**

Techniques for opening one's awareness to the subtle worlds beyond the Physical Plane. Includes exercises for traveling to these inner worlds while sleeping, and how to remember your dream experiences.

Gopal Das

Select a class. Then look up and notice an angelic figure stands before you. He or she is wearing the brown tunic of an Askleposis 'prefect'.

The prefect's job is to answer questions and guide students through the registration process. He or she also helps new students find their way around. When you have made a selection, the prefect will submit your name to the appropriate teacher.

To attend the class, feel your desire to be there. Just before sleep, remind yourself: 'Ah yes, my class on Dream Travel is at 4:00 a.m'. Then tell yourself: 'I will be there'.

You will indeed attend. *Gopal and I smiled at each other in delight at the thought.* The prefects will help you locate the class during your first visit. And if you sign up for a class at a certain time, six nights a week, he or she will help remind you to attend each night, just before class begins. Although it is up to you to keep your commitment, they are willing to help you leave your physical body while it sleeps and travel to class.

You always have the option, of course, to go with the prefect or not. Furthermore, you can stop attending a class whenever you like. But teachers usually ask you to make such a decision during the first one or two sessions, so a stable group consciousness can be formed.

Many first-time students have no conscious recollection of their dream classes. But they may notice an inflow of knowledge on the subject of their interest.

There is a part of you that is always awake. As your physical body sleeps, your spiritual self awakens. This is the part that dreams, not your mind.

Your mind muddles your dream experiences in an attempt to maintain sovereignty. It wants to contain these experiences within its limited state by translating them into symbols. You may not remember what you experienced because of this mental censorship. But for many, dreams offer the only true glimpse into Soul's reality. Soul never sleeps, even when Its lower bodies do.

The purpose of these sheaths is to teach Soul Self-awareness, even while dwelling within the illusionary lower planes. Eventually Soul learns to retain and expand this consciousness in the lower worlds. The goal is to be awake in the physical body while dwelling in the God-worlds as Soul.

If a class is not comfortable or 'right' for you, Soul will drop out. You may not know this has happened. But you might lose interest in your topic, or forget about it in the rush of daily activities.

Everyone who signs up for a class is urged to also sign up for a self-renewal session, which is the Astral Plane's answer to homework. Instead of studying, the information you receive in class becomes a part of you during this special session. Hence there is no need for tests or examinations.

During a self-renewal session, you are led to a special spot in the gardens or buildings that assures you privacy. Some choose rooms of light, while others prefer soothing dimness and music. You may be given certain exercises or therapies to practice. There is also personal, private time for contemplation and energy re-balancing. During these sessions, all that you have learned in your class sinks into Soul, the very fabric of your being, as well as into your heart and mind.

One may ask: What is the price of a class at Askleposis? The price should not be looked at as a cost. A class is more like a reward for good deeds done: for giving of oneself without thought of return. Students do not have to be saints to attend classes, however.

To earn the attentions of a teacher, one need only open one's heart to Spirit and give love, compassion, understanding, and joy, rather than expressing a negative emotion of the ego, such as jealousy, resentment, or the desire to self-punish.

It is indeed a blessing to be able to attend classes here. If one accepts even the possibility that Askleposis exists, the heart is probably open enough to attend.

Let me repeat: if you can get to Askleposis, you can attend a class. To get there, think about the subject you would like to explore. Say firmly to yourself, 'I want to take a class on (your topic)'. Do this for several nights in a row.

Then re-read the information about how to register. Look at the sample catalog listing printed in this book, to help you visualize the one at Askleposis. Then, say aloud, 'Yes. At 3:00 a.m. every morning (or whatever time you choose to take the class), I will attend this class'.

That's all you have to do. It is that simple. When you go to sleep, you will be studying here. If you doubt your eligibility but still have a desire to learn, practice selfless acts. Do something for someone else that you wouldn't normally do. But do it for love and love alone.

Gopal Das stood up, leaned over the table, and rested his hand on my shoulder, It is time to return to physical consciousness. One last word: be careful not to sign up for too many classes at once. You must allow time for your inner bodies to play and rejuvenate, just as your physical body needs rest periods.

I nodded and rose to follow him out of the reading room, glancing one last time at the beautiful Temple of Golden Wisdom as I closed the door. Together we left the building.

"There are so many subjects I would like to explore," I said. "It's hard to choose only a few classes. And yet, I want to continue studying Diamond and Gemstone Therapy."

You do a great service in passing along what you learn on this subject, *Gopal Das replied.*

"Thank you," I said.

We can talk about gemstones tomorrow if you like, *he offered.*

I nodded gladly.

He raised his right hand to shoulder height, with palm outward, and said, May the blessings be.

I watched as his image slowly blurred into a soft blending of colors. As I strained for focus, my bedroom swam into view. The experience seemed like a dream. I switched off my tape recorder, my only proof that indeed, it had all been real.

Chapter 17

The Role of Therapeutic Diamonds and Gemstones

I anxiously awaited my next contemplation time. I wanted to hear what Gopal Das had to say about gemstones. For reasons I was only beginning to comprehend, Diamond and Gemstone Therapy was a large part of my life.

I sang HU and entered the Astral Plane a few hundred feet from the main university building at Askleposis. As I set out briskly toward the courtyard, I spied Gopal Das approaching from the opposite direction.

Welcome! *he called out when we were still a few steps apart. He reached for my hand and shook it warmly.*

Is there anyplace in particular you would like to go for today's discourse? *he asked.*

"Since you're going to talk about gemstones, I want to be sure to record your words accurately. So I'd like to go someplace where I can be particularly open and clear."

Very well. Follow me.

We walked up the steps into the entrance hall. The master's energetic stride carried him across the large foyer. I had to jog a few steps as he ushered me through the doors directly opposite the entrance.

I stepped into a small but striking room with a metallic black floor. The walls looked like sheets of white crystal, which illuminated the room from all sides. The ceiling was crystal also, making it hard to judge its height. But it was at least twelve feet.

White block-like seats with black cushions were positioned at the center of the room. We made ourselves comfortable on them.

I was exhilarated by the energies of this room. My sinuses, eyesight, hearing, and thoughts cleared. I took a deep breath and felt the air fill every corner of my lungs. I inhaled again and my crown chakra opened with a faint popping sound. My head felt weightless.

At the next breath, my brow chakra also opened, giving new depth to the expansion I felt in my head. A few normal breaths followed, during which my heart chakra gently unfolded, followed by the other chakra centers. My heart poured out gratitude for this experience.

Each chakra center registered the effects of this new state of consciousness, and communication lines opened between all my inner bodies. This allowed me a much more full expression of my gratefulness.

I realized in a flash that I interacted with life mainly through my heart chakra. It bore the brunt of my emotional expressions and the incoming emotions of others. No wonder my chest sometimes felt burdened. And how much easier it was to connect with life through all Soul's chakra-windows!

By dividing the workload, other chakra centers could share in the intake and outflow of physical and emotional expression. My heart was free to exude clear, divine love.

I could have remained in this state indefinitely. But after a few moments, questions about the spirituality of gemstones came to mind. "Sri Das, many people are attracted to gemstones and experience their amazing therapeutic and spiritual benefits. But others dismiss gems as psychic tools, or useless jewelry, adamantly labeling them 'non-spiritual'. Why?"

Many people misunderstand gemstones, *Gopal Das began.* Down through history, crystals have often been misused. The last widespread period of misuse on Earth was at the end of the Atlantean Age.

About this time, the negative energies destroyed the Temple of Technology here at Askleposis. This unleashed destructive forces into the Physical Plane. These forces perverted the minds of those who worked with gemstones and crystal technologies. As a result, the great continent of Atlantis sank into the ocean, convulsed by earthquakes.

This event was imprinted into the consciousness of all who were there. So some people unconsciously associate gemstones with the horrors of the malevolent forces which were amplified and directed by Atlantean crystals.

Without being aware of it, they link gemstones with destruction. They have very sincere reservations about using gemstones and may react very strongly against them.

"Did diamonds play a part in the Atlantean era?" I asked.

Diamond Therapy and Technology was unavailable then. Until now, it has never been introduced on the Earth planet. The secrets of diamonds are only now being brought to the Astral Plane from the Causal World. The information is gradually being released into the Physical Plane as Souls there become ready for it.

Usually, information must be well established on the Astral Plane before it can be brought into the Physical. But there are enough clear vehicles to allow Diamond Therapy to flow directly from the Causal World into the Physical Plane. Many people on the Astral World, as well as a few on Earth, have devoted their lives to this knowledge.

There is also an interdisciplinary effort among enlightened physicians, therapists, scientists, spiritual seekers, and spiritual masters in the Astral World. They are helping to bring this knowledge to the Physical Plane. Such a group is also assembling on Earth. These individuals not only use diamonds therapeutically, but take the responsibility to record their experiences, observations, and results with Diamond Therapy.

Gaelil Kibran Jhonès, your Diamond and Gemstone Therapy teacher, is responsible for collecting Diamond Therapy information on the Astral Plane. He oversees the beings who sort, organize, and catalog the data on this healing therapy. It is then stored in the Medical Hall of the Science and Technology Library.

Similar work can also be done on the Physical Plane, if you wish to initiate it. You will also need the cooperation of those working with you. Compiling information on what works and what doesn't in Diamond Therapy is important. It will allow Diamond Therapy research in future generations to progress more directly and easily.

Diamonds are used extensively in the healing centers of the Causal Plane. Practically every patient there interacts with diamonds. Some receive Diamond Therapy treatments; others are tested or treated with instruments empowered by diamonds.

Suddenly, I was startled by the low rumblings of an earthquake. Although they were mild, it was the last thing I expected to experience at Askleposis.

I looked uneasily at Sri Das, who explained, The negative forces have tried to crumble the Hall of Science and Technology several times since their last successful attempt in the eighteenth century. Waves of negativity come and go here. Do not put your attention on them. Instead, feel the love that meets them and soothes the planet's struggle for balance.

I did as he instructed, and after a few moments the ground felt calm again. "Please, tell me about the spirituality of diamonds," I asked.

Gemstones belong to the mineral kingdom, as you well know. Plants make up the herbal kingdom, while animals form their own realm. Human beings, however, belong to a spiritual kingdom. Many individuals consider therapeutic-quality diamonds to be members of this same kingdom.

"Perhaps that is because Therapeutic Diamonds carry seven-color-ray spectrums which resonate with human blueprints," I surmised.

An individual may include in his spiritual kingdom anything that gives him life, that lights his spiritual fire, or leads him onward toward his spiritual goals. Therefore, what one person uses in his spiritual kingdom can be remarkably different from what another brings to hers.

One of the greatest blessings a master can offer is to allow his students the freedom to consider anything as a spiritual tool. Validating another's tool doesn't necessarily mean, however, that you advocate or use it yourself.

The spiritually wealthy know that Spirit provides whatever they need on the path to God. Even if what is needed is rare to the masses, it will still be obtainable.

Your task is to wade through the mass of misconceptions about what is truth. This task not only applies to your work with diamonds, but to your entire existence in the lower worlds. In other words, as Soul you must realize yourself as a spiritual being, while living in the midst of lower vibratory rate reflections.

Those who successfully release their own narrow and limiting viewpoints are able to open to higher consciousness. Eventually they recognize their true beingness as Soul. A spiritual student releasing limiting viewpoints and concepts can be likened to a hot air balloon that drops bags of sand. Each rises to new heights.

Negative attitudes about diamonds and gemstones—or anything at all—form the ballast of life. Release the ballast, and the true nature of things comes into perspective. As far as diamonds and gemstones are concerned, people may regard them as jewelry, therapeutic aids, or spiritual tools. Though some may never use a diamond or gemstone for healing, perhaps they can at least accept the possibility that diamonds and gemstones can serve man in this way.

I have something to show you. Come, let's take a quick trip to some of the major spiritual temples of the lower worlds.

Instantly, we projected beyond the walls of the university and flew through the air. Within moments, we were hovering over a temple protected by a dome of white light. Golden beams radiated from the walls, and the indescribable music of stringed instruments filled the air.

Without time for further inspection, we passed through the walls and into the building. Our entrance surprised me, but there was no time for questions.

Observe carefully so you'll remember later what you have seen, *Gopal Das instructed.* The spiritual energy is not evenly distributed in this temple. Look for concentrations of it and take note of their locations.

The master spoke in hurried tones, so I scanned the room quickly. Its ceiling, walls, and floor were all made of a smooth, slightly reflective, golden-yellow material.

Evenly spaced along the walls stood large rectangular columns which supported the roof. Several sets of steps led to platforms where individuals or small groups contemplated and received discourses.

The whole architecture, however, focused the eye toward a central platform. It featured a pedestal wrapped in a glistening shaft of golden-yellow light. A large book rested atop the pedestal, which I assumed was another section of the Book of Golden Wisdom. The light from its pages illuminated the entire room.

Here, certainly, was a concentration of spiritual energy. But there were other handfuls of concentrated Light and Sound. They were of various colors, in nearly equidistant locations on the floor, walls, and ceiling.

Without warning, I was again swept through the temple walls and into the atmosphere. Within moments we arrived at another temple, which I was again asked to study.

Our journey continued to temple after temple until they became jumbled in my memory. The entire experience was like a travel film played at high speed. Yet the movement from place to place and from plane to plane was distinct. Finally, we returned to our seats in Askleposis. My dizziness from the swift travel calmed almost instantly.

Tell me what you noticed about the concentrations of spiritual energy you saw, *Gopal Das requested.*

I searched my memory of each temple. "In each, the most notable energy came from a distinctive column, sphere, or dome located either in the center of the room or off to one side. Sometimes it encompassed the Book of Golden Wisdom.

"Smaller concentrations of energy were present in strategic locations along the ceiling, walls, and floor. Often, but not always, these manifested as gemstones."

What else do you remember about the energy concentrations which took the form of gemstones? *he asked.*

I thought carefully and studied the pictures in my memories. Suddenly it dawned on me. "All the gemstones I saw were faceted!" I exclaimed. Though they were of every color and size, each was faceted. The shapes of the faceted stones also varied, but most were round, oval, or square.

The atomic matrix of certain gems holds energy, as you noticed in the temples. Their locations on the ceilings, walls, and floors preserves the strength of the temples.

"I was surprised to see gemstones on the floor," I commented.

Every Soul who walks upon these floors is destined for Self- and God-Realization. Therefore, the floors are blessed by the feet of those who walk upon them. Naturally, these floors are worthy of jewels.

Faceted gemstones freely express the energies they contain. Their flow is uninhibited unless contained by metal, such as the prongs of jewelry mountings. Furthermore, faceted gemstones don't need to be enlivened by a wearer's aura, like gemstone spheres do, in order to express their limitless state.

Raw, crystalline gemstones also have unfettered energies. Crystals, which grow within the ground, serve an important purpose in the life of the planet. Yet, blessed are those that are faceted or shaped into spheres, for they can best assist human beings.

Perhaps you noticed that some of the people at the various temples held faceted gemstones or wore gemstone sphere necklaces. In fact, some of the beings you saw had energetically-implanted spheres. This therapy is commonly performed at the healing center on the Causal Plane.

Gemstone Implantation Technique

The essential properties of a gemstone sphere can be implanted into one's being. Not by surgical methods, of course, but by a spiritual implantation technique. This allows the gem's energy to affect the implantation location of corresponding areas in all subtle bodies. A new level of balance is attained throughout the individual's entire being.

When a gemstone sphere is energetically implanted, the limitlessness of the Light and Sound it carries resonates with the limitlessness of Soul. This forms a bridge between Soul and the afflicted area implanted with the gem. Anything that prevents Soul's expression in the target area is released as fast as the individual can adapt to the new state.

By the way, an implanted gemstone does not feel uncomfortable. Contrary to what you might think, it doesn't feel like you have a rock inside your body.

198

We both smiled at the thought.

Gopal Das continued, The implant is an energetic one, made of the essence of the particular gemstone chosen.

There is a way to implant one or more gemstone spheres, within seconds, using two diamonds of a special kind. However, the technique I will give you employs the imagination instead. It can be done with or without a manifested sphere.

First, decide where on your body you would like gemstone therapy. If you have a whole body condition, find out which organ, if it were working normally, would best help the entire body's return to health. If you don't know, I suggest implanting the gemstone into your heart center. Spirit flows through this center circulating good will, love, and blessings to you and all life.

Second, decide which gemstone you wish to implant. Gemstone therapists are trained to help, or you can look inwardly to receive a suggestion. Individuals might select a stone based on the descriptions in your book, *Gifts of the Gemstone Guardians.*

Reading about a particular gemstone sphere may give you enough of an impression of its energy. Otherwise, obtain at least a single sphere of the gemstone you want to try. An entire strand would be even better, because it would provide more mass, and its essential properties or vibrations would be more obvious.

Third, perform the implantation technique as follows. Begin by placing the sphere or strand of spheres (either imagined or manifested), on your heart center and hold it against your body with both hands. If you are working just with your imagination, envision the spheres as best you can. Close your eyes.

Develop a rapport with the gemstones by expressing gratitude for their beingness. It is important to hold them close, so your body heat can warm them. This generally takes just a few minutes.

When the spheres are warm, move them to the organ or part of your body you wish to treat. Hold them next to your skin, covering them with your right hand. Your hand should be cupped, as if it's a dome guarding the spheres.

Now, cup your left hand and place it over the top of your right hand. If you are using only one sphere, hold it in position with the thumb and forefinger of your cupped right hand.

Imagine the gems slowly growing to fill the dome created by your cupped right hand.

Experience the sphere's presence.

Then, keeping your fingers touching your body, slowly flatten your hands as if you were pressing the sphere into your body. Keep your hands flat over the area for a few minutes.

To maintain the presence of the implanted sphere's energy, keep your right hand in place while using your left hand to remove the physically manifested spheres if you have been using them. If you are working with a strand of gemstones, place it around your neck. Also remove your left hand if you are using non-manifested spheres.

Keep your right hand pressed against your skin. Then, without lifting it, slowly and gently move your hand in a very small circle, either in a clockwise or counterclockwise direction, whichever seems most comfortable for you. The movement stretches your skin slightly. Do not lift your hand off your body or rub your palm over your skin.

This circular motion helps embed the energy of the stone into your astral body counterpart. Spend five to fifteen minutes doing this.

Now, stop the movement, open your eyes, and look at the back of your right hand, which is still resting on the target area. Imagine the sphere is embedded beneath your skin there. A sphere of light the same color as the gemstone is now centered inside or encompassing the organ or area treated.

After you've focused on the region beneath your hand with your eyes open, close them.

Wipe your hand off the area as if you had peanut butter on it and wanted to spread it onto your body. Be careful to get all the 'peanut butter' off your thumb and fingers, especially the little finger. It helps to flex your hand backwards as you wipe.

As soon as your fingertips leave your body, open your eyes. You have just implanted a gemstone.

If you wish to enhance the sphere's effects, go lie in the sun and allow its rays to beat upon the skin. As a general guideline, do this for fifteen minutes daily. If the weather is cold but sunny, you may lie indoors near a sunny window. If it's cloudy, you can visualize the sun's energy radiating into the sphere.

Water can be used to cleanse the disharmony being released at the site. A simple way is to take a shower and let the water beat upon the area. If you can, alternate the temperature of the water from hot to cold and back to hot again. Another way to help release any disharmonies is to apply hot and cold compresses to the area.

If you enjoy the effects of a particular sphere, leave it implanted for as long as you wish. This can be for a few minutes or several weeks. If you forget and leave it in place after that, its energy will gradually dissolve. However, if you wish to remove a sphere or replace it with another, follow this procedure carefully:

Close your eyes.

Put your right hand over the area where the sphere was implanted.

Now open your eyes.

Stretch your fingers apart as far as they can go. Brace them as though they are preparing to lift a heavy sphere from the inside of your body.

Imagine the sphere attaching itself to the palm of your hand, and grip it with your fingertips. Now, very gently and slowly lift your hand away from your skin. As you do this, the sphere will leave your body.

When your hand is about twelve inches away from your physical body, turn it so that your palm faces away from the skin. The energetic manifestation of the sphere will remain in your hand, facing away from your body.

Now, close your eyes. With a thankful heart, let go of the sphere and release it into the ethers. It will dissolve back into the spiritual essence from which it was born.

To implant a different sphere into the same area or another area, repeat the procedure given earlier.

I had a question. "What if the placement area is difficult to reach, such as the right shoulder or arm, or one that the eyes can't focus on, such as the back?"

Use your right hand whenever possible. But if you can't reach a target area, use your left. If you can't see the target area, have another person perform the technique for you. In this case, however, have him use his left hand. Bio-magnetic laws dictate that a person's right hand is more effective when implanting a gemstone in his own body. Conversely, the left hand is better when performing implantation on another.

Gopal Das stood up. I rose also and accompanied him to the door.

Tomorrow you will resume your discourses on Soul's lower bodies. Although your experiences here may have seemed like an interruption in the flow of that information, they have served a definite purpose. Those who read about your experiences here have an opportunity to release limiting attitudes about diamonds and gemstones. Attitudes limit one's understanding of physical existence as well as growth of the spiritual consciousness.

We entered the foyer and walked toward the main entrance. The Master stopped near the middle of the hall and turned toward me. He had a reflective look on his face. If you're going to be honest, why not be completely honest? *he said.*

Avoid holding back information about diamonds and gemstones just because you think others may have attitudes about them. It is human nature to resist new ideas, and the mind complains. But if Soul wins, the mind and heart open and the individual is blessed with new opportunities and understanding.

The master's expression changed. He smiled and love poured from his eyes and Light and Sound flowed freely from every atom of his being.

Then he erupted in a full-hearted, healing laugh and I couldn't help but join in. I think he laughed for the pure joy of it.

I returned to my physical body still chuckling. I may never know why we were laughing. But I felt truly happy. That's all that seemed to matter right now.

Chapter 18

What Controls
Your Physical Existence?

It was early afternoon, not my usual time for contemplation, when I recognized the familiar inner tugging sensation. I could not disobey or ignore it. The only solution was to sit down and start a spiritual exercise.

"HUUU," I sang, wondering who would present the next discourse. It was hard to focus. My physical body kept fidgeting in the chair—first with an itch, then an ache. Even though I was compelled to contemplate, the slightest noises distracted me.

I struggled on for ten minutes before I remembered a technique that usually overcame my restlessness. It was simple: I would recognize, acknowledge, and make peace with each distraction, one by one.

My foot was itching, so I asked it to join me in my spiritual exercise. In a few moments the itch disappeared. Then I turned my attention to the various household noises. I came into harmony with each one by listening for the HU in its sound. This also helped bypass sleepiness, as I kept my mind busy.

Finally, the physical distractions diminished. I caught the faint strains of an unusual music, different than anything I'd ever heard. Gradually it became louder.

Then a man of medium height appeared in my inner vision. Robed in brown, maroon, and gold, he sported the black felt hat and leather boots of a Gaucho.

I didn't feel I had traveled anywhere. My physical surroundings were still present in my awareness. Just to make sure, I peeked through squinted eyes and saw my familiar bedroom. But a few feet in front of the chair stood the man's nearly transparent form. His lively brown eyes sparkled in contrast to his weathered, brown skin. I opened my eyes fully.

I, Shamus-i-Tabriz, will now share a discourse about important factors that influence physical existence, *he announced.*

I recognized his name from my spiritual studies. Shamus-i-Tabriz was a sage and poet who lived on the Physical Plane during the thirteenth century in Persia. He is presently the guardian of a section of the Book of Golden Wisdom on the Causal Plane.

As I contemplated his nearly physical presence, the music became deafening.

You hear the music of the spheres, *he said.*

I had heard of that expression before, but never understood what it meant. Different notes, each corresponding to different spheres of consciousness, were all played at the same time. The notes were separate, yet joined in harmony. The resulting sound was divinely beautiful.

When the sounds had died down a little, he spoke again. When individuals hear this music, they are able to understand paradoxes such as these: We are all together, yet we are separate. Life just is, yet it is not. God is here, yet It is nowhere.

Such concepts are especially hard to grasp in the physical consciousness. However, paradoxes do not exist above the lower worlds, and this music helps to transport an individual beyond them—beyond conflict and paradox.

I listened carefully to the music of the spheres again, surrendering to its upliftment. It carried me deeper into the in-between zone, where the inner and outer worlds overlap.

After a few minutes, the master again spoke. At the beginning of this contemplation, it took you a long time to take your attention off your physical surroundings. Do you know why?

I didn't think it was appropriate to go into detail about my itches and distractions. Fortunately, he replied before I had time to answer.

It was because I kept you in the physical state of consciousness, *he said.*

"Why?" *I asked.* "It was really uncomfortable."

Tabriz sat down on the corner of the bed. I am here to speak to you about the physical consciousness. I wanted you to experience what it's like to be trapped here, out of contact with Soul.

The physical consciousness does its best to maintain your constant attention. For example, your physical consciousness employed several distractions to delay this discussion.

If Soul is meant to do, learn, or experience something, the physical consciousness may contrive excuses to avoid it—perhaps even for a few lifetimes. But one day the experience will be drawn into the individual's aura, regardless.

Sometimes, just one aspect of the physical consciousness keeps a person from this next spiritual step. It is usually associated with a deep-seated trauma that makes us fear or resist change.

However, all limitations must be released on Soul's journey home to God. When you are ready, life will expose the tangled energies of an issue. As they bubble up to the surface, your life may be filled with turmoil. But once the release is completed, your whole being leaps forward in consciousness.

After a long pause, the Master said, As it is written, so shall it be.

These words seemed to come out of nowhere. Because they were unexpected and didn't make sense to me, I didn't relay the words into the tape recorder.

You didn't record what I said, *he admonished.* Let me repeat myself: As it is written so shall it be.

"I apologize, sire," I said. I made a mental note to be more careful in the future.

Never mind, *he said.* We are developing an inner-outer relationship and this banter of ours is a means for doing so.

The saying, 'As it is written so shall it be', has three meanings: one superficial, another deeper, and the third most significant of all. I shall explain these in order, beginning with the first.

At this superficial level, that which 'is written' refers to the seed patterns, or cause-blocks, in the causal body. These contain lessons all Souls must learn. Seed patterns are destined to manifest as experiences, for our unfoldment. A Soul cannot leave the lower worlds until every cause-block has been resolved.

However, once an individual develops a conscious relationship with the Wayshower, his spiritual life comes under the master's direct guidance. The adept oversees and regulates the student's lessons. They are organized in a more orderly fashion so he can get the most out of each experience.

As a result, Soul is often able to learn the lesson of a particular seed pattern without having to go through outer experiences that would have been otherwise necessary. Or one experience may take care of several seed patterns, instead of just one. Therefore, once this linkup with the Wayshower occurs, Soul's unfoldment accelerates.

The deeper meaning of the phrase, 'As it is written so shall it be', refers to the records of Soul. The records I'm

208

referring to are not contained in the Causal Plane, but in the Golden Kingdom. These list Soul's unique characteristics, expressions, and potential. They shape Soul's sojourn in the lower worlds.

The deepest meaning of 'As it is written...' lies in the heart of God. One cannot fathom the scope of God's intention when It created Spirit. Spirit is the current that flows out of God and into all the worlds of Its creations. Yet, each of us responds to the message of love written in the heart of God, which calls Soul back to Itself. So shall it be.

Soul's return to God starts in the physical consciousness. From that severely limited viewpoint, all is muddled. And yet all is clear. I shall explain this paradox.

All is muddled, because the human consciousness takes all the awareness of the inner bodies and considers it one consciousness—the physical one. Of course, you know each lower body is as separate as each organ in your body. All one's bodies and organs are required for life; they are separate yet they function together.

All is clear, because according to physical consciousness one's inner bodies don't exist. The physical body is all there is. It is born, it lives, and it dies. After this, some expect to go to heaven or hell, while others think they will cease to exist.

The earthly body cannot be truly understood when viewed only from the physical consciousness. One is unable to see the whole of the individual, since the physical body is only a fragment of his beingness.

In this series of discourses, you have been given brief sketches of each inner body and its functions. You may have tried some of the techniques for gaining greater awareness and control of them. Now this knowledge will come together in the study of the physical form.

Let's begin at birth. When a Soul living in an astral body wishes to enter a physical body, It must first place Its attention on the physical realm. Before It can do this, however, It must be shown how. This help is provided by inner guides, who belong to special orders of spiritual masters.

This guidance is necessary because the Physical World is much more finite than the astral realms, and fewer physical forms are available. Each Soul must wait Its turn and be guided to just the right baby's body.

The spiritual value of having a physical body is often overlooked. It allows Soul to experience a much wider spectrum of experiences and environments than any of the other lower forms. And since the physical form deteriorates fairly rapidly, Soul can experience many lifetimes in a relatively short period of time.

Karma can also be dealt with quickly in the physical body. All the inner bodies directly influence the physical body, allowing for rapid cause-and-effect learning.

In the Astral World, a wide gulf of time separates an effect from its cause. This makes it hard to recognize that you reap exactly what you sow. Physical life makes it easier for Soul to realize and learn from cause-and-effect cycles.

If I impress only one thing upon you, let it be this: the physical body is Soul's most precious and valued tool. With it, Soul's return home is practically guaranteed.

There is a waiting list, so to speak, to enter the physical realm. Those who have already lived there have priority over novices. One of the functions of the spiritual guides is to ensure that Souls are taken to their proper place at death—and that only those who are eligible to incarnate again do so.

After dropping the physical body, Soul may spend much time in Its astral form. Or It may go directly to the Causal or, more rarely, the Mental World.

To an individual who has spent lifetimes on Earth, the Astral Plane may seem like heaven. Some believe they have entered the highest region of the God Worlds. In fact, entire religions are based on reaching this heaven. They mistake it for the ultimate region of the Divine. But anyone can prove these areas are not the ultimate. Simply enter the Soul consciousness and explore them for yourself. Such travel can awaken Soul more effectively than years of religious study. There is no better teacher than direct experience.

As I mentioned, when Soul is eligible to enter the Physical World, a spiritual guide shows It how to focus Its attention there. This focus is a key to entering a physical body. Sometimes, the spiritual guide may have to provide this focus for an individual. In these cases, the astral being is reluctant to return to Earth. Perhaps he had just left physical existence, but must return immediately to reap the effects of some negative or violent action.

Most of the time, however, Soul wants to incarnate into the Physical World. Its attention is directed at several pairs of carefully selected parents. Each of these couples offer experiences Soul requires. They might help It unfold and resolve Its karma in the swiftest way possible.

However, just because an astral being places its attention on a couple, it doesn't mean that they are obligated to have a baby. It is their choice. But if a baby's body is conceived and carried to term, Soul and Its inner bodies can enter into it at birth. It cannot incarnate until the sheath is manifested enough to protect the Physical World from the higher vibratory rate of the astral form.

The sheath must also have complete life systems. These allow the astral and other inner bodies to communicate with the physical body for survival.

Some fetuses cannot house Soul until they reside in the mother's uterus for a week or two past term. Others are ready sooner. The time required in utero depends entirely on the genetic makeup of the parents, and the strength of the fetus's life systems. By the way, this strength may or may not remain with the child later in life.

211

Until the fetus leaves the mother's body, it receives color-ray nourishment from her. When it first leaves her body, it is nothing more than a clay shell.

An instant later the baby's body receives a jolt of spiritual energy. This jumpstart of Light and Sound is like the breath of God giving life to the newborn. It occurs when the Soul places Its attention on the new body. This jolt awakens the baby's physical sheath to receive color-ray nourishment directly, as it normally does when Soul is housed in it.

If a fetus can't handle the strength of this spiritual shock, the jolt will upset an already weakened or imperfect organ or life system and the sheath will die.

"What happens when a fetus dies in utero?" I asked.

Sometimes color rays are blocked from passing through a mother's cells to the fetus. Remember, a fetus receives color rays indirectly. They must be channeled through the mother's atoms to her baby.

If a mother's life is in question while she is pregnant, the Soul in the mother's body usually takes preference over the Soul waiting for the baby's body.

It is only when the body receives its spiritual jolt that a Soul is wed to a particular body. Then, within seconds, It enters the baby along with all the inner bodies It already wears.

Over the next forty years or so, the individual's physical body develops special energetic connectors to each of the inner bodies. These connectors link the color-ray frequencies in the physical body to those of each inner body. They allow the inner bodies' color-ray spectrums to influence the physical body and shape the individual's experiences.

It takes days or even weeks before the astral and physical bodies are fully interconnected. Weeks after that, the links between the causal and physical body begin to develop.

It takes many months, or sometimes years, before mental-body connections begin to be established, and then often many more years—until the individual is a teenager—before this connection is fully intact. For many, the development of the connection with the etheric, or subconscious body is completed at age thirty. Around the age of forty, the connection between the Golden Kingdom and the physical body is made.

This is not to say babies don't express emotion before their astral connectors are in place. Or that children cannot have full contact with their causal or mental aspects. Nor does it mean that one cannot become self-aware before the age of forty! Each of the inner bodies can directly affect the physical body in specific situations.

Remember, the connectors I am speaking of involve the interrelationship of color-ray frequencies among the lower bodies. They are another component of an individual's 'spiritual anatomy', so to speak.

The development of color-ray interrelationships between the astral and the inner bodies is governed by cycles that correspond to seven Earth years. This cycle presides over color-ray relationships for as long as the astral body is the lowest sheath Soul occupies.

When Soul takes on a physical body, the formulation of these color-ray relationships is dictated by ten-year cycles. Years ago, these cycles were twelve years long. But the times have sped up. Haven't you noticed? *Tabriz grinned.* The cycles have been in transition for the last several centuries.

Ten-year cycles don't necessarily begin at birth. The astral body must first complete one of its seven-year cycles. The astral body may be in the middle of a seven-year cycle when it enters a physical body.

So the child's first ten-year cycle begins sometime between birth and age seven. The beginning of this ten-year cycle is marked by a spurt of spiritual activity. Parents may

213

notice in their children an increased consciousness of Self when this cycle begins. The child recognizes his own identity apart from the family. He might experience a sudden burst of emotional, mental, or physical growth that is greater than what is normally expected of children that age.

Once the child embarks on his or her first ten-year cycle in the Physical World, the influence of the astral body's seven-year cycle diminishes.

At the beginning of each ten-year cycle, the color rays that nourish the physical body's atoms are re-evaluated. Information written in the causal body and the Soul records is re-evaluated in light of what is written in the heart of God Itself.

Spirit then determines what will be manifested in the person's life during the next ten-year cycle. This is done by giving the individual's color-ray spectrums an opportunity to change, and perhaps become more like his blueprints.

A golden opportunity for making changes in your life is therefore at the beginning of a ten-year cycle. But don't worry if you don't know when your next one begins, or if you have just missed the beginning of a cycle. In your regret, you may overlook what is happening in your life right now.

There is no better time than right *now* to initiate whatever changes you want in your life.

Each cycle gives you a unique opportunity to understand a particular part of yourself. Try to get the most out of it. When the next cycle comes, your attention will shift to another part of yourself.

Knowledge of cycles gives you a greater awareness of the spiritual flows that affect life in the physical body. The ten-year cycle is only one of many cycles that affect the physical body. There are others that last from seconds to lifetimes.

"What is the significance of numbers in regard to cycles?" *I asked suddenly.*

Shamus leaned forward. Numbers are divine inspirations. They are not just counting inventions. Numbers are spiritual reflections. Much of the truth about numbers can be discovered through a study of geometrical shapes. Not only three-dimensional forms, but also those which incorporate a fourth dimension.

"I've often wondered about the fourth dimension. Where is it, exactly?"

One question at a time! Tonight I will explain what the fourth dimension is. Then we will continue our discussion about numbers tomorrow.

Imagine a sphere in space. Its surface can be considered the Golden Kingdom, and its center the Physical Plane. Beyond the perimeter of the sphere is the infinite home of God. This is a reasonable, three-dimensional model of the Planes of Existence.

The surface of the sphere contains an infinite number of points, since geometrically speaking, a point has no properties of size or dimension. It only has a location. Spirit flows toward the center from every point on the sphere. And since there is an infinite number of points on the surface, there is an infinite number of spiritual currents flowing toward the Physical Plane. These add up to one—the singular current of Light and Sound that feeds the lower worlds.

The amount of Light and Sound flowing along this current remains constant. However, as it nears the center of the sphere, it is compelled to slow down. Pressure builds as it meets the increasingly limited space at the center.

Where does Spirit go once it reaches the center? The pressure catapults it into the fourth dimension!

The fourth dimension is highly unpredictable. It is continually being recreated as energy flows from the center of the sphere. It is malleable like clay. Just as the physical body is influenced by inner bodies, the Physical World is very much influenced by the fourth dimension. All inner worlds directly connect to the physical. However, the Physical World only expresses three dimensions.

"So, where is the fourth dimension?" I persisted.

Tabriz answered patiently, It is enveloped within every atom of the sphere, and yet it is also the envelope itself. Here again is a paradox. Remember, a paradox only exists when you tap into a greater awareness from the confines of the physical state of consciousness.

Philosophers love paradoxes. These Souls are making their first steps out of the physical consciousness. They have not yet gone far enough to resolve the paradox and understand its meaning.

So the fourth dimension exists both within and without each atom of the sphere. From a three-dimensional viewpoint, that's the only answer I can give you.

Exploring the Fourth Dimension

Contemplating the fourth dimension is a good exercise. It stretches the mind and makes it more flexible. It also expands the human consciousness and exercises the connectors between the mind and the physical body. These connectors should be elastic, like bands that can stretch and contract as needed.

Your exercise for tonight is to contemplate the fourth dimension. As you know, contemplation is very different from passive meditation or mental gyrations. It might be described as an 'effortless effort'.

To contemplate on the fourth dimension, hold the thought of it lightly in your mind, like a butterfly on your palm. Take an active interest in the subject without analyzing it. Just give it your loving attention.

View it from all sides, as if it were the middle of a circle and you were observing it from all 360 degrees of the perimeter.

Now let's see what you can learn about the fourth dimension through your own personal experience. If you'd like, launch your contemplation with the following visualization:

Imagine you are sitting in a bubble-like spaceship on the surface of a large golden sphere. Soon your ship rises above the surface. Then it dives into the heart of the golden orb.

Keep your ears open to different sounds and colors as you penetrate the globe. You may feel a gradual increase in pressure. There is no need to worry. Your consciousness is completely protected by the spaceship. Notice you are amidst a crowd of vehicles moving toward the center.

Suddenly, you are caught in a silent explosion! All measurement of space and time are ejected from your consciousness. You become one with your spaceship at the center of the sphere and with the infinity that exists beyond its surface, all at the same time.

A world of possibilities is now open to you. The fourth dimension is the place where dreams come true. If you go there with an intention, question, or yearning, the substance of the fourth dimension will respond to you.

To return to the three-dimensional world, you need not perform a visualization technique. Just think about the Physical World and you will be there. In the fourth dimension, wherever you put your attention, you are.

Shamus stood up to leave. Give life to this visualization, for it can provide dramatic results. Tomorrow our topic is numbers, *he reminded me as his form faded.* May the blessings be.

"May the blessings be," I answered.

My mind felt like bread dough that had been kneaded and stretched by the awesome, unlimited possibilities of Shamus-i-Tabriz's exercise. I sat back and shook my head in wonder.

Chapter 19

Mastering Numbers and Cycles

It was a gorgeous autumn day, so I decided to go outside and prepare for my next meeting with Shamus-i-Tabriz. I knew nature held the answers to many of life's questions, and wondered what secrets they might reveal about numbers. But after several minutes without inspiration I turned back toward the house. I knew Sri Tabriz would be here soon.

I brought a snack to my room, planning to eat it before returning to the inner worlds. To my surprise, Shamus was already sitting by my desk as I opened the door. His semi-transparent form glimmered with the soft glow of warm light.

I brought my lunch, *he smiled.* We both could use some nourishment before we begin—so I thought we'd eat together.

I enjoyed sharing this new and very human experience of eating with a master. I could feel my false concepts about spiritual adepts melting away with every bite.

As soon as we finished, Tabriz began. I promised to talk about numbers today. As I mentioned before, numbers are divine inspirations. They are not just mental devices used to count things. Of course, when expressed in three-dimensional terms, numbers are subject to the same limitations of the Physical Plane as everything else. They abide by the laws of the lower worlds.

But numbers can also be expressed from higher states of consciousness. When this is the case, they can actually affect the fluidity of the inner worlds. Furthermore, they can be expressed in fourth-dimensional terms, which allows them to defy physical numeric laws.

Suddenly I noticed that although Shamus-i-Tabriz was continuing his discourse, I could no longer hear him.

My mind was in the way. It resisted his information about numbers because it could not logically accept the concepts. I struggled in silence. My desire to convey new, fascinating information about numbers wrestled with the mind's need to hold onto all its old ideas. The mental body was sure it needed to keep its old state intact—the very stability and predictabilty of my universe depended on it.

I fought on, but Tabriz stood up to leave, his form fading from my room. I felt bad—I didn't want to lose this one! Despite my inability to bring the information through, I decided to follow him into the inner worlds. But I couldn't budge without giving up the struggle. So I took a deep breath and let go.

With my attention on the sound of HU, I slipped into the inner worlds. Tabriz had already mounted his large, tan camel, which was now walking away from me.

"Forgive me, Master," I called out.

The camel stopped walking, but the Master sat motionless in the saddle. I jogged toward Tabriz and looked up at him.

"I do not know if I can accept what you were trying to tell me, but perhaps by filling my heart with love, my mind may be more receptive." I wiped the tears from my cheeks with the back of my sleeve.

Shamus-i-Tabriz sat silently for a moment, then dismounted. I see you were able to let go of your mind enough to follow me here, he said. That is a good indication that one day you may indeed be ready for this information.

As it is with all battles of the mind, there is no real winner. The mind only thinks it wins.

Tabriz led his camel toward a small grove of trees near a field of thick grass. I walked by his side.

"I apologize for allowing my mind to interfere," I said.

You were tested to see whether you could control your mind. As you know, you didn't pass the test. This may seem unfortunate, in that this information will not be presented to the readers of your book. However, we can find a way to turn this seemingly negative experience around.

You see, the positive forces respond to each situation— even those which seem to be negative. They twist our failures into experiences to present or teach something positive. At the very least, they provide a mirror—so the lessons presented can be perceived.

We reached the trees. Tabriz tied his camel to a branch and sat down on a fallen log. I sat on the grass next to him and leaned my back against a tree.

Let's talk about cycles instead, *he suggested.* Information about them will be understood and appreciated by a much wider audience anyway.

I'm not exactly changing the subject, because numbers and cycles go hand in hand. Numbers help to shape and define cycles. In this way, they influence all aspects of life. Cycles govern our lives, dictate our experiences, and keep the Physical World running smoothly. There are yearly cycles, as well as monthly, weekly, daily, minute, second, and momentary cycles. We live within these rhythms, and each plays a role in our lives.

Each cycle repeats itself based on a numeric value. For example, there are two-year, three-year, four-, five-, seven-, nine-, ten-, and twelve-year cycles. Which of these numeric cycles will have the most impact on an individual depends on which numbers have the strongest influence in his life.

A cycle is the Sound's quality of rhythm in expression. Since the Sound is responsible for forming the matrix of all atoms and non-atoms in the Universe, everything expresses a rhythm. A thing's rhythm is defined as its own unique pattern of beats. It can be likened to a unique sequence of taps on a drum. Every rhythm also has a particular number associated with it. Cycles associated with that number will have a particularly strong affect on the rhythms of that number.

In the lower worlds, individual atoms are combined to form elements, molecules, and cells. Each express their own unique rhythms. They are the sum of the atoms' individual tempos. When atoms combine, some of their beats are cancelled out, some are amplified, and of course, other pulses are added.

The organs in one's body also express individual rhythms. These are the sum of all its cellular, molecular, and atomic cadences. Each organ's rhythm also resonates more closely with a particular number. It is most influenced by other rhythms and cycles associated with this number.

The organs comprise the physical body's overall rhythm. Ideally, the organs' rhythms should act in harmony with one another. Then the body's overall flow is expressed with harmony. This assures health.

The physical body's overall rhythm is not just a sum of the rhythms of its parts. It is also influenced by the rhythms of the individual's inner bodies—and vice versa. This is why inner turmoil can create physical troubles, even when the physical body is relatively strong and healthy.

Cycles in the environment can also influence us, especially if they resonate with the body's own rhythms. Events, circumstances, and people with rhythms similar to ours will also have a more influential impact on our lives.

This is true not only for the body as a whole, but also for the individual organs and cells. For example, the rhythm of foods and medicines are also associated with specific numbers. When this number-association matches that of a particular organ or cell, the substance will naturally be drawn there. Foods will also more effectively nourish cells when both food and cell share rhythms that correspond to the same numbers.

The rhythm of a medicine may differ from an organ's. But if they both correspond to the same number, the medicine's rhythm can encourage the organ's cadence to be more like the medicine's. This can have either negative or positive effects, depending on the nature of the medication.

Of course, if they are strong enough, outside rhythms can alter the body's cadence without sharing a numerical influence. Therefore potent healing tools such as medicines— or Therapeutic Diamonds and certain gemstones—must be used with care, knowledge, and responsibility.

Besides opening the door to greater health, knowledge of cycles is the first step to gaining control over the Physical Universe. It helps one become a master of the human consciousness. Consciously working with cycles in your life helps you realize your power in the physical dimension. I'm not referring to the power of the human consciousness, but to Soul's power in this world—It's ability to be the master of the human reality.

Through an understanding of cycles, one can influence the Physical Universe. In fact, such knowledge can be dangerous unless used exclusively for Self-mastery.

To attain physical-body mastership, you must understand cycles: what they are and the role they play in your life. You can employ cycles to both create positive changes in your life and to become less influenced by negative cycles.

Of course, physical-body mastership is only a step on the path to spiritual mastery. Awareness of cycles is actually a way to recognize the rhythm of Spirit. In order to be an adept of Spirit, one must know and understand all of Its aspects. Rhythm, which manifests as cycles, is one of these aspects.

"There are so many cycles. How can one possibly become aware of all of them?" I asked.

223

I will give you two methods to help you recognize the cycles which influence you most.

Identifying Your Physical and Inner Cycles

To perform the first technique, obtain a large calendar with plenty of space for daily notes. Then each evening, jot down what occurs in your life, both positive and negative. Record your physical, emotional, causal, mental, and spiritual well-being.

When you describe your physical well-being, note any injuries, pains, or physical disharmonies you may experience. Next, write about your feelings and emotional life.

Causal well-being can be recorded when you notice your attention turning to the past. This might happen when you receive a letter from a friend you haven't heard from in years. Note if you are spending much time daydreaming about the future or planning future events, which also affect your causal life.

Your mental well-being may be taxed at some times more than others, such as when you need to take a test at school or solve a complex problem at work or home.

Take note of your spiritual well-being as well. Have you had any special dreams or contemplative insights? What about the class or seminar you went to on a spiritual subject, or the religious ceremony that uplifted you? You can also record days when you experience a spiritual awakening or a special insight into life.

After logging this information for several weeks, look back at your notes. Have events in your life followed any patterns? For example, an emotional cycle might go like this: when you began recording your emotional well-being you felt balanced and happy. Then, the next day, something happened and you felt hurt or sad. The following day the sadness turned to anger and you reached the climax of your emotional expression regarding the issue. The day after, you felt balanced, but on the succeeding morning you again felt sad and then angry—this time about a different issue.

Examine the cycles for one inner body at a time, to try to spot their rhythms. At first, I suggest you make a study of weekly cycles in your life. Work up to an overview of all your subtle sheaths over longer cycles.

Spotting these patterns can be easier and more fun if you record your experiences in five different-colored inks. Use a different color when writing about each of your physical, emotional, causal, mental, and spiritual events.

Expanding Your Awareness of Cycles

The second exercise for becoming aware of cycles lasts only a week. Begin by writing several notes to yourself, to remind you to think about cycles. Then, tape the notes to various places—your bathroom mirror, the refrigerator, the dashboard of your car, and your desk, for instance.

During the week of this exercise, take time to contemplate the seasons and other cycles in nature. Wind, for example, expresses a rhythmic cycle, as do ocean waves and river currents. You can also contemplate on your body's rhythms—your breath and heartbeat. Be aware of the cycles of your daily habits and rituals of living. When do you eat? When do you go to bed, and when do you awaken?

Fill your life with thoughts of cycles—so much so that they spill over into your dreams. Dream symbols that indicate the technique has been successful are wheels and circles, especially those that turn or spin.

After placing this much attention on cycles, information about them will begin seeping into your consciousness. Watch for realizations as they surface during your daily life. If you

225

record them as they happen, you will note two things: a record of the success of the technique, and new information to apply in daily life. Otherwise, a heightened understanding of cycles will just become a part of your being, as if you always had this awareness. This makes it harder for your mind to identify the knowledge as new and useful.

Using Cycles to Change Your Life

The second thing you must learn is how to use cycles to create change in your life. You can harness the power of cyclical repetitiveness to cement positive changes.

In order to do this, identify a cycle associated with the behavior or situation you wish to change. The previous exercises can help you do this. Or the cycle may become apparent just by reflecting upon when the behavior or situation manifests.

After you become aware of the cycle influencing an undesirable experience, change just one thing that you do in it. It's as simple as that. By changing just one part of it, the entire cycle is interrupted, and a new cycle is set into motion.

Here is a great secret of life: it is much easier to make simple changes at the start of a new cycle than to make alterations in the middle of an old one.

This technique is especially helpful to make new cycles out of well-established ones, such as eating habits. If you want to change your diet to more healthful foods, examine the times when you eat. They are probably influenced by daily or hourly cycles.

Let's say you skip breakfast every morning, eat a snack mid-morning, have lunch around 1:00 p.m., then eat dinner around 7:00 p.m.

Now, to use the power of cycles to change your diet, first change the times that you have your meals. Instead of keeping your regular schedule, eat breakfast before you leave for work, move lunch forward to noon, and plan dinner for 6:00 p.m.

Once you have set a new cycle in motion, you are freer to rethink its components, such as the foods you eat.

At first, it may take effort to set a new cycle into motion. But after an initial adjustment phase, the repetitive power of the cycle itself will establish new, positive behaviors in your consciousness.

Diminishing the Undesirable Effects of Certain Cycles

Now, let's say something unpleasant regularly happens in your life. You want to change the intensity of its impact on you, but don't want to (or cannot), alter the cycle itself. This brings us to the third point you need to know about cycles: how to diminish their effect on you.

One method is to employ the imaginative faculty. By mocking up the situation and playing it through in advance, you can diminish the intensity of the experience before it manifests physically. Of course, the cycle must first be identified. Then you must determine when it is scheduled to occur again in your life.

For instance, let's say that your husband's aunt comes to visit you every three months. This has always been a tense experience for you, because of your attitudes about her. You decide you'd like these visits be more enjoyable for everyone.

Look up the day of her next visit on your calendar and visualize the events of that day unfolding. Play the visualization over and over in your mind until you determine what one thing you could do differently that would most improve the entire outcome. Visualize yourself making this one change. For instance, you could give her a gift of flowers as soon as she walks through the door.

227

"Sometimes an undesirable experience is part of a cycle that's hard to predict," I mused. "Since I can't pinpoint what the cycle is, it's hard to anticipate when it will happen again."

Sometimes more than one cycle influences a situation. When this occurs, it may seem like no one number shapes the cycle. Indeed, many cycles could be involved and the numeric influence could be complex. In such a case, just use the imaginative technique without trying to guess exactly when the situation will come up again.

Rhythm Alteration Method for Cycle Mastery

Another way to soften the effects of a cycle is to alter the rhythm of your being—so it responds to a different number. This changes the way all outside cycles and numeric influences interact with your life.

Overall rhythmic evolution occurs naturally in life, but it can be greatly hastened by practicing spiritual exercises to uplift your consciousness.

It is also possible to work with an exercise to change the rhythm of just the undesirable situation or behavior. This diminishes the effects of the cycles directly involved with it.

One final technique will help you do this. It gently transforms a large cycle by starting with its smallest cyclical component. This allows one's atoms to adjust swiftly and easily, wisking you gently from one balance point to the next.

Once again, the purpose of this technique is to help you realize that you, Soul, have greater control over your physical life than the human consciousness or the mind.

To begin this exercise, sit in a comfortable position so your body is relaxed. Close your eyes. Contemplate on the situation or behavior you'd like to improve, and its corresponding cycle. Now, think of two or three words that reflect the overall feeling the situation evokes within you.

Choose only positive words, as if speaking from the new, desired state of consciousness.

Let's say you'd like to adjust behavior that manifests from low self-esteem. Rather than assigning the words 'I am unworthy' to the cycle, say 'I am worthy', or 'I am Soul'.

You may discover that a shorter version of the statement fits the situation better, such as 'I, Soul', or even just 'Soul'. Or a more complex set of words may feel right, such as, 'I am worthy of having my physical, emotional, and spiritual needs fulfilled'.

You will be working with the smallest, moment-to-moment, rhythmic increment of the chosen situation. As you work with this mini-cycle, every larger cycle that incorporates it will also change.

The next step is to repeat your chosen words until they develop a strong rhythm in your consciousness. As you repeat the words, continue to think about the situation in question. Soon, the rhythm of the words will begin to resonate with the rhythm of the situation.

Continue the repetition until the words lose their meaning and become nothing more than a rhythm. *Feel* this rhythm of the words. Know that the part of you experiencing the deeper meaning and pulse behind the words is Soul.

This technique snares the mind in a repetitive loop generated by Soul. In doing so, you separate Soul from the mental body and can play a little trick on the mind. This is the next step of the exercise.

But first, let me share another secret about cycles. Even though they manifest physically and keep the Physical Universe running smoothly, the root of every cycle is in the mind. Once this secret is understood and Soul recognizes Its control over the mind, It can control and change any cycle.

This Self-recognition is being experienced by more and more individuals within Earth's society. People in general are looking beyond the human state and into the spiritual realms for answers to daily problems. This upliftment in consciousness can be seen in the fields of science, medicine, music, and other creative arts.

Changes in the weather cycles are just one result of this spiritual opening. Once regular and predictable, weather patterns across the Earth are now quite capricious. The weather and seasons, as well as many other cycles of nature, are directly affected by the mental and spiritual activity of the planet's inhabitants.

But let's get back to the exercise. Listen to the words until you, as Soul, feel the rhythm behind them. Then use your imagination to shine a ray of light toward your mind. This light-ray can take whatever form you wish. It could just be the light of your attention focusing on the mind. Or, it could be a burst of music or a lighthouse beacon.

The purpose of the beacon, whatever its form, is to disrupt the repetitive sequence of the words you have used in this exercise, and alter it. Let the beacon of light change the words. Instead of repeating 'I am worthy', say instead: 'I, I, am worthy', or 'I am worthy, worthy'. Or stretch or contract the time between the syllables as you sing them.

Try several variations of the words. Then go back and sing the old rhythm just one or two times. Continue to alternately sing the new variations and then repeat the old, original version until you are unable to remember or precisely duplicate it. At this point, pick your favorite new version and repeat it several times.

By doing this, Soul has generated a modification in the rhythm of the issue being addressed. The ramifications will be felt in all the larger cycles it is a part of. Furthermore, these changes will be beneficial to the individual's whole being, since they were initiated by Soul.

In the days following this exercise you may notice shifts both in your behavior and in your perceptions of time—first in minutes and then in hours—as the component cycles are altered in larger and larger increments of time. If your life is very busy, you may not be aware of these shifts. But at some point, you will realize your life is no longer as limited by the behavior you were trying to change.

So, be aware of time after you do this technique, especially for the first several hours. Also be alert to any shifts in perception. This exercise can help expand your awareness. You may discover the Physical Universe is much more changeable and movable than you may have previously thought!

The longer the cycle you are working on, the more constant and resistant to shifts in time it will be. The shorter the cycle, on the other hand, the more easily manipulated. Shifting a years-long cycle, for example, is practically impossible until one first alters many of the smaller cycles within it. When you alter the short cycles first, the longer ones reflect those changes.

One note: there is a price to pay if you try to force changes through willpower. Willpower is generated by the mind. Rarely does it succeed in making permanent changes. It can also cause imbalances if evoked. If the imbalances are left unresolved, they can sink into the cells and affect their function.

The disrupted cellular function may not manifest until several months later. Usually the individual has no idea that his decreased health relates to trying to force a cycle to change. But indeed it does. This technique, on the other hand, can help ease transitions between cycles and does not force changes. It allows the individual to move gradually into a new state by following a natural order for change. This order is dictated by Soul and starts with component cycles first.

As the smaller cycles are altered, the larger one is affected through a ripple effect. Then, its next scheduled occurence is delayed or hastened because of the shifts in the smaller cycles.

When that larger cycle shifts, it will be affected by different smaller cycles than before. It will resonate differently with all the other significant cycles in the individual's environment, as well as within the person's physical and inner bodies.

When a larger cycle is altered, it doesn't necessarily alter other major cycles as well. Only those that overlap with the changed cycle are affected. However, all events associated with the shifted cycle change. Experiences are the result of many different cycles converging in a single time and space.

For example, let's say you change your eating cycle. Now instead of routinely eating a breakfast of eggs, sausage, and pancakes at 7:00 a.m., you now eat a simple bowl of fruit at 6:00 a.m. As a result, other events—which may not seem to have anything to do with food—will change also. Yet in some way, they are associated with the numeric factors of your new habit.

Once you become aware of cycles, you don't need to keep your attention on them all the time. It's like learning to add the numbers between one and ten. Once you learn them, you know them. It's not necessary to continue focusing on adding one plus one over and over again. You simply incorporate the principle and apply it to more complex mathematical problems.

Try to do the same with cycles. Recognize their existence, learn how to use them to your benefit, and realize that their impact can be altered. Remember: Changing what happens within a cycle is usually much easier than trying to change a cycle itself.

This ends my discourse on cycles.

I would like to lead you now to another being who will share some insights with you on the organization of the physical and subtle bodies.

Tabriz stood up, untied his camel, and led the animal away.

I knew from past experience with this master that he would disappear if I took my attention off him. Sometimes he simply vanished, while other times he rode off on his camel.

This spiritual adept simply didn't have time for those who faltered in their attention, or whose love for God was inconsistent.

I riveted all my focus on his back and followed him to my next appointment with as much inner alertness as I could muster.

Chapter 20

Life Systems

I *followed Shamus-i-Tabriz's quick step as he tramped through a forest. The vegetation became more dense and tropical as we made our way along. After what seemed like hours of travel, we finally stepped into the light of a clearing. A small temple stood nearly hidden by the surrounding vegetation. It was made of pure gold and ornately encrusted with jewels. Beams of white light emanated from almost every gem. My mouth dropped open in awe of the beautiful little building.*

Shamus smiled at my expression, tipped his black felt hat in farewell, and vanished again into the thick foliage.

Soon, I felt someone's presence behind me and turned to see who it was. There stood a nearly bald master at least seven feet tall. He wore a creamy, short-sleeved robe of straight and simple style. A gold cord bound the garment at his waist.

Light and Sound concentrates so strongly here only the crystalline matrix of gemstones can contain it, *he commented.*

I wondered who he was, but he didn't offer to introduce himself.

The gold you see is not metal, *he continued.* Its color and the beams of white light are created by the intensity of the Light and Sound of Spirit swirling within.

"Are the jewels also a product of the Light and Sound?" I asked. "Or were they built into the temple so the Light and Sound could concentrate here?"

235

On the Causal Plane, where we are now, images and substances are easily molded. These jewels were spontaneously manifested to house the spiritual energy converging at this place.

Regardless of which plane they exist on, atoms arranged into crystalline matrixes can contain concentrations of Light and Sound that stagger the imagination. This includes those gemstones found on Earth.

Each crystal type has a distinct purpose. Its matrix channels the spiritual energy to create unique effects. Moreover, Therapeutic Diamonds and gemstones can be placed in certain configurations to create specific and highly individualized vortexes of spiritual energy. Just as each gem has a distinct purpose, so does each configuration of diamonds and gemstones.

Combining Therapeutic Diamonds in specific ways, with or without gemstones, initiates precise transformations in the physical and subtle bodies. Diamonds have this capability only if they resonate with the life systems of the human being.

Not all diamonds harbor this affinity. A diamond that is not therapeutic can rob the human body of life energy.

Gems transmit concentrations of spiritual energy. This energy is the catalyst for profound change. If applied correctly, Earthly diamond and gem configurations can emulate the healing effects of an inner-plane center such as the one before you.

Yes, this is a place of healing and great change. The presence of a spiritual master can also manifest spiritual energy so powerful it can change another's atomic structure. Above all, there is the eternal, inner presence of the Wayshower. This is the most powerful vehicle for the Light and Sound in all the planes of God. The Wayshower's inner presence is felt to the degree that the spiritual student opens himself to it.

The Master paused, then continued. I want you to know that I, myself, do not use diamonds and gemstones. I do not need physically manifested tools to help me work directly with the Light and Sound. However, I no longer occupy a physical body either.

Men and women today can also work directly with Spirit, without the need for tools. But first they must transcend self-imposed limitations, weaknesses, and spiritual poverty which cloud and inhibit this ability. They must overcome past life karma and settle scores of unresolved issues. These hold the individual back spiritually. Each tightens the heart, and prevents the seeker from soaring through the lower worlds back to the Golden Kingdom and beyond.

There are masters today, however, devoted to helping one tap the Light and Sound directly. They are opening doors and manifesting new ways to release all burdens and limitations.

Gemstone therapy is one of these doors. A gemstone, or any spiritual tool for that matter, is simply a container of spiritual energy. Working with gems is indeed like working directly with Spirit. Hidden knowledge about gemstone therapy is now being disclosed on Earth. The door to Diamond Therapy has also been opened. Therapeutic Diamonds have an affinity with the physical and inner body structures like no other diamonds or gemstones.

The seven harmonious color rays expressed by a Therapeutic Diamond are powerful, yet invisible healers. Soon you will complete the rigorous training required for identifying these colors. You will be able to distinguish the eight different color-ray-bearing Therapeutic Diamonds from those with harmful frequencies. However, you will continue learning new ways to treat the physical and inner bodies with these Therapeutic Diamonds.

Diamond Therapists require knowledge of the inner bodies because Therapeutic Diamonds do not limit their work to just the physical shell. They uplift all aspects of the individual when applied. However, the therapist may focus a diamond's effects on a particular inner body for healing.

My purpose here is to share information about how the anatomy of the lower bodies is organized. This anatomy can be divided according to life systems. Each system spans the physical, emotional, causal, and mental bodies. Seven specific life systems comprise one overall system. Each corresponds to a particular color ray and is named for that ray. These seven are: the Red, Orange, Yellow, Green, Blue, Indigo, and Violet Life Systems.

The cells and organs in the Red Life System take their nourishment from a precisely-dictated spectrum dominated by the red ray, and so on. The overall life system, however, responds to a spectrum in which all seven colors are present in relatively equal amounts. No single ray dominates the others. This is called the White Life System.

Life systems span and connect all man's inner and outer bodies. Hence it is difficult to describe their components. They correspond to subtle-body anatomy unknown to medicine. Therefore, I will largely relate the life systems to physical body parts.

Keep in mind, though, that the organs of a life system have more than a physical manifestation. Each has a corresponding aspect in the inner bodies. Man must realize he is much more than just a physical being. The physical body is just a part of who you are.

I detect information about life systems in your aura, *he commented abruptly.*

"Yes," I replied. "I learned something about them in my Diamond Therapy classes at Askleposis."

Very well. For the benefit of those who will one day read of your experiences here, please describe some physical organs belonging to each life system, and their energetic functions.

"I'd be glad to," I replied.

"The Red Life System includes all parts of an individual that provide strength and protection. Muscles, tendons, and fascia are physical examples of its components.

"Metabolic functions and the production, regulation, and distribution of chemicals in the body is governed by the Orange Life System. In the physical body, this includes the endocrine and lymph glands, as well as the lymph itself. These body chemicals regulate protein, fat, carbohydrates, vitamins, and minerals.

"The yellow spectrum harmonizes the inner and outer bodies when vibratory rate changes occur. Such changes can be the result of therapies, foods or medicines, or spiritual experiences, to name a few. Yellow helps the body adjust to higher and lower vibratory rates. It helps the physical body eliminate waste. It also adapts the body chemistry to the new vibrations of an awakening consciousness. The skin and the organs of the urinary tract are members of this system.

"The Green System helps each part of a body retain independence while functioning harmoniously within the whole. All of the visceral organs as well as the eyes and brain are members of this system. The green-predominating spectrum helps its components maintain their unique functions while communicating openly and freely with the body that houses them.

"The blue spectrum aids circulation or movement of energy within and between bodies. This can be a circulation of color rays, energies, fluids, or information. The Blue Life System has three components which support each other in a triangular fashion. The first is the sense organs, which bring knowledge and nutrients to the body. The second includes the nerve sheaths, cerebrospinal fluid, blood, and blood vessels. They use the knowledge and nutrition provided by the first group to protect the information and nutrient-transfer mechanisms in the body. The third group consists of the

neuro-connectors between the physical and supra-physical body. They use the second group's protection devices to shield members of the first group—the knowledge and nutrient transfer mechanisms.

"Indigo governs the structural system. It supports the shape and integrity of each body, including the connectors between the sheaths. Physical body manifestations include the bones, joints, and ligaments.

"Communication is essential between all aspects of an individual. The Violet Life System provides direct means for Soul and the innate intelligence of each body to remain awake and able to communicate. Violet governs information transfer and feedback mechanisms, including the nerves and the brain.

"The White Life System has no predominant color. It supports the entire individual as a whole, integrated being. The White System connects all aspects of the individual into the unbroken continuum of vibratory rates that make up the lower world sheaths."

The Master nodded when I finished speaking.

All body parts consist of cells, molecules, and atoms, *he continued.* These can belong to any of the seven life systems. Each individual organ and cell has Red Life System components that provide strength and protection. It also has Orange System elements to aid chemical transfer, Yellow System influences to help it adapt to new vibratory rates, and so on.

Although each life system has specific areas of influence, they often intertwine and overlap each other. All of the systems work together within the lower bodies.

Life system interaction follows a specific sequence within the physical and subtle bodies. This circle of communication is comprised of the seven colors in this order: red, orange, yellow, green, blue, indigo, and violet.

Each spectrum and system is intertwined with the one next to it in an unending circle. The Indigo System is closely allied with the Blue and Violet Systems, while the Red System affects the Orange and Violet Systems more closely.

The life system components appear the most distinct and separate in the physical body. For example, your bones, which are of the Indigo Life System, are highly differentiated from the sense organs or nerves, which are Blue and Violet System components. Yet energetically, the bones interact more closely with Violet System elements than those of the Yellow Life System. These system interactions are more apparent in the subtle bodies than in the physical.

He stopped speaking and we stood in silence for a while. Then my attention was drawn to a huge vortex that suddenly appeared above the temple. It funnelled spiritual current into the building in a dazzling cascade of Light and Sound. I felt energized just watching it.

An Imaginative Diamond Therapy Technique for Rejuvenating Life Systems

Now, I would like to present an exercise to strengthen, nourish, and heal the components of any life system.

First, choose the system you would like to work with. Then cup your hands. Imagine you are holding a baseball and trying to cover its entire surface with your fingers.

Now, keep your hands in this position and imagine the ball replaced by a star. See its intense beams of color, as they radiate through your fingers. The light forms an energetic cloud or halo which extends several feet in all directions. Although each of the color rays are present in this cloud, it expresses one color in particular. This color corresponds to the life system you chose to work on.

Enjoy this star and its light for as long as you wish. When you are ready, try to detect the boundary, or farthest perimeter of the light-ray cloud surrounding your body. Now use your imagination to draw the perimeter in closer and closer to your hands. As you do, the light rays will become increasingly concentrated.

Use all your inner strength to compress the mighty light rays until they are completely encompassed within your fingers. The star you hold in your hands is now a dense mass of color rays.

In fact, the rays are so dense, the star necessarily transforms into a supra-physical faceted diamond—the only non-living manifestation that can contain such a powerful concentration of Light and Sound.

The diamond will be therapeutic because the frequencies it carries are a harmonious balance of all seven color rays. However, one color ray dominates its spectrum. This is the ray that corresponds to the life system you decided to work on.

Let the diamond be as big as you wish. Open your thumbs slightly and look at it. It may look brilliantly liquid and colorless, as all physically-manifested Therapeutic Diamonds appear to the physical eyes. But know that it contains all seven color rays.

Your diamond is one of eight different kinds of Therapeutic Diamonds. Each strengthens, nourishes, and heals the components of a different life system. If you imagined a blue cloud or blue colors radiating from the star at the beginning of the exercise, call your gem a Therapeutic Blue Diamond. It will heal and support the components of the Blue Life System. Likewise for the other six color rays: red, orange, yellow, green, indigo, and violet.

The eighth type of Therapeutic Diamond is, of course, a Therapeutic White Diamond. All seven color rays are present in relatively equal amounts, with no one color predominating. This diamond's spectrum will support the whole individual, although it will focus its energies on any parts in need.

A Therapeutic Diamond has special and unique effects on the body. Just like the human body, it is based on carbon atoms. The Therapeutic Diamond is a very special, physically manifested tool. It awakens the body and its components to their own blueprints for optimal health. It also provides color-ray nourishment in a form both blueprints and body components recognize as food.

The diamond's rays provide the body with a pure form of nourishment. They also enhance the body's magnetism, so it draws energy not only from the diamond, but from the atmosphere as it should. A Therapeutic Diamond can prove vital to cells so weak they cannot attract color-ray nourishment through the surrounding clouds of disharmony.

The Therapeutic Diamond in your hands can nourish and strengthen all the components of its corresponding life system. When combined with another Therapeutic Diamond, the two can help resolve limiting patterns, remove accumulations, and release blockages.

The Master stopped speaking. We held a magical silence between us, thick with the Light and Sound of Spirit. I had nothing to say or ask, yet there was no awkwardness or shyness in his presence.

The diamond remained in my hands. I felt its energy seeping into every atom of my being. Its color rays cleared my head like sunlight melting clouds. I felt whole and complete. Life danced through every cell. I felt every part of my being joining me in my quest to return to the Golden Kingdom.

When you are finished with the diamond, *the Master advised,* imagine it dissolving back into the ethers from which it was born. You can reconstruct the diamond whenever you need it.

Now, I have been instructed to lead you to the Temple of Golden Wisdom at Askleposis. There you will peruse the pages of its Book of Golden Wisdom, and read aloud what you see.

I quickly outlined a clear mental impression of the bejeweled temple before us. I wanted to catch some of its beauty as a precious memory—and perhaps anchor its vibration in my awareness for a return visit someday. Then the Master extended his energy field around me and we stepped into the air. Forests, fields, and valleys blurred beneath us as we flew toward one of the most enormous mountain ranges I had ever seen.

Soon we landed among its rocky foothills. My mind wondered if the mountains were too high to fly over as I watched my guide scratch his chin and scan the walls of the nearby cliffs.

Ah, there it is! *he exclaimed.*

Without notice, he plunged between two boulders into a tunnel almost hidden by the rocks.

Chapter 21

A Book of Golden Wisdom

I stood hesitating before the tunnel. Dark waves of claustrophobia washed over me as I faced its dark and uninviting maw. My mind was already weary and stretched from two masters' discourses. And now my fears were being tested.

The tunnel's shadows had swallowed the Master. I knew I had to follow quickly, but my feet were rooted to the ground.

A thought of the Wayshower crossed the screen of my mind, and I called for help: Please send a light to guide my path!

As I stood helpless, an unexpected answer swirled in front of me. It was a baby vortex of gentle, golden wind. With motherly instinct, I reached out and cradled it in my arms. At the heart of the wind lay a transparent, golden book.

It was a clear reminder of Sat Nam's assignment and gift. As I clasped it to my heart, a renewed sense of excitement filled me for this project I had accepted.

My heart swelled with love, confidence, and determination and I dove into the tunnel. After a few steps, I sent a flash of heartfelt thanks to the Wayshower, as I discovered the golden light of the book dimly illuminating my path.

The Master stood waiting when I finally emerged at the tunnel's end. The astral sunlight lent a beautiful pink glow to the cream of his robes. The book in my arms dissolved into the ethers as I stepped out into daylight again.

Silently, we again took to the air and flew toward Askleposis from the northeast. I had only passed this way once before. It was in a dream long ago, when I was first learning how to travel in the inner worlds.

As we approached the temple, the Master spoke.

Many people are able to visit this temple and gaze at the sacred book within, which radiates such magnificent light. However, few are curious enough to actually read from the book. Although all are welcome, many wait for a direct invitation to decipher its wisdom.

And so I offer thee an invitation. Whosoever comes to Askleposis can attend its classes or read from the Book of Golden Wisdom.

It is a spiritual blessing to be here. When you attend a class, you are accepting a gift that has already been granted. In the same way, it is a blessing to see this book. And it is a form of acceptance of the gift to take the steps and read from its pages.

We landed near the Temple and walked up its white marble steps. The Master's aura began to glow with warm golden light that enveloped me. Perhaps it is for protection, I thought. But I noticed that my own aura was beginning to radiate a similar light as well.

The Master had given me a precious gift. I would be allowed to absorb some of the wisdom in the Golden Book and translate it into words for my physical tape-recorder.

We passed between six towering, marble-white columns encircling the small temple. At the center of a circular platform rose an ornately-carved gold pedestal. The Book of Golden Wisdom rested atop, illuminating the temple with the blinding light of its pages.

The Master beckoned me up the platform. I proceeded slowly, filled with reverence. Could I read the book through all the blinding light?

My guide spoke, his face illuminated by the liquid pages. This book shares a characteristic with the university catalogs. Readers perceive different passages, depending on their need and level of understanding. The text of this book, however, cannot be compared to any other. It speaks with the melody of life itself. It communicates directly to the reader about his life—sharing wisdom, lessons, and guidance as needed.

Each reader will grasp something different from this sacred text. Some find stories of great adventure and healing, while others receive spiritual techniques or instructions for their daily lives. Still others discover golden waves of poetry within the book's pages.

Some may even experience the book as a series of images, as if watching a movie. Others may see blank pages of blinding white or golden light that is intensely purifying. The cleansing is exactly what is required at the time. You may have a different experience with the divine book each time you gaze upon it.

At times, you may read the Golden Book as you would any other. On later visits, the words may be unfamiliar. They may appear in another language, or as symbols.

However you experience it—even if you just imagine looking into its pages—the Book of Golden Wisdom will impress its knowledge and wisdom upon you, whether you are conscious of it or not.

Reading from the Book of Golden Wisdom

To read from the Book of Golden Wisdom does not require any ritual. At this point, I'd like to share a contemplation technique to guide the reader to this spot as well, so he or she may gain enlightenment too.

First, lie down. Take a few minutes to relax your mind and emotions. Now, focus your attention within. You may

247

sing 'HU' or any other word or name that brings you spiritual upliftment.

Imagine you are walking through the gardens of Askleposis toward the circular, white temple on the hill. See it glowing with a golden light.

Climb the steps and enter the temple. Behold the sacred volume. Brilliant white light pours from the book. You may also hear a divine symphony more glorious than any earthly orchestra.

Walk to the book and gaze at its pages. Visualize and feel its presence as clearly as you can. Let yourself bathe in the Light and Sound emanating from it.

To fully experience the information it has for you, relax even more. Let yourself fall into a daydream or even a light sleep.

Before you look into the pages of the holy book, take a deep breath. Clear your heart and fill it with love. Love for life itself, and for the Spirit out of which your atoms were born. If you wish, extend this love to your parents who combined and nurtured your atoms until they formed the sheath in which you now reside, and the Wayshower, for his love, guidance, and protection.

With a heart filled with the purest love within you, approach the book. Watch its pages turn by themselves, as if an unseen hand is finding the exact chapter you need to read. Be open to any experience. It will be exactly what you need.

Don't worry if you fall asleep. Know that Soul has read from the Golden Book, even if your physical consciousness is unaware of it.

With these words, the book became less blinding. Or perhaps my perceptions adjusted to it. A divine message began to swim into focus on the pages beneath my face...

Chapter 22

On the Road to
Self- and God-Realization

Sing 'HU' with me now, *the Master suggested.*

Our voices blended and resonated in dual harmony.
"HUUUUU."

Can you see the words on the pages more clearly now? *he*
asked.

"Yes," I replied. "But they seem to be written in a lan-
guage other than English."

Never mind. Understanding is not limited by the language skills of your present physical brain. Besides, in your
numerous lifetimes you have spoken many languages.

The truths found in the Book of Golden Wisdom lie
beyond language. The book speaks directly to the consciousness. Trust in your heart. Know you will understand what
you read and communicate it!

I pushed all doubt from my being and looked at the
strange yet somehow familiar writing on the pure white pages
of the glowing book. Any doubt and unsureness would have
foiled my efforts; if allowed even a small foothold, they would
spread quickly throughout my consciousness.

I closed my eyes and relaxed into a dream-like state, as
the Master suggested. I imagined my heart filling with love. I

saw it circulating throughout my entire being and radiating out from every atom. Satisfied my outflow was sufficient, I opened my eyes and looked at the book once more.

The title of the chapter before me was 'The Ways of the Physical Body'. Here is my best translation of what I read:

The physical body is made of atoms and their fundamental particles. These particles are manifestations of the positive, negative, and neutral qualities of Light and Sound. Light simply responds to what the Sound formulates. Therefore, atoms are not particles of matter at all, but formulations of energy. When they are amassed in particular combinations, these energy packets are perceived as solid, material forms.

Another energetic component of the body is its blueprints. Blueprints organize the formulations of energy and direct their function. Blueprints blocked and clouded by negative, entangled, or misaligned energies serve a purpose. They teach Soul the lessons It needs to be free of Its lower bodies and return to the Golden Kingdom. They help It correct spiritual imbalances and immaturities which caused the disharmony to manifest. Blueprints also link Soul to its lower bodies, including the physical. Without this connection, people might choose to leave their physical bodies when life became difficult, in the hope that the after-life would bring joy.

Actually, the more difficult Soul's experience in life, the more rigidly It is attached to the physical body. Conversely, an individual in harmony with his or her lower bodies will experience life as a fluid reality-agreement. The connection between Soul and the physical body is supple and free.

The ability to explore heaven and move among the lower bodies lies in direct proportion to one's neutrality. True spiritual masters have mastered this neutral state to move at will from one arena of consciousness to another.

Therefore, if you are in the face of great difficulties, whether they are illnesses or disharmonies with loved ones, business associates, or friends; if your mind is wrought with confusion or your emotions are knots of grief, jealousy, or anger, take heart. Your salvation from these states lies in your ability to become neutral.

Relax and recognize you are not your physical body, your tumultuous emotions, nor the machine which is your mind. You are Soul.

Soul has physical and subtle bodies because It has made an agreement with Its Creator. Soul was not forced to take on lower bodies. This narrow view of life is sometimes adopted to shirk responsibility for difficulties. 'Ah,' some say, 'it wasn't me who wanted these problems. No, it was God. God demanded that I take on these lower bodies and because I am God's servant, I obeyed. So, here I am. Woe is me.'

Soul, thou art not a servant of God nor are ye God Itself. Thy destiny is to be a co-worker with It.

To attain such a position, you go to school. Liken this to a son or daughter who aspires to be a full partner in his or her father's law firm. Let's assume the ambition is not just born of family tradition. It is born out of Soul's desire to pursue that goal.

Such a child cannot become a partner in a law firm without the proper schooling. He or she must pass all the necessary years of classes and then graduate. The school knowledge is first put into practice during an apprenticeship. As experience gradually builds in the 'real world' of law, the son or daughter rises through the ranks of the law firm as a full attorney.

Eventually the lawyer is seasoned by experience, toughened by failure, and encouraged by successes and accomplishments. He or she gains stamina after learning the value of persistence and unfaltering attention to a goal. Only then, perhaps, will the son or daughter become eligible for partnership. This period of eligibility, however, may stretch on for some years without apparent fruition.

251

During these years, the candidate's focus on the goal must be at the forefront of both heart and mind. Others with seemingly less experience and achievements may attain partnership first. Patience and a true love for the law are tested and developed during this period.

Finally the candidate passes all the inner and outer tests leading to the goal. The partnership committee and his or her father, who is the president of the firm, grant a full partnership in the law office.

Soul is the child who wishes to work in partnership with Its Creator, (which actually has no gender). The position of partnership represents a state of consciousness called God-Realization. Soul may periodically visit this state for many years. But when It finally dwells there, It is recognized as a co-worker with God.

To fulfill this goal, Soul willingly takes on lower bodies and attends the earthly academy of life. While there, each spiritual achievement signifies the completion of a cycle of intensive schooling. Each represents more advanced levels of education. At the Fifth Spiritual Achievement, it is finally time for Soul to 'practice' what It has learned.

To further the partnership analogy, Soul's classrooms are all Its many lifetimes and experiences in the lower worlds. There It unfolds Its relationship with Its lower bodies. Eventually It becomes aware of Its true nature and relationship with Spirit and Its Creator. This is Self-Realization.

But this understanding, or awakening, is not all that is required. It is only one graduation. Now Soul must enter into life, in the same way the law student must apprentice with the partners in the firm. Soul must apply what it has learned to everyday life.

Can It survive the attention-detractors? Can It keep Its goal—the God-Conscious state—clearly in mind? It requires unwavering attention and loyalty.

Self-Realization, which Soul can enter fully at the Fifth Spiritual Achievement, is only a step. One must master more and more of the tools Spirit has provided for unfoldment. These include the lower bodies themselves. Gradually Soul works more and more directly with the Sound and Light Current, while mastering balance, control, and beingness in Its physical, emotional, causal, mental, and subconscious bodies.

At times, mastership may seem an eternity away, as you continue to practice co-workership. With so many lessons to sort out from Soul's past incarnations, it seems there can't possibly be more to learn. Yet life repeats situations you thought you'd mastered before.

If you feel this way, you probably have learned certain parts of a lesson. But a cycle will return until you have mastered it fully. Each time it touches your life, you have another opportunity to expand your viewpoint and advance on the spiritual path.

In your despair while going through these experiences, you learn patience, yes. But the true lesson behind the grief, the feelings of abandonment, and the questioning, is that of neutrality. Soul must become a loving force for this great quality and characteristic of Spirit Itself: loving detachment.

There is a prayer one can say, to invoke this spirit or state. It is to simply whisper, 'Thy will be done', as each event or situation arises in life. This allows Spirit to enter the liquid moment and uplift it.

Eventually, Soul learns how to partake of all experiences without getting caught up in them; to be in the lower worlds but not of them. The individual does this by keeping his heart open to the divine love of the Creator.

After wanting God-Consciousness and co-workership with God more than life itself, even these goals must be released. This is a crucial test, to be detached not only from what one lives and dies for, but from the purpose of life itself.

When this final attachment is released, a flood of Divine Spirit consumes Soul, in glorious admittance into true co-workership.

At this point, it might seem Soul's long story, which has spanned thousands and thousands of ages, has come to a close. But the entrance into an order of spiritual masters is only another chapter in Its story. There is always a plus element to Soul's unfoldment. Soul constantly extends Its awareness into greater and greater realms of consciousness. There are many spiritual goals beyond that of mastership.

Now Soul's goals are no longer personal. It works for the good of the entire law firm, to continue our analogy. The new partner now confers with the head of the firm to carefully formulate the overall design of his job. All the details of creating an effective and successful practice are worked out with each of the other partners, both individually and collectively.

In this uncharted territory, Soul's journey becomes entirely unique. During schooling, apprenticeship, and early work, Soul participates in a largely pre-determined round of lessons, just as at a school. Fellow Souls share similar experiences, although from an individually-tailored viewpoint. But once Soul becomes a full-fledged member of the partnership, It walks on new creative ground.

It is impossible to speak of the journey of Soul beyond the Golden Kingdom. Indeed, the heart of God lies far beyond this heavenly point. Although the path may be charted in the beginning, the further It reaches into God Consciousness, the less travelled it becomes. There is only Divine Spirit to rely upon, calling Soul ever home to God.

The Light and Sound Current provide Soul with all It needs. The Light illuminates Its path, and keeps It moving forward. The Sound is the path itself. It helps Soul stay in balance on the razor's edge of life. Soul learns the value of not leaning too far to the right nor to the left, but staying in the middle ground of strong and loving neutrality.

When this neutrality is allowed to flow freely through It, Soul takes on the qualities of a powerful gyroscope. It can not be easily swayed or knocked over. The more Soul seats Itself in this force, the stronger and broader its service as a vehicle for God. Its spinning vortex becomes so refined nothing can move It from Its course and mission.

As the Golden Kingdom comes into conscious focus, the individual begins to recognize the Light and Sound of God as the only reliable direction in his lower worlds. However, as long as he lives in the lower worlds and has lower bodies, Soul must deal with many distractions. It must consciously and constantly work at communication with the Divine.

The coarse vibrations of the lower bodies prevent direct communication with the undivided Spirit Current. Instead, Soul's sheaths must communicate and work directly with the Light and Sound, as it manifests dually in the lower worlds. After all, the lower bodies are comprised of these same dual energies.

Those who wish to communicate directly with Spirit can start by learning to work with Light and Sound. Eventually, Soul learns to open Itself to pure, undivided Spirit and communicate with It directly.

Regardless of where Soul is on Its path to Self- and God-Realization, It works best with the Light and Sound Current by surrendering to It. Detachment and loving neutrality are required for this surrender. The greater one's expression of neutrality, the greater one's ability to surrender. Then Spirit, in the form of Light and Sound, can easily flow through the individual, facilitating clear communication between Itself and Soul.

This clear communication often manifests subconsciously through creative expression. A person might be oblivious to his spiritual unfoldment. Yet his uplifting ability to create reveals a true connection with God. Creativity is merely spiritual energy in expression.

Spiritual mastery is mastery of Spirit. It occurs when Soul enters into a conscious, intimate agreement with the forces that created It. These forces are the Light and Sound of God. It then works consciously with these divine currents.

As one nears spiritual mastership, he becomes more creative about how he lives each moment. This creativity is as valid a measure as any of his ability to work with Spirit. It may manifest in artwork or writing, or less tangible gifts like happiness, a facility for business, or a loving relationship. The ultimate creativity is to make each moment one of inspiration—to polish it until it shines like a diamond. No matter the manifestation, a concentrated focus of creative love is the mark of a master or a master-to-be.

The first goal of a spiritual apprentice is to find his true, spiritual identity. Then he must operate the lower bodies as best he can from this viewpoint. How can he find this identity? Where does Soul exist? In the heart? No and yes. Soul exists in the Golden Kingdom.

But, Soul also exists in the heart as love. We are not speaking here of physical or emotional love, but rather a God love, a divine love laced with gratitude and surrender. With this love, one can move beyond physical laws and limitations and view the lower worlds as a useful illusion.

The material realms are mocked up to help Soul become a co-worker with the Divine. Space, time, energy, and matter are gifts to Soul, for Its benefit. These elements of the lower worlds only exist for Soul's use.

Grade-schoolers rarely reflect on pre-school. And high schoolers seldom return to dwell on their grade-school experiences. So too, Soul, when It graduates from the lower worlds and releases Its lower bodies, no longer reflects on the laws of space, time, energy, and matter. It has no need of them. They become nothing more than a distant memory or impression. Only the effects, the culmination of Its experiences in the lower worlds accompany It into the Higher Worlds.

The Master placed his hand over the words. You have read and absorbed more than enough for what is needed now.

Self-discipline is necessary on the path to spiritual mastership. Too much of anything, even spiritual energy, can be harmful. You must remember your goal of spiritual mastership in all that you do. This streamlines your efforts and enables you to work within the spiritual Law of Economy.

The Law of Economy dictates that everything we do, think, or say is aimed toward the best spiritual advantage of not only ourselves, but of the Whole. In this way, nothing is wasted and all our energies are pointed toward God.

Your purpose in reading from the Golden Book is to present yet another chapter of Soul's story. That purpose is fulfilled.

The strange words in the book were once again replaced by brilliant white light. I left the great book open and accompanied the Master down the temple steps with a grateful heart. My thoughts lingered on what I had read.

"It's a paradox that Soul exists in the heart of the lower bodies and yet it does not," I said.

We reached the bottom of the steps and started walking back across the field, toward the tunnel.

Soul's home is in the Golden Kingdom, *the Master replied.* However, It extends a part of Its consciousness into the lower bodies to enliven and activate them for Its spiritual unfoldment.

It remains connected to these bodies until the consciousness expands beyond them into mastery of all lower-world realities. After that, It is free to release the lower bodies and unfold further into the heart of God.

One way to increase your awareness of yourself as Soul is to let your natural happy state bubble to the surface.

I'll let you in on a secret. Happiness is not an emotion born in the emotional body, even though it is *felt* there. The truth is, happiness is an inborn expression of Soul; it is one of Its most innate qualities.

Yes, derivatives of happiness arise in the emotional body. But the kind of happiness that promotes balanced contentment and sublime joy, and that nurtures divine love, neutrality, and surrender, comes from Soul.

Liberate Your Wellspring of Happiness

To liberate Soul's wellspring of happiness, try this self-reflective exercise.

Part 1

Contemplate how much you are expressing yourself as Soul by the degree and quality of quiet happiness or inner joy you feel in your daily activities.

Think about the physical activities and situations you are involved in, as well as the conditions and circumstances your physical body is currently experiencing. Are they imbued with an underlying happiness?

If so, your experiences are teaching you valuable lessons. If not, they may merely be a continuous replay of old records. Judge by your happiness. If your body is experiencing disease, sift through the fear, discomfort, and inconvenience of it all, and ask: am I truly happy?

Spiritual happiness does not come from the emotional body or ideal mental scenarios. It is possible to feel emotionally sad, unhappy, or depressed, yet underneath it all, connect with the refreshing joy of Soul. Soul delights in change, challenge, and growth. It delights in life itself.

If you feel joy, you are unfolding, resolving karma, and taking priceless steps home. Of course, this happiness does not mean you should sit back and accept your discomforts. Rather, it should be a wellspring and inspiration to do what you can. By all means, strive to diminish pain, bring situations into balance, and make life less difficult. Use whatever tools Spirit has provided for healing and knowledge.

Part 2

Then contemplate on happiness itself. Nurture it and let it spread throughout your being.

If you feel unable to let happiness flow, a spiritual tool may help remove the limitations and disharmonies that block it. Many such tools are provided by the Light and Sound for this purpose. They include creative visualizations, gemstones, exercise, herbs, vitamins, acupuncture, and massage, to name just a few.

Part 3

From the point of happiness that you have nurtured in the first two parts of this exercise, ask yourself these questions: what is your life's goal? How well do your physical, emotional, causal, and mental aspects support this goal? To what degree does everything that you do lead you toward your highest purpose?

Does your mind work for you? Are karmic patterns tying you to certain experiences? Does the way you express emotion create the environment you want? Does your physical environment facilitate your goal?

After evaluating the answers to these questions, take steps to change whatever is getting in the way of your goal. If you realize that your mind, for example, does not work the way you want it to, practice the technique given earlier for adjusting the dials in the mental body. Change the dials so your mental body can give you the kind of life you wish.

Work with the tools available to change other aspects of your life. Alter your diet, for example, if it is hindering your spiritual life. Evaluate all that you experience in life with this criterion: Is this helping me toward my spiritual goal? This one question will help you unfold a greater happiness in life.

259

Magically we had traversed the countryside and now stood at the entrance to the tunnel from which we had arrived. Although we had been walking as we talked, our bodies seemed to glide over the many miles of grassy terrain. What would have taken days of travel on Earth, took only minutes.

Our ways part here, *said the Master.* But I have one more aspect of this exercise to share. Try it when you return to the Physical Plane.

Part 4

To nurture and practice the joy of Soul, think about something you do in life that makes you truly happy, sparks divine love, and encourages detachment and surrender. Once you have identified it, then partake of the activity.

"Yes, I'll do that," I promised.

Good. I have shared all that Spirit has guided me to. Farewell. Perhaps we shall meet again. *The Master bowed respectfully and said,* May the blessings be.

"May the blessings be," I replied.

Chapter 23

Introducing the Supra-Physical

*M*oments *after I began my spiritual exercise, a familiar spiritual master met me at the threshold of the inner worlds. The halo of light surrounding him was so strong I could only catch a vague outline of this angelic, golden being. Yet the warmth and joy of his presence was overwhelming. His outstretched arms beckoned me to him, pulling me like an irresistible magnet of love. His bright head was smooth and without hair, and his white robes were so luminous they seemed to be woven of light itself.*

Where are you? *he asked.*

"I'm not sure," I replied.

Look around you.

We were standing in what appeared to be a desert. The rocky yellow soil was barren except for a few scrubby plants, which had somehow gained a toehold among the stones.

"I feel very close to the Physical Plane, but there's a quality to the air that is clearly non-physical." I said.

Actually, you are in the Supra-physical World, very close to physical manifestation. This place is only unfamiliar because you see it now with conscious eyes. You have been here before, during spiritual exercises and dreams. Perhaps this will refresh your memory. *He gestured straight ahead.*

I looked again and saw a familiar city. It was nestled behind a wall which I had mistaken for cliffs at first glance.

261

This is Agam Des, *the Master confirmed,* the spiritual center located in the remote mountains of Tibet. It is only accessible to those invited to learn or teach here. Most come in their supra-physical body while their physical body sleeps.

As you know, a highly-important volume of the Book of Golden Wisdom is housed here. However, Spirit has guided me to direct you instead to a special lecture which is about to begin.

I accompanied the golden being as we walked swiftly through a doorway hidden in the cliff wall and onward to the city. We followed a dusty road to one of the first buildings in Agam Des. Stepping inside was like entering a different world.

Sunlight sparkled through the clear, domed sunroof that spanned most of the ceiling. The sparkling white marble walls and floor were accented by brass planters supporting delicate ferns in each corner. Adorning the walls were several vivid paintings of enticing gardens, ponds, and fountains.

We passed through a set of broad french doors at the far end of the entry way into an open-air hall, punctuated on the left by white marble columns. The passageway ceiling was molded into large, concave squares adorned with lavish, oil-painted murals.

Looking between the columns, I recognized the beautiful garden depicted in the foyer paintings. It was thick with exotic plants and unusual flowers. Here and there, water fountains and marble statues rose from the leaves. A shallow pond filled with smooth, round rocks bordered the walkway. Dozens of large orange, yellow, and white Japanese koi fish lent their living color to the grey-green water.

I followed the Master up a set of stairs at the end of the hallway. The entire second floor consisted of one gigantic blue-carpeted room, with white walls and ceiling. The wall to my right had small windows, which I assumed looked out over the city. On the left, the room overlooked the magnificent central garden, which accounted for the soft, perfumed quality of the air. One could also see a small lake from the upstairs balcony which reflected the nearby hills and the blue sky. Near the middle of the far wall, about twenty people sat in a circle on the floor. Their attention was on a woman about to give a presentation.

There is much more for you to learn and share about the puzzle of physical existence, *said my host.*

He led me to the gathering, exchanging a silent nod with the Master in the center of the group. I knelt to join the circle.

The Master was a petite, gentle featured woman with shoulder-length brown hair. Her simple clothing consisted of a creamy, long-sleeved knit shirt, plainly tailored, over a floor-length full skirt of the same material. A woven blue belt encircled her small waist. It was fastened with a shiny blue buckle fashioned into an unusual, six-pointed blue star.

She spoke in a quiet voice of great clarity and strength. The Physical World is full of mysteries, *she began.* The human consciousness cannot contain all this world has to teach. However, the Physical Plane doesn't need to be thoroughly studied, dissected, and analyzed. That isn't Soul's purpose here. Eons of study would reveal only a fraction of what this realm has to offer.

The quest for physical knowledge is alluring. But the desire and curiosity it awakens may be misdirected. You see, the Physical Plane can become a dangerous trap. It can siphon Soul's natural curiosity into meaningless pursuits. Only by the grace of the Divine does something occur to once again redirect Soul's attention toward Spirit.

Those who strive for mastership must only put enough attention on physical phenomena to gain self-control in this plane. One of the phenomena you do need to understand is your supra-physical body. While it resembles your physical body in every way, it lies just beyond physical sight—between the body and your astral sheath.

263

Each of you is here in your supra-physical body. This means your physical body is lying elsewhere without benefit of the supra-physical sheath's protection.

This protection is constantly required by most individuals. However, you have earned the right to be here tonight. Therefore, Spirit Itself is protecting your physical body. You have opened yourselves to serve as a conduit for the Life Flow, bringing you that privilege.

Let's look at the development of the supra-physical body. It is formed within several weeks of Soul's entrance into a new, infant physical form. It reflects this form and develops from it like an outgrowth. Eventually it extends about six inches in all directions from the physical body.

Beginning at birth, the physical blueprints magnetize a continuous flow of color rays to nourish the body. These color rays collect in a thin energetic layer around the physical body as they are released into the atmosphere.

The color rays pass through the body's atoms, molecules, cells, and organs, collecting information about the physical body. This information is then deposited in the newly-formed supra-physical aura. Throughout the individual's life, these color rays, as well as other energies released by the body, continually update the supra-physical form.

The supra-physical body is also nourished by the subtle bioelectrical field emanated by the physical sheath. Sandwiched between the physical skin and the lower regions of the supra-physical body, this field is at its strongest within one inch of the physical body. It is a source of the physical body's magnetic pull, and contributes to the currents of energy pictured in Chinese acupuncture charts. Some people call this energy 'chi' and have charted the meridians of its flow and movement.

Individuals who explore the inner worlds develop an additional current or meridian in their supra-physical aura. It runs along the sides of the body, becoming stronger as an individual matures spiritually. This extra meridian helps provide protection while the supra-physical body explores the Supra-physical World.

The Supra-physical World is unseen by physical eyes, yet it harbors the keys to many of the mysterious, energetic components of the Physical Plane. These include subtle magnetic pathways which span the planet and the physical universe like a precisely-organized, complex highway system. These pathways flow between planets and various other points to connect the physical universe in an invisible, but well-traveled grid.

The Earth has its own set of energy meridians. Various flows, including electrical currents, travel these major highways. Supra-physical bodies can ride on them as well. Smaller highways branch off from the major paths, and divide into even smaller roads.

The major meridian lines, through which the Earth's energies flow, are required for the life of the planet. Some of the smaller roads, on the other hand, lead to individual houses. They are created by the people in the house, who use them for travel. For instance, those of you who travelled here in your supra-physical bodies needed a means by which to arrive. A temporary path was established.

How did this happen? Your spiritual Self caused your supra-physical body to become extra magnetized. This increased flow drew a portion of current from the nearest supra-physical highway. Thus a side road of sorts was created to connect your house to a main supra-physical artery. This side road was probably established within minutes, and although it is not permanent, could remain in place for many months after its last use.

Supra-physical travel is much faster than any kind of physically generated, propelled, or fueled vehicle. It is possible to move even more swiftly than light in your supra-physical body. But not all individuals travel at such speeds.

When you first step on to a meridian, you may choose to go slower.

This mode of transportation also differs from Soul projection. This is when Soul simply takes Its attention off the Physical World and places it on an inner body to explore one of the inner worlds. Such inter-plane travel can be accomplished outside the boundaries of time, movement, and energy. Soul can be in the inner worlds as quickly as It pictures a desired destination.

On the other hand, intra-plane travel, or travel within a plane, uses entirely different mechanics. In some worlds, it is inappropriate to instantly project from one place to another. It would upset the local inhabitants to simply appear or disappear!

This brings up an interesting point which you must also be aware of. The beings who populate the Astral, Causal, and Mental Worlds are not necessarily conscious of Soul and Its ability to instantly move from one place to another. Whole populations in these inner worlds confine their awareness to their immediate surroundings. This is the same as on the Physical Plane, where most people are entirely focused on their outer, so-called reality.

However, awareness is growing in a number of individuals that there is more to life than meets the eye. This insight is more wide-spread in each subsequent inner world. Souls on all planes are learning of the limitations of the laws that govern their respective realities.

Each plane has an entire set of laws to serve many important purposes. They maintain the balance of each realm and preserve the sheaths of the Souls who live there. The laws allow Soul to learn many important lessons, and they also support the interdependent continuum of all the lower worlds.

Of course, these rules only exist in relation to Soul's awareness of them. The spiritual guardians of each plane carefully monitor the local laws, fine-tuning the 'dials' that regulate them as necessary. It could be disastrous if one tried to make unauthorized adjustments to these dials.

Instead, one need only adjust one's own relationship to the laws of each plane. This in turn alters how and if they affect you.

Each world's laws exist for the learning purposes of the Whole. Yet the Whole is uplifted each time even one Soul in millions—just one—can disentangle Itself from these laws. Soul then rises in awareness above the lower planes, to work in greater harmony with Spirit and Its universal laws. These laws are much broader and supersede those of the lower planes. Thus Soul is liberated from the limitations of materiality.

When this happens, all Souls are lifted a little higher. We are all part of the Whole. When one Soul frees Itself, the rise in consciousness may only be a fraction of a vibratory rate. But it still makes its indelible mark.

Sometimes that tiny fraction of upliftment is all that is needed to spark another's spiritual liberation. It can open a door so the Divine touches and uplifts thousands of Souls. These doors of knowledge and inspiration sweep one's attention away from the physical and back toward the true home. Souls who catch this current are momentarily freed from physical limitations, to reorient themselves towards the Golden Kingdom.

As one rises in a state of consciousness, he finds himself increasingly detached from physical laws. If he can maintain an attitude of neutrality, this newfound freedom can be used to eventually loosen the cords that bind Soul to the lower worlds. Gradually, as Soul explores higher realities, the physical body becomes not a limitation, but the sharpened tool and the clear channel it is meant to be. Soul receives the experiences and education It needs to build spiritual strength and stamina for Its return journey home.

267

One of the first laws Soul masters is that of simple, physical gravity. Consciously or subconsciously, you have transcended gravity to be here now. Soul has extended Its consciousness beyond the basic physical laws.

One day the technique for supra-physical travel will probably be mapped out in earthly equations and mathematics. But first man must hypothesize that such movement is indeed possible. Then when the possibility is accepted, the equations and formulas will follow.

Defying Gravity to Travel
the Supra-Physical Highways

Here is an exercise to help you move beyond the law of gravity: Close your eyes and think about what your house would look like from above. If you were looking down at it from a helicopter, what would the roof and yard look like?

Just by imagining looking down at your location from above, you have superseded the law of gravity. It's that simple!

Gravity keeps your physical body on the ground. Therefore, when operating within the physical laws, you need some type of fuel or propellant to transcend this force. But when you are working in other sheaths and beyond the physical laws, external energy is not needed.

The technique I just gave stretches the imagination and gives you a momentary experience of rising above physical laws.

Let's take this creative visualization a step further. From the vantage point of twenty-five to fifty feet above your house, look around you in all directions. Search for a golden ribbon several feet to several yards wide. The actual width of this ribbon depends on your perception and where you live. If you live near a major meridian, the ribbon will be quite wide.

If you cannot find one, raise your vantage point to several thousand feet above your house. When you look down toward the Earth you may notice many golden ribbons which form a delicate grid. Notice where the closest ribbon to your house lies. Is it just beyond your driveway or does it run through your back yard?

Over the next several days, continually remind yourself of the existence of this roadway near your house. It is unseen by physical eyes, yet very real. Periodically imagine it being there, or just know that it is present. This acknowledgement is an important step to consciously construct a side road from your doorstep to one of Earth's meridian lines.

As you unfold spiritually, your supra-physical body will collect magnetic energy. Eventually, this magnetism will be strong enough to attract supra-physical energy lines as needed. Side roads branching off Earth's main meridians can automatically be constructed. However, not every spiritually-evolved individual has a road connecting his house to Earth's energy lines. Not at all. These roads are constructed as needed, for intra-plane travel in the supra-physical body. But a measure of spiritual maturity is a requisite for their construction.

These magnetic roads serve the same purpose as physical highways. You can travel on them just to explore or to get to a specific place. When you become adept at this mode of travel, you can arrive at your destination within seconds. Often it takes more time for the physical consciousness to pick a destination than it takes to get there! However, it is also possible to take your time and explore the planet at a slower rate of travel.

Again, inner travel or Soul projection 'moves' you via the attention of Soul. When travelling the Supra-physical Plane in this way, your supra-physical body will automatically follow Soul's lead.

At the conclusion of our class, you are free to return home by any method you choose. You are all knowledgeable about the different forms of travel. I assume each of you has a favorite mode you routinely use.

I suggest that today, when you return home, you try a different method. It is important to remain versatile in all aspects of your life. Habit breeds complacency, and often sets the mind into ruts.

No one method of travel is more spiritual than another. I assure you, even the highest spiritual masters often use the common automobile when traversing the Physical Plane.

That is all.

The listeners in the circle stood up to leave. A few approached the Master individually for a private word or two.

Gazing out at the sparkling blue waters of the lake, I decided to consciously travel home on one of the golden energy lines. This would certainly be a change from my preferred method of instant Soul projection.

To my surprise, my desire immediately pulled me onto a nearby supra-physical line. I was immediately caught up in its swift-moving current, speeding over the mountains and plains of China.

Traveling these highways was quite different from driving on a physical road. There was no vehicle to provide impetus. The golden road propelled me itself, via magnetism. After some experimentation, I discovered that one's thoughts and desires determined the rate of travel as well as the destination.

What is it like to travel these highways? Well, each road is similar to a two-way street, with traffic moving in both directions. Each lane is made up of a series of magnetic points alternately aligned toward the south and north poles.

I experimented with using the magnetic quality of my supra-physical body to leave and return to the current. To float away from the road, you focus on one of its alternating magnetic points. Then you shift your supra-physical polarity so it is matches the polarity of your chosen point. The two similar poles—that of your body and the road-point—repel each other, and off you go. It feels somewhat like pushing off from the side of a swimming pool.

I left the main highway but wanted to keep moving. As soon as I manifested my desire, a new road sprang up instantly before me. Regardless of my speed, it was always several feet ahead.

When I was ready to return to the main road, I again reversed my polarity. Now my magnetism and that of the point from which I launched my exploration were opposite. This set up an attraction which drew me back into the main road's current. Of course, I could have also just matched polarities with any point on the new road I had made, and returned to the main highway wherever I wished.

To remain stationary within an energy road and examine it, I had to suspend myself between its two currents. It felt like I was perching atop a concrete meridian separating two lanes of a major highway! Energy swept around me in both directions.

When I was ready to go back to my home in Oregon, I hopped onto a current going East over the Pacific Ocean, surrendered to it, and quickly found myself back in the physical body. My supra-physical sheath immediately surrounded and protected my physical form. I was home.

I sat still for a long time afterward, marveling at the possibilities of physical craft using these lines for travel, both on Earth and between planets. Even more fantastic was the idea of a vehicle able to manifest its own magnetic pathways, just seconds before it traveled them. Why, it could travel anywhere in the physical universe!

My mind stretched with possibilities, dreams, and the hope I might be able to contribute, even in some small way, to humankind's advancement toward such technology.

Chapter 24

Keys to Self Expression

The next day, I anxiously awaited an opportunity to return to the Supra-physical World and practice moving along the Earth's magnetic lines. Spirit, however, had something else in mind. As I sang the word HU, my consciousness floated from my physical body. I entered the astral realm to find Peddar waiting to speak with me. He was sitting on the rocks on the grassy fields by the cliffs' edge.

How are the interviews progressing? *he asked.*

I took a seat next to him. "I am learning valuable information from the beings Spirit has led me to," *I replied.*

Is the picture complete yet?

"No, definitely not," I said. "There are still many questions that have to be answered."

'Have to be'? *he repeated with a smile.*

I also smiled at the inaccuracy of my words. "That I would like to have answered," I corrected myself.

Yes, that's more accurate. Choose your words with care, to clearly express the meaning you wish to convey. The written word often harbors a dual vibration or meaning. First is the meaning the author wishes to communicate, and second is the meaning the words themselves express. If they are at odds, the latter invariably overpowers the author's intent, for readers tend to use their minds to understand what they read instead of their hearts.

To express himself accurately, an author's or speaker's words must parallel his deepest meaning and intent. As concepts are spun into words, their energies actually join to form delicate clusters of waves. The energy of the author's meaning represents one set of waves. The energy of the words is another.

If the peaks and valleys of one set of waves correspond to those of the other, they undulate together in a single synergistic, larger wave. The author's intent and the meaning expressed by the words become part of a larger whole.

If they interfere with one another, the conflict may cancel out the writer's intent. Or it may leave the reader or listener feeling confused or vaguely dissatisfied. The conflicting waveforms produce a dissonance that frustrates the reader's attempt to construct new insights for himself.

On the other hand, when the waveforms parallel each other, their sum touches a chord in the heart. This is accomplished through a certain synergistic rhythm of syllables, which resonates with the very rhythm of an individual's atoms.

This resonance, however, can serve an overall negative effect if the author's underlying intent is less than positive. This is seen all the time in television commercials and advertisements, which stir the heart for empty purposes. But when the intent behind the rhythm is pure, the written or spoken word can resonate with Soul and be profoundly uplifting.

Pay attention to the waveforms and rhythm of your own and other's words. If you feel harmony, then the meaning you perceive is parallel to the author's intent. If the overall feeling doesn't ring quite true, you should not form attitudes or conclusions about the author's information. Perhaps he just didn't choose the right words or take the time to carefully edit his concepts into the proper word-clothing.

Now I'm not talking here about technical correctness. Writing can display terrible grammar, reprehensible English, and a total lack of internal organization. But if the rhythms of the author's meaning harmonizes with that of the words he chooses, the end result will still ring true to Soul.

Look for this ringing effect when ever you write or speak. If the resonance is weak in a particular paragraph or idea, look inwardly to refine your true meaning. Then re-form the concepts or sentences until they ring with harmony.

There is a difference between this inner approach to expression and the outer-directed method of most editors. If you allow grammatical rules to be the sole dictator of your correctness, the inner rhythm of golden communication will never be right. One must approach the process from a spiritual, resonant viewpoint. Editing or speaking from this perspective can make a world of difference. The end result speaks to Soul.

Words and rhythms can also resonate with specific chakra centers. Through the exercises in this book, your chakras are gradually being attuned. The goal is to harmonize these energy centers, without one being domineering over another.

Peddar stopped and smiled, Now there's a good example of bad grammar upsetting the rhythm of communication. The words 'being domineering' in the last paragraph upset the rhythm. It could have been stated as 'without one dominating another', for a tighter rhythm and clearer understanding.

For proof that rhythm is more important than tight grammar, recall our discussion with Sri Jhonès. During his discussion of blueprints he said that if they are freely expressed, 'you are in harmony with all around you, above you, and below you'.

This could be more economically expressed as: 'you are in harmony with vibrations around, above, and below you'. But some of Jhonès essential rhythm would be lost without the poetic repetition of the word 'you'. This is just a small example of what I mean by inner-directed communication.

For best results, it is important to experience the adventures in this book and the series of interviews with balanced and harmonious chakra centers. Then they can work their highest, divine alchemy. This alchemy or rhythm allows the essence of each Soul concept to be planted firmly into your heart by the Masters.

When words resonate with and align a reader's chakra centers, he becomes more receptive to their underlying truth. Certain concepts may be new, different, or beyond his mental understanding and social system—but something about them rings undeniably true.

To produce literature that resonates in this way, the author's chakras must be in a state of harmony and balance. So be sure to write and edit from a state of balance. The same is true for your spoken words. Let them come from your highest, most resonant state.

Speaking and Writing from Harmony

The next time you wish to communicate something important through the written or spoken word, begin by balancing your chakra centers. One way to do this is by breathing deeply into each individual chakra center. This is described in detail in our discourse about the emotional body, under the 'Chakra Center Clearing Technique'.

When you are finished breathing into each chakra separately, feel all seven energy centers breathing in synchrony. Hear their sound of divine harmony—like seven intertwined instruments playing a gentle piece of music.

This will align the chakra centers so they are open, alert, receptive, and in tune with each other. Continue breathing gently into all seven chakras until it seems they are breathing and responding as one.

Now try writing or speaking while lightly holding your attention on your breathing chakras. Do not be concerned with grammar and punctuation. Instead, focus on how clearly and truly you are expressing yourself. Let the breath of your chakras inhale and exhale into your words.

Okay, enough about that. I know you want to learn more about the supra-physical body. Tell me, who would you like to ask about this aspect of the Physical World?

Several masters and guardians came to mind. "The supra-physical body is an outgrowth of the physical one and develops as the physical body ages. Therefore, I'd like to ask someone with an exceptionally well-developed supra-physical body—someone who has retained a physical body for a long time."

A wise choice, *Peddar replied.*

I shall escort you to the abode of a spiritual master who has retained his physical body for over five hundred years.

To get there, we can ride upon the supra-physical currents that you enjoy so much.

Come. Follow me!

Chapter 25

Healing Winds in the Himalayas

*P*eddar and I leaped onto a supra-physical current of gold and sped across oceans, plains, and mountains.

In less than a minute, we found ourselves halfway around the world, in the vast wilderness of the Himalayas.

A howling blizzard enveloped us as we stepped down onto the Earth's surface again. The fierce wind and snow tore at my skin as my eyes searched out a small wooden structure just a few feet ahead.

Peddar indicated he would not be joining me for the discourse awaiting me in the remote hut. He motioned me forward and waved goodbye, leaping back onto a golden magnetic current with a jaunty wink and a smile. Shivering from the cold, I watched as the current disappeared behind him.

I braced myself against the strong, icy winds, and struggled toward the doorway of the snow-bound hut. It opened and I dashed in from the howling snowstorm. My host refastened the heavy swatch of leather that served as a makeshift door.

Welcome, he said simply.

As my eyes adjusted to the dimly lit room, I made a quick inventory of my surroundings. To call it a house would be an overstatement. A rudimentary cot occupied one wall; a small, well-stocked bookshelf leaned against another. In the corner lay the bare essentials for preparing a simple meal. Another leather square blotted out the small window.

279

Yet I found something soothing and familiar in this humble abode. I had read about this dwelling in other books. It belonged to the Tibetan Master, Rebezar Tarz. I had always hoped that one day I would be invited here.

Rebazar walked over to the small fireplace, with its single chair resting to one side of the simple hearth. But he lowered himself on to the large, soft rug in front of it instead. After staring meditatively into the flames for a moment, he motioned for me to seat myself on the rug across from him.

As I made myself comfortable, I was surrounded by a toasty warmth. Did it come from the fireplace, or from the love emanating from the Master before me? He had short black hair and a closely cropped beard. Instead of the knee-length maroon tunic described by other visitors, he wore a pair of simple woolen trousers. Two shirts were layered above for warmth, topped by a leather vest. His feet were swathed in thick hide boots strapped with leather laces.

I noticed a heavy fur-and-leather coat next to the door. I couldn't contain a question about his attire and broke the silence.

"Sire, I thought you were impervious to cold. Haven't I heard stories of you roaming the mountains in sandals and a tunic in the coldest of weather?"

A part of me couldn't believe I had blurted out such a trivial question. But instead of admonishing my boldness, the Master laughed. People perceive me as they wish, *he smiled.* Often they project qualities they themselves would like to have.

Rebezar took my hand and placed it on his arm. I am as human and as physically manifested as you are. *He squeezed my fingers against his flesh so I would pinch it. Then he squeezed my hand so I could feel the pressure of his strong grip.*

You know, I even get the sniffles sometimes. *His tone was serious, and I believed him.*

280

Yes, there are times when I am seen in my maroon uniform in the snow. But let me ask this. When have I been seen in such attire when the sky hasn't been blue or the weather mild?

In these high mountain altitudes, the snow lasts well into July. But when the sky is clear, temperatures can reach the seventies. A sprightly wind off the snows is not bitter on such days, but refreshing and invigorating.

The howl of the wind became more insistent. We listened to its song for a few minutes before it subsided again.

You are here to learn of the supra-physical body, *Rebazar announced.* This is a most important aspect of physical existence. This sheath must be understood, at least in part, in order to ease many presently-incurable diseases.

You have already heard how the supra-physical body is gradually manifested from birth. It never stops growing, developing, and maturing—unlike the physical body which reaches its prime and then begins to deteriorate.

Some people's supra-physical bodies may encounter decade-long plateaus in their growth. But those individuals on an active spiritual path will find these plateaus last only minutes or days instead of years.

The Master poked the fire with a long wooden stick and removed his vest, for the room had become uncomfortably warm.

Instead of continuing, he suddenly closed his eyes in motionless contemplation. Perhaps he was needed elsewhere in another state of consciousness. I waited quietly, gazing into the dancing flames.

Ah, yes the supra-physical body, *he continued abruptly, as soon as he opened his eyes.* Perhaps the best way to describe it is to call it a magnetic reflection of the physical body. Like the astral, causal, and mental bodies, the supra-physical sheath functions independently, yet is interdependent on each of the other bodies of Soul.

Human bodies are not the only objects which manifest magnetic, supra-physical counterparts. Indeed, all physical things have such a complement. These manifestations exist in a realm of their own. This realm, which is called the Supra-physical World, is based on and closely mirrors the Physical World.

Yet time can play differently in the Supra-physical World. Let's say you are walking through a forest and switch your awareness to your supra-physical surroundings. You may suddenly find yourself strolling along a desert floor! Where have the trees gone? They are there physically. But thousands of years ago this particular forest was a desert.

Supra-physical reality may become out-of-step with physical manifestation for many reasons. Electromagnetic anomalies and atmospheric disturbances are only two reasons. The Earth's guardians also freeze time in some areas with a dome of protection. But in most cases, past environments are preserved through the desire and agreement of communities of the supra-physical inhabitants who live there. You exercise this same control over your own, immediate physical environment. You could plant your yard with trees and ferns, while your neighbor may prefer landscaping with cactus and pea-gravel.

When such differentials in time occur between one's physical and supra-physical bodies, they can affect the physical body's health—to our benefit or chagrin. Let's say your past health was poor—yet the physical, emotional, causal, and mental reasons for the illness are totally resolved. If the supra-physical reflection of ill health remains, the condition will continue to afflict you.

Other conditions caused by out-dated, unhealthy supra-physical reflections can manifest in a variety of mysterious symptoms, which respond reluctantly to treatment. Lingering pains may move from place to place. Or you may be haunted by a nagging fear of disease.

Such problems are impossible to accurately diagnose, because they have no physical reason for existing. They are physical manifestations of a supra-physical condition. Or, more accurately, physical reflections of outdated supra-physical information.

In an opposite scenario, the supra-physical may hold on to a clear reflection of when an organ was particularly healthy. If that organ is subsequently hurt or injured, its strong, supra-physical picture of health can guide the body to an unusually swift recovery.

Time lags between supra-physical and physical realities can therefore be of benefit or not. In the human being, such lags exist for two basic reasons. Either you initiate them as Soul, or there has been a disturbance in the magnetic flows of the supra-physical body.

Supra-physical disturbances can cause this sheath to fall out of touch with current physical-body conditions. Electrical interruptions become ingrained as distorted patterns in the millions of minute, magnetic, bipolar particles of the supra-physical body.

Such magnetic disturbances are usually caused by habitual, coarse-vibration activities. These are often physical actions whose negative energies eventually penetrate the supra-physical mechanics. They include the misuse of alcohol and drugs, animalistic expressions such as profanity or sexual lust, or repeatedly watching certain low-vibration images.

You will note that in general, these activities are self-initiated. The individual is, in essence, inviting low vibratory rates and difficulties into the supra-physical body.

A single expression of profanity, for example, could start a subtle, negative chain of events. First, the low-vibratory rate expression disrupts the magnetic pattern and energy flow of the supra-physical fibers. Then the individual acts out from this distorted pattern—let's say by watching a disturbing movie. The imbalances caused may then prompt a sudden urge to indulge in another coarse activity or craving.

One by one, these actions deposit low energies into the supra-physical body. Eventually, the accumulation causes a split perception of time as it unfolds in the supra-physical body. The supra-physical sheath becomes slowed or anchored in time, so it no longer reflects recent developments in the physical body. This split can occur throughout the whole body, or with regard to just one organ.

Of course, sometimes you may enter an environment of low vibratory rates over which you have no control. You are not necessarily inviting the effects of these vibrations into your Supra-physical World. Through your conscious choice, the door can remain closed to coarse influences in your life.

However, if you do open the door to these experiences by partaking of them yourself, the effect of their low-vibratory rates can be profound on the supra-physical body. Ignorance is no excuse. Knowingly or unknowingly, participating in low-vibration actions is somewhat akin to smearing peanut butter into the cog wheels of a clock. Time stops—and the supra-physical body becomes frozen in whatever state it is in. This is why one often sees cases of arrested emotional and inner development in those who use drugs, for example. Their habits have locked them into a static reality of zero growth.

From what I have just said, you may deduce that one of the primary functions of the supra-physical body is to protect the physical body from the effects of such harmful lower vibrations and habits.

"Excuse me sire," I interjected, "can you explain how Soul can initiate a time-stop in the supra-physical body? And if one has 'peanut butter' stuck in his supra-physical body's 'clock-works', how can he remove it?"

Soul rarely stops time. This would be somewhat akin to slamming on the brakes of a fifty-car train. It is hard to accomplish without complications, such as impeding the momentum of unfoldment, which could obstruct or harm the lower bodies' maturity and evolution. But it is possible in some cases, and that is why I mentioned it.

Peanut butter in the clockworks, so to speak, also causes a growth plateau. Supra-physical growth slows or halts when drugs, alcohol, or low-vibration habits are indulged. And do not be fooled. Many coarse habits are not recognized by society as at all dangerous. High-sensation activities such as watching horror movies, listening to hard rock music, scaring oneself with thrill-seeking amusement rides, or inflicting cruel peer-pressure jokes on others, for example, are ways people can unknowingly slow supra-physical development.

Whenever such activities are indulged, the supra-physical body's strength, stamina, and ability to protect the physical body are impeded for a time. This sheath also loses its ability to detach from the physical body and explore the Supra-physical Plane.

That, by the way, is another purpose of the supra-physical body: To protect Soul and Its other lower bodies when It wants to journey to other places in the physical and supra-physical realms. This can include trips to other planets or cities, where It leaves the outermost physical sheath behind.

As you know, any sheath is designed both to protect Soul from coarse vibratory rates—and shield the lower worlds from the radiance of Soul. You may wonder how spiritual Masters can manifest a physical body in more than one place.

Likewise, how is it possible to leave one's body behind and travel in supra-physical dimensions? These are accomplished in the supra-physical body. The stronger this sheath becomes, the more consciously you can explore the physical realm. For example, you might go to secret and hidden spiritual centers of the Earth world—one of which you visited last night for learning.

Therefore, the question is not how Soul can learn to stop time in the supra-physical body. It is: How can one clear blockages in this body, so one's supra-physical time-clock is in sync with current, physical-body time/reality?

I asked, "Let's say the supra-physical is stuck in a time when a certain organ was at a peak of health. And in current time that organ is diseased. What is the benefit of bringing the supra-physical into current time? Wouldn't it be better to allow the strong, past reflection of health guide the body to a swift recovery?"

A healthy supra-physical reflection could aid physical healing. But an even faster and more thorough recovery from the illness is possible if the individual is fully aware of the illness in every sheath. This allows him to work through all the lessons and opportunities of his condition.

If the supra-physical is not operating in current time, it cannot relay accurate information about the cause of the affliction among the physical and inner bodies. Nor can it communicate the moment-by-moment changes associated with the condition, as they occur in any of the lower bodies. Without this information, learning and true healing occurs much more slowly. Causes cannot be resolved if part of the individual is living in delusions of the past.

A wise humorist once identified this recipe for disaster: 'The illusions of the present, that are befuddled with delusions of the past, make the future nothing but mud'. *Rebazar shook his head and chuckled to himself.*

Do you want some tea?

Without waiting for an answer, the Tibetan Master got up and headed toward his meager kitchenette. It consisted of little more than a basin, a holding tank for water, and a few cooking utensils. Rebazar lit a small propane burner with a match, filled a tea kettle with water, and reached for two cups hanging from their hooks on the wall.

"I don't think I have ever eaten or drunk anything while outside the physical body," I commented. I was expecting this to be a very interesting experience.

If the Master heard me, he didn't reply. He put the cups on the counter and checked the temperature of the water with his fingertip. This won't take a minute, *he predicted. I knew he meant exactly what he said. At this altitude, it probably wouldn't take one minute—but several—for the water to boil.*

What does your supra-physical body feel? *he asked as we waited for the tea.*

"I feel the pressure of the howling wind and the intense energy of the storm," *I replied.* "Yet I know I am protected by the four walls around me."

Good. That leads me to my next point. The supra-physical body is the source of the sixth sense. This sixth sense is different from intuitive hunches which Soul uses to express a direction or decision to your human consciousness.

Instead, your sixth sense provides you with information from just beyond the physical.

This sixth sense is particularly sensitive to the weather and the subtle energies of others. Animals use it all the time. Have you ever seen a dog react with hostility to a seemingly kind stranger while expressing warmth to an indifferent passer-by? This sense allows them to perceive the truth about people, who often mask their true nature with false words and actions.

Healing and Clearing the Supra-physical Body with Sound, Wind, and Warmth

Now, going back to your question about clearing the cogs of the supra-physical machinery. I will now share a technique to clean this sheath. It exercises your sixth sense or supra-physical perceptions of sound, wind, and warmth to heal and clear the supra-physical body.

First, sit or lie down in a comfortable position. The technique will be easier if your eyes are closed.

Now, imagine you are outside on a windy day. Let the wind be warm as it sweeps across your body. Notice in which direction the wind is blowing. Does it approach you from the right or left, from the back or front?

If it approaches you from the left, do this exercise many times throughout the day for periods of about five minutes. If it approaches you from the right, practice this technique only once or twice in a day, for a long period of time. Do it for half an hour to an hour—or as long as two hours if you wish.

If the wind approaches you from the back or the front, change your position until it is approaching you from either the left or the right. Neither direction is better than the other, they are just different.

We were interrupted by the whistle of the tea kettle. I continued to listen to the blowing wind while I watched the Master's quick and efficient preparations. Not an ounce of energy was wasted in excess motion.

As he flashed a glance toward me, his piercing eyes awakened a memory of the first thing he had said to me that day. 'People see qualities in me they wish to see in themselves'. I wondered if that had anything to do with spiritual masters being perfect mirrors.

Yes, *he replied aloud. Evidently it didn't matter if I spoke aloud or via telepathy.*

The perfect mirror not only reflects that which is, but also that which could be.

One can be a mirror with divine or negative intent. However, the price one pays for being a negative mirror is too dear to contemplate.

The Divine Mirror is a quality even spiritual students possess. It is unconscious. The clarity of your own Divine Mirror is proportional to your surrender to Spirit. One never knows when the Divine Mirror is shining, nor for whom it is reflecting.

He handed me a cup of tea and told me to hold it to my heart with both hands.

Yes, very good. Now feel the warmth of the tea radiating throughout your body. This is, by the way, the second part of this supra-physical healing and clearing technique.

Feel the warmth of the hot tea as it melts the blockages and accumulations of negative energy in your supra-physical body.

At the same time, continue to imagine the wind blowing through you. It will sweep away that which the warmth of the hot tea has melted.

As the tea cools, begin the third phase of this technique, which involves sound. Imagine the beautiful song of a flute. Allow its haunting melody to replace the wind, until there is nothing more than a gentle breeze or stillness.

The wind, the heat source, and the flute can either be imagined or mocked up in the physical.

To employ physical stimuli, perform the exercise outside on a windy day, or turn on a fan. Fix yourself a hot beverage and play a recording of a flute. The song of the flute is more effective for this technique than that of other instruments. It has a special clearing quality and resonance with the subtle bodies.

To perform this technique with physically manifested tools, sit near the fan so it blows toward your right or left side. Hold your mug of tea between your hands, close to your heart. Let it touch your skin or your clothing.

When the tea cools, get up, turn on the music, and return to your place in front of the fan. As the music plays, slowly move away from the fan so it affects you less and less. When you are out of the wind's reach, shut the fan off and enjoy the music of the flute.

Now you must know why and how this technique works. The wind gently realigns the supra-physical body's magnetic particles so they all point in one direction. As the particles align themselves with the direction of the wind, they loosen their hold on various blockages and accumulations.

The heat source activates the heart chakra, which regulates many supra-physical body functions. It also relaxes the magnetic particles, encouraging them to swing free and release negative energies.

The music anchors the magnetic particles in alignment with the wind. It also stirs up love in the heart. When the wind subsides and the particles reorient in a more flexible, healthier pattern, this love is a powerful force for anchoring this higher state.

Once the accumulation has been removed and the new magnetic orientation found, the sound of the flute replaces the old vibratory rate with a new one.

Any music can suffice if its vibration is high enough. This vibration does not depend entirely on the type of instrument played. If the musician has aligned heart, mind, and Soul with the Divine Sound Current while he performs, you can be assured of the music's spiritual nature.

Nevertheless, the flute is a worthy representation of the spiritual Sound Itself. As I've said, this is because of its clarity of intent and expression.

Yes, the sound of the flute is clearing and cleaning. It purges negative accumulation from the supra-physical body. But it also provides a framework for higher vibratory rates to enter.

It is also the instrument of choice when using music to reconstruct physical or supra-physical matrices, as in this exercise.

Drink your tea before it gets cold. We have much more to discuss. But you must leave now and come again tomorrow.

I downed my tea, took the cup to the water basin, washed it and replaced it on the hook.

The Master accompanied me to the door and lifted the leather covering. May the blessings be, *he said.*

Bracing myself, I plunged out into the cold again. Following Peddar's exit, I adjusted my supra-physical polarity and hopped onto a nearby meridian line. I didn't want to spend any time exploring the Earth tonight.

My warm bed at home awaited me—and besides, I wanted to see just how fast these supra-physical lines could move.

Chapter 26

Imagination and Reality

It was snowing heavily when I arrived again at the little hut in the Himalayas. The wind was quieter than yesterday, but huge drifts were rising by the meter. Only a fire-warmed roof protruded above the deep white blanket layering the mountain.

As I shuffled toward the door, I was enveloped in an aura of profound peacefulness. But when I raised the flap, the Master was stirring his tea almost impatiently before the fire. I had an inkling that his movements were calculated, however, as if only to give the appearance of no-nonsense urgency.

He got right to the point. Tonight we will discuss another of the supra-physical body's protective functions. I also wish to talk about the distinctions between imagination and reality. Are you ready?

"Yes," I replied taking a seat across from him on the rug.

Good. Then let's begin.

Many people today know a relationship exists between their inner dimensions and their day-to-day, outer circumstances. They can see a connection between any physical problems and their emotional, causal, and mental states. So they seek therapies to clear out repressed emotions, resolve past hurts, and reprogram their thinking. But at the end of this beneficial process, they wonder why all their physical problems still aren't resolved.

The physical body is considered the most inflexible aspect of a person's being. However, in previous discourses you have learned that like the other sheaths, it is also comprised of atoms of Light and Sound. You have seen how profoundly the mental, causal, and emotional bodies can affect the physical body. Why then, can't an individual completely mold and control his health and physical temple by altering his thoughts, emotions, and past and future patterns?

The perplexing blockage lies in an inflexibile supra-physical body. Soul can indeed clear this sheath so the mental, causal, and emotional bodies are able to directly heal the physical body. But this can only occur when the whole of the individual is ready for a major step forward.

Spiritual maturity and self-responsibility are required before Soul will clear the supra-physical body and allow it to be an open channel. If the individual employs certain therapies that prematurely clear the supra-physical, the physical body will bear the brunt of every misdirected, undisciplined, or rampant emotion, thought, and pattern.

Clearing-therapies that use the crystalline form of gemstones can cause just such a problem. I mention this because I know you are interested in gemstone healing.

When crystals are used therapeutically, they naturally clear the supra-physical body. However, unlike the gemstone sphere, the crystal cannot analyze the holistic state of the individual's inner bodies, and self-regulate its effects to provide a balanced overall outcome.

Energetic changes initiated by most other therapies are gentle compared to those possible through gemstone therapy. A gemstone's crystalline matrix can be a vehicle for intense, purifying concentrations of Light and Sound. When the crystalline shape of a gemstone forces this energy into the aura, it can initiate imbalanced change. As an aside, this is why gemstone spheres are generally safer for the layperson's use.

Let's say the individual is not at a point where he can completely discipline his thoughts, emotions, memories, and patterns. As I have stated, a non-regulated supra-physical-body clearing would then turn the physical-body into a battle ground for the inner bodies.

Mental, causal, and emotional imbalances would flow unimpeded right through the opened supra-physical and into the physical body, causing havoc.

On the other hand, gemstone spheres radiate their energies in all directions. The changes they initiate consider the entire individual and work from that holistic viewpoint.

Gemstone sphere energies combine with, add to, cancel out, loosen, or interweave with the individual's energies to facilitate a higher, overall balance. With balance there is harmony. Harmony supports further growth, unfoldment, and well-being.

Clearing the supra-physical body by any method should be approached carefully. The individual must be able to assume complete responsibility for a freer, more open state.

"What about using faceted gemstones?" I asked.

Sometimes the student will see a faceted gemstone in his inner vision. Or perhaps it will come into his outer life. This is often a symbol of a spiritual gift from an inner master. Occasionally these gifts are represented by spherical gems— but rarely are they offered in the raw crystalline form.

The Earth is abundant with crystals, but it is arrogant to think that man locates mines or finds single specimens on his own or by accident. Earth shares her containers of Light and Sound as needed.

In this troubled era, the planet requires her crystals now more than ever. So as ever, she also hides certain gems for her own purposes.

The very presence of gemstones on this planet is a gift of the Divine. Those in tune with gemstones can use them for spiritual benefit. Each has an application and a special mission or purpose for being.

Again, faceted gemstones represent a gift of Light and Sound. Such a gift will hold a unique meaning for each individual. But in general, the presence of a gemstone signifies a greater ability to accept, work with, and be a vehicle for the spiritual current.

The mission of faceted gemstones is to refocus the consciousness. This occurs in a number of ways. They can open awareness for healing or resolution, stimulate the intelligence within each cell, or provide energy for change.

A faceted gemstone also helps one to experience or enter certain spiritual states. These include humility, love, surrender to Soul, and true honesty. Faceted stones can open one's consciousness, preparing him to accept the love of the Wayshower or another spiritual master. They also help one reach directly into the Golden Kingdom to experience Divine love and joy—and bring these qualities back into everyday life.

Of course, one doesn't need gemstones to accomplish these things. I'm only saying that when a gem is presented to you, especially inwardly, it can help you realize these goals or symbolize your readiness to achieve them.

It is indeed a blessing to receive such a spiritual gift. However, it is not presumptuous to seek out gemstones in the Physical World. To own one is a gift manifested. Knowing how to apply the gem as a concentrated container of Light and Sound is perhaps the real secret behind the gift. Knowledge of its applications transforms the merely beautiful into the tool of invaluable worth.

To be fully realized, any gift must fulfill a need or niche in the receiver's heart. Have you ever received a pretty but useless Christmas present? How long did you leave it on display before tossing it in the attic or shoving it in a drawer? Or did it collect dust on some shelf for years, never drawing your attention again?

When the gift was received, the love of the giver was acknowledged and accepted. And yet, since you had no practical use for the gift, it was set aside. A useful or meaningful gift, on the other hand, is fully treasured. The love of the giver is remembered over and over as the gift is used. If you receive a gemstone from someone or purchase one yourself, it is well worth learning what spiritual need it fulfills and how you can apply it.

As the human race evolves, gemstone applications will change and unfold. Some of their inner gifts are just now being made available for healing and growth. I believe your mission with Therapeutic Diamonds demonstrates this.

It is also possible to own gems in the inner worlds, whether they are received as gifts or acquired. The mere ability to have one in your presence means you have passed certain tests and experiences. Sometimes, simply taking responsibility for such an inner-world possession entitles you to enjoy one.

I will share a technique to locate a gem on the inner planes that involves the imagination. But first, I want to talk about the difference between imagination and reality.

Imagination acts as a springboard into creative reality. Where does imagination end and true reality begin? At the exact point where stored images turn into scenes with a life of their own!

When you imagine something, you are looking at preconceived images, built from previous experiences. True inner reality—that state beyond imagination—has a quality of the new and the unexpected.

You cannot be surprised by your imagination. When you imagine something, you are constantly out ahead of yourself. You are fabricating what you imagine and planning every move. When you leap into the world of Soul-reality, however, you participate in the journey first-hand. What you perceive is new, surprising, and unexpected. You still use your imagination to embark, but this visualization-process merely sets up a framework for the true experience to follow.

As you listen to the following visualization, and your readers one day read it, the imagination will be given ample food to produce ideas and images. But hopefully these will just act as a springboard.

How you eventually take part in this experience is personal. The results lie between you and Spirit. Expect the unexpected. Anticipate something new, something different, something specifically designed for you.

How to Obtain a Gemstone in the Inner Worlds

Sit in a comfortable position and close your eyes. Be sure your surroundings are quiet and you will not be disturbed. Take a few deep breaths to relax and center yourself.

You may wish to sing a holy word, such as HU, to help seat your attention and relax your mind.

Now on the screen of your mind, imagine a small, rectangular building. It is made of a golden light so concentrated it forms itself into illuminated walls and a roof.

Notice the faceted gems embedded in every golden board and shingle. What color are they? Each shines and hums with the glory of the Light and Sound.

Approach the entrance of this small edifice. Guards posted on either side of the doorway cross their spears in front of you.

'Speak the holy name, and then you may enter', declares one.

Here is where you must prove your eligibility. My suggestion is not to think about your virtues but to clear your mind and just be yourself. Rest your attention either on God or his agent, the Wayshower.

Sing a holy word that means something to you. Sing 'HU', 'Love', or 'God', if you wish. The guards will part their spears and return to attention. As you pass them, notice their uniforms, and the fact that their gaze does not waver from some distant focal point far behind you.

Perceived or not, as you enter the building a spiritual guide will be stationed nearby. He or she is there to ensure your subtle bodies remain in balance.

The small entry way may seem dark at first. But continue walking. Within a few steps, you will pass into a room of breathtaking light and brilliance.

Shelf upon shelf of neatly arranged gemstones line every wall, from floor to ceiling. It spins the mind, purges the eye, and fires the heart to be in the presence of such energy. Many of the gems are as big as your hand—clear, brilliant, free of inclusions, and richly colored.

If this is the first time you have entered such a place, I suggest you make haste in your selection. Otherwise your energy may quicken to the point of imbalance.

Briefly scan the shelves. Ask your guide for assistance if you wish. He may direct your attention to the exact gemstone to fulfill your present spiritual needs. Otherwise, simply allow yourself to be drawn to the vibration of the most compelling gem.

Before touching it, focus your attention on the face of this gem. The 'face' is its largest facet. You will know if this is the one for you. As you remove it from its cushion on the shelf, be warned: Nothing but gratitude and love must be in your heart!

Allow this gratitude to overflow as you cup the gem in your hands and turn to leave this golden place.

Just before you exit the dark entrance hall of the building, the guards' spears will once again cross before you. This signals your spiritual guide to perform yet another function.

He or she will make a record of the gem and its new owner.

Once the information is recorded in the book in the hall, the spears will part and you may leave.

Enclose the gem in your hands. You may remain in the inner world or return to the physical. Either way, contemplate on your gem and enjoy all its gifts.

If you know how to apply the gemstone therapeutically, you may do so. Some people simply hold the gemstone to their hearts. Others plant it at some needed site inside the body, or let it rest on the skin. Since it is a non-physical manifestation, it will remain in your aura for as long as you agree to its presence.

When you are done, think of a place to store your gift. It must be a distinctive place that you will later remember. If you wish to keep it in the inner worlds, your storage site could be under a rock or near a tree so unique you will be sure to find it again. You may also store it on its shelf in the gemstone temple.

Or be creative. You may want to go to an inner-world bank and place your gem in a safe-deposit box. You might even find a place in your physical home to keep your supra-physical gem; perhaps in your jewelry box, or a favorite drawer.

If you have no perception of the gift, I would suggest simply knowing you have it, and then implanting it within your heart. This way, you will always know where to find it.

It is your responsibility to remember the whereabouts of your gem. At some point, you may be completely finished with it. Return it to the little golden building, and choose another if you wish. Although no one will ever ask you to return it, the gem is your responsibility. It is best to put it back where you found it, so another may benefit.

Opening Your Heart to Receive the Gifts of Spirit

Being able to receive the gifts of Spirit is just as important as being able to give them. Here is another approach to finding a gem. It opens your heart to receive spiritual gifts, which will be symbolized as a faceted gemstone.

Begin once again in a relaxed position. Sing over and over the name of a spiritual master. If you are unfamiliar with any, imagine what he or she might be like and sing a word that means something special to you. Again, a word like 'Love', 'God', or 'Holy' will work. At the same time, think about the spiritual master.

As you sing the master's name, imbue your song with the love of Spirit. Feel your love-filled heart pouring an abundance of this divine expression into your voice.

As you sing, your readiness to accept the gifts of Spirit will be made known. Hold your hands together, as if preparing to receive something. It will be a gemstone—one that is right for you.

Fill your heart with worthiness and gratitude. If you can see the master presenting you with such a gift, you are indeed blessed. You might even partake of a conversation with him or her.

If you have no conscious awareness of the transaction, you may feel a warmth in your cupped hands, or the presence of a special energy. Know the gift has been given.

If you feel no results at all, see if your heart is filled with true gratitude. If so, after about twenty minutes of practicing this exercise, assume that you have indeed received a gem. The test of your readiness now will lie in how you take responsibility for its well-being.

Then go out into the world to share your gratitude. Practice being thankful for even the slightest gesture life or another person extends to you.

301

Practicing the art of gratitude is one of the most effective exercises for developing a perception of realities beyond the physical!

We will continue our discussion tomorrow, *the Tibetan abruptly announced. He picked up his cup of tea and drank its contents.*

Good night, *he concluded warmly.*

My heart filled with gratitude for this special being who had shared so much. I nodded my thanks.

As I reached the doorway, I was filled with the image of the sentries who stood at the golden entrance of the gemstone temple on the inner planes. I imagined the doorway of the Master's hut protected by similar guards. They parted their spears as I exited into the snow.

Chapter 27

Gifts of the Sun

I *placed my attention on the Master who had taught me so much over the past couple of days. Before I knew it, I was standing waist-deep in snow only a short distance from his hut. I plowed through the snow to a narrow walkway leading up to the door.*

With a shiver, I knocked on the doorframe and waited for an answer. The evening sky was thick with clouds, but it had stopped snowing. I shivered again, and suddenly I was clad in a heavy woolen coat. It had appeared out of 'nowhere'! I was grateful to Spirit for providing the coat but continued to hop up and down for warmth and circulation.

After a few minutes, the Master finally pulled back the door covering. But he remained standing at the threshold, watching me stamp my feet and slap my arms.

Are you really cold? *the Master asked.*

I stood up straight and took a quick self-inventory. "Funny thing, I don't really feel that chilly," *I suddenly admitted.*

The really funny thing is that your actions are born out of habit, *he replied grinning. He motioned for me to step inside.* You didn't feel cold, and yet given the snow and the altitude, habit told you that you should be freezing. So you acted out the motions of a very chilly person.

Temperature is a funny thing. What warms the Earth? The sun? Have you ever thought how hot this star you call the sun must be, to provide heat from so far away? And what an interesting coincidence that the Earth is just the right distance from the sun to make it habitable. Have you ever wondered why it's so much cooler in the shade than in full sunlight?

What science doesn't understand is that temperature is interrelated with magnetics. Each of these affects biological cycles, seasons, and species populations. The living creatures of Earth are one component of a life triangle. The other two components are the Earth and the sun.

It is arrogant to think that people are the only intelligent portion of this triangle. I am not saying the Earth and the sun are self-directed like human beings. But they are part of an intelligence governed by Spirit itself.

Actually, Earth's sun throws off more than just heat and light. It also has a supra-physical sheath—an unseen sphere which surrounds the physical manifestation of the star and bombards the Earth with electrons.

Earth's supra-physical sheath protects the physical atmosphere from this electron assault. The bombardment is not intended to destroy Earth. In fact, it serves a purpose relevant to our discussion. The sun's rays help keep the Earth's supra-physical sheath alive, by providing it with cyclical exercise.

When sun-bombardment increases, the planet and its people face the potential danger of excess radiation. Earth's supra-physical sheath must compensate to protect its inhabitants. Like a muscle, the supra-physical sheath becomes stronger and more vital with exercise.

Solar flare is unpredictable. So the Earth must call upon its energetic resources without warning, to strengthen its protective sheath. In between these surges, Earth's supra-physical sheath rests. The unpredictable cycles of radiation keep the Earth's supra-physical sheath alert, toned, and flexible.

I brought up this subject today because it leads into a further discussion of the human being's supra-physical body.

The Master paused, and I thought about removing my coat. It was growing uncomfortably warm.

Your atoms do not feel warmer or colder depending on the temperature. But they do respond to your changed perception and needs. That coat manifested because you thought you needed protection from the cold. Change your perception of yourself and your needs, and the coat is no longer necessary.

As I caught his words, something shifted within me. I wasn't sure exactly what it was.

There you are, very good, *the Master declared.*

I looked down at myself. The coat had vanished! I knew the principle was an important once, since the Master had chosen such a dramatic illustration. "I wonder if I could change my appearance or state of being just by changing my perception of myself," I exclaimed.

Yes that is possible, *he replied with an enigmatic smile.* Now, let's not stray any further from the topic of this discussion.

Your supra-physical body is a reflection of your physical state. Yes, it can function apart from the physical body when Soul so chooses. But it is intricately tied to the physical body and the cycles of the Earth and sun. Just as the sun keeps the Earth's supra-physical body toned and in shape, it also flexes your supra-physical form. Of course, the effect is significantly less because the Earth's supra-physical sheath acts as a filter.

"You say the sun and Earth have supra-physical sheaths," I interjected. "Do they also have other inner bodies, like human beings?"

They have inner-plane counterparts. But these do not reflect the physical manifestation like your inner bodies resemble your physical appearance.

Counterparts are energetically connected but can appear vastly different. Your inner bodies, for example, contain counterparts of physical-body organs. They are energetically linked, often perform similar functions, yet their anatomy can be quite dissimilar. A traveller from Earth probably would not recognize Earth's Astral-Plane counterpart.

But let's get back to your supra-physical body. It shields you from atmospheric radiation, but it can also protect you from your immediate environment.

If you trip and fall, your supra-physical body often collects energy from within itself to cushion your impact. This happens with children all the time. Have you ever noticed your young ones take a nasty fall and come out unscathed? Children are often more flexible and adept at gathering this supra-physical energy than adults.

The Physical World is harsh. Without this protection, we would be hurt many more times than we are, or more severely. People are unconscious of the hundreds of times their supra-physical bodies save them from pain.

This protection can also occur when you are driving a car. Your supra-physical body can extend itself into the physical to provide a cushion between your car and another vehicle. Sometimes this averts an accident or lessens its impact. A well-exercised, well-nourished, and healthy supra-physical body is a great asset.

This does not mean that every time you get hurt, your supra-physical body has failed. When there is a lesson to be learned, Soul—or one of the inner bodies associated with the lesson—flicks off this function of the supra-physical body for an instant. And lo and behold, you have an experience to learn from.

What is the protective mechanism of a healthy supra-physical sheath? It is similar to the lymphatic system, in that lymph does not circulate except when the body moves and exercises. Likewise, supra-physical energies provide the best protection when exercised and allowed to circulate by repeated stimuli.

The best stimuli for strengthening the supra-physical body are unexpected challenges—when every ounce, so to speak, of protection is required. On the other hand, continual, non-stop dangers, such as living in a heavily polluted environment, whittle away supra-physical reserves.

The supra-physical body itself contains a multitude of magnetic particles. Each has a positive and a negative pole. These are the reflections of the physical atoms' positive and negative components.

Physical atoms rotate continually. The faster and more smoothly they spin in your body, the healthier you are. Exercise provided by the sun's radiation keeps these particles well oiled, flexible, and able to turn.

If all of these little magnets are free to move in all directions, they can offer great protection. If one part of the body is in danger—say from a fall—they can instantly reorient themselves toward the point of probable impact.

Energies are relayed from one supra-physical particle to the next. They rush to the area of probably impact and collect there to form a cushion. In an optimal situation, these magnets can provide the ultimate of pathways to protect any area of the body. Some martial artists have developed this cushioning effect to a high degree, allowing them to break bricks and boards with their hand.

To protect the body from a blow, the supra-physical body must react before the object hits the physical body. Fortunately, anything approaching the body first passes through the mental and emotional sheaths, which signal the supra-physical body. This allows enough time to form an energy cushion. But it's not until the actual impact that the cushion takes its effect.

The supra-physical can also orient all its magnets so they point outward. This protects the entire physical body from pervasive negative influences. These might include coarse or harmful thoughts and emotions, as well as pollution, heat, or noise.

Supra-physical particles also syphon off excess energies that accumulate in the physical body. This is necessary to prevent toxin deposits, edema, or a build-up of fat.

I had another question. "Can the supra-physical body protect us from our own negative thoughts and emotions?"

No, *Rebazar replied,* because it does not recognize them as something foreign, something to react to, or something to protect the physical from.

This non-recognition is by design. Otherwise, the physical body could not benefit from lessons regarding negative images, thoughts, and emotions. These include not only derogatory thoughts and emotions about others and oneself, but also those which limit free expression and growth.

Strengthening the Supra-Physical Body

Now it seems appropriate to offer you a technique to increase supra-physical flexibility. This exercise will also gradually remove blockages and accumulation from this sheath.

It is important to keep the supra-physical free of excess blockages and accumulations. When you take the time and effort to do this, great strength and stamina develop. This in turn allows you to handle a greater spiritual flow.

The supra-physical body can grow quite inflexible when forced to protect the physical sheath from an unvarying stream of energies. Remember, the unpredictability of the sun's ever-changing radiation exercises the Earth's supra-physical sheath best. But constant levels of pollution, noise, and negative mental and emotional energies are steadily debilitating to your planet.

The same is true for your supra-physical body. Unexpected stimuli offers the ideal strengthening exercise. But if the supra-physical is burdened by excess baggage or weakened by inner-body negativity, even beneficial exercise can cause stress.

Accumulations prevent the supra-physical from fulfilling its protective duties. These negative energies eventually seep through to the physical form as well. This in turn stresses the supra-physical body more, rendering it even less effective.

Our technique today is based on the principle that the supra-physical body mirrors the physical body. Therefore certain physical stimuli can also exercise the supra-physical.

You, as a conscious Soul, will be initiating this exercise. The supra-physical will therefore anticipate the stimuli. But the exercise will still strengthen this sheath—without the stress of unanticipated change.

We will not only exercise the supra-physical's protection mechanism, but also expand and contract the supra-physical body itself for increased flexibility. During the expansion, accumulations stuck in the supra-physical matrix can be released. Contraction will move the blockages out of position. This helps the sheath recognize and begin to resolve them. As a result, the supra-physical body will be strengthened.

I recommend that one begin practicing this technique slowly, gradually increasing its intensity. A key to making it work is your awareness of the purpose of the exercise. Keep your attention on the reality of your supra-physical self.

Harsh demands on its protective mechanism can stress the physical body. So go slow. If the supra-physical does not have good strength, incoming stimuli can throw the physical body out of balance.

The supra-physical body does more than simply repel negative stimuli. It also monitors what is allowed to enter the physical aura. It is selective even of things of a positive nature, to maintain your body's balance and order.

309

Let's describe this somewhat unusual technique.

First of all, you need to practice it during your daily shower—a bath will not work. While you are washing at normal temperatures, make the water just a little bit cooler. Wait a few seconds, and then adjust the faucet to hotter water. After a few seconds, fluctuate the temperature again from cool to hot.

Start gently, with just a few, minimal water-temperature fluctuations. Then over the next few days, swing the temperature back and forth a little more.

Now, if you already love hot showers, don't make your shower burning hot. Work from hot to a few degrees cooler. Each time you take a shower widen the temperature extremes.

Eventually, try to spend about fifteen to thirty seconds at cool and hot, moving between them three or four times.

As you build your supra-physical strength, you will be able to widen the gap between hot and cold. Do this gradually, and you will know when you are ready for the next level of fluctuation.

When you reach a point where it's too uncomfortable to make the water any colder or hotter, maintain this technique at the same level. If the supra-physical body is functioning well, your physical body will feel invigorated by this exercise, and you'll enjoy it every day.

The Master paused momentarily, Next, I would like to talk about the supra-physical body's role in sleep and dreams. But I think you need a stretch break before we resume tonight's discussion.

I agreed. My imagination was captivated, but I needed some time to absorb what I had learned. I decided to take a walk outside. Perhaps it would exercise my supra-physical body's ability to perceive warmth—even in the appearance of cold.

The sun was just below the cloudy horizon as I stepped outside. The jagged mountain peaks cast eerie shadows, making the landscape surreal.

As I stood in the snow, my thoughts wandered back to the mission at hand. How many more discourses would I receive on the subtle bodies?

There was so much yet to learn. The information I had gathered so far seemed barely introductory to these Adepts.

The Master quietly called my name, and I returned to the little hut refreshed and ready for more.

Chapter 28

Sleep and Dreams

*T*he *fire was burning brightly when I entered the small Himalayan hut. The Master and I watched the dancing flames for a few moments before seating ourselves on the rug before the warm hearth.*

The Tibetan studied my aura. I want you to realize something as you edit this series of discourses. Wisdom cannot be imparted whole. It's an ongoing, unfolding process. The difficulty my associates and I have is that there is so much information to share. Volumes could be written about each of the subtle bodies and their interworkings. It takes years for a physician to explore just some of the workings of the physical body. And yet here you are, accepting the task to lay a foundation for all of the bodies in just one book.

This project, therefore, should simply be considered as a framework for an intricate puzzle. Future works by you, as well as others, will fill in more and more of the missing pieces. As this occurs, a greater picture of life will unfold.

Now, back to the supra-physical body.

The supra-physical's functions are so natural they are often overlooked. Today I shall tell you a few of its other duties, to help round out your understanding of this fascinating sheath.

The Physical Plane is a harsh environment for the physical body, especially when the Soul it houses is awakening to Itself. The supra-physical body envelops the physical body to constantly adjust the various energies which both enter and leave the physical form. It acts like a buffer zone—an area of transition between the harshness of the physical environment and the rising vibratory rate of a spiritually-evolving individual.

The supra-physical body plays another important role. It has to do with the bio-electric currents or 'chi forces' which continually flow around the body.

The physical counterparts of these bio-electric currents are the body's meridian lines. These lines, which flow throughout the body, were first identified thousands of years ago by the forefathers of Chinese Medicine.

I call meridian lines 'physical manifestations' though they are energetic, non-physical, non-dissectible components of the body. Still, they are more physically-oriented than their supra-physical counterparts.

Physical meridian lines affect physical organ function, while supra-physical flows affect behavior. This behavior includes one's ability to magnetically attract desired experiences or members of the opposite sex. It also includes the ability to interact on an unconscious level with one's surroundings.

The supra-physical body's overall magnetic quality does attract circumstances and experiences. However, the continual flow and movement of supra-physical currents of electricity is a much more fundamental force for drawing them.

An individual may desire, have earned, deserve, or need a certain experience. But if the experience is somehow out of harmony with his physical surroundings, his physical expression, or the unique nature of his physical body, then his supra-physical magnetism cannot attract it. The supra-physical body's electrical flows search for common threads between the individual and the needed experience. They provide the bridge or means by which the experience can enter a person's life.

314

And as I mentioned, the bio-electric currents play an important role in one's ability to attract a mate. This is the root of biological attraction, and provides the urge to seek out a partner for physical reproduction.

The supra-physical's bio-electric currents also play an important role in sleep and dreaming. For most individuals, sleep allows the physical and inner bodies to re-balance their chemistry. They process and assimilate, record or erase, and release or store stimuli from the waking hours. Nothing more. But for the God seeker, there is yet another purpose for sleep: to allow the consciousness to expand at a rate faster than the physical awareness can allow.

"Wait, what do you mean by 'erase' stimuli?" I asked. "I thought all experiences were recorded."

Experiences are recorded, yes, *the Master replied.* But all the peripheral stimuli associated with them need not be. In fact, the stimuli associated with certain experiences can become a needless burden. For example, after you see a movie, your mind records all its images and the emotions you felt.

But the mental body has a difficult time distinguishing between reality and what you experienced via the movie. To the mental body there really is no difference between 'real life', and that which is imagined or viewed.

Soul, however, can make such distinctions. It will direct the mental body to erase such clutter. Clutter comes from real life too. All unnecessary images are erased to make room for storage of the significant happenings in one's life.

Clutter accumulates, for example, when one watches television or visits the grocery store with its bombardment of advertising, lights, smells, colors, and people. Most of this is erased. However, images with emotions attached to them are not so easy to dispense with. They must be processed if Soul wants to resolve and release them.

For example, if you see something you want at the store and it arouses a desire, you may feel sad if you don't buy it.

315

Now you have a feeling attached to the experience. That night when you sleep, all the stimuli you picked up at the store will be erased except that which applies to your desired object.

If you get enough sleep, or if your mental body isn't overburdened with other work, the image with its attached emotion may be processed, released, and resolved. Otherwise, you may buy the item or make a conscious decision to forego it.

Dreams are essential to one's health. Why? First of all, dreams smooth disharmony between the physical and inner bodies. Remember the sublime interconnectedness of your physical and inner sheaths? Dreams are a good way to painlessly work through emotional issues, karmic debts, and limiting concepts, desires, or attitudes.

Second, your inner bodies often see what lies ahead for you. This doesn't mean time plays itself out any more swiftly in the inner worlds. But the inner bodies have a broader viewpoint on life than you can gain in the physical body. A dream might warn or prepare you for events to come.

Third, during sleep, harmony is re-established among and within the inner bodies through processes of cleansing, healing, and relaxation. I believe the re-balancing of some metabolic chemicals during sleep has even been measured and studied in the physical body. Dreams are a key to this processing.

Fourth, dreams are a means of communication between Soul, Spirit, and the physical consciousness. Sometimes an inner body will use a dream to communicate with the physical. It may send a dream instructing you to avoid certain indigestible foods or alerting you to an upcoming emotional test. This is why it is enormously beneficial to record and study your dreams.

Most dreams are clouded in symbols. These symbols are one of the inner bodies' natural defense mechanisms. The human consciousness may not be ready to instantly perceive

316

all that exists in the inner worlds. But dreams are a way to gently remind the mind and heart that these worlds and realities exist.

Some people do not accept the presence of the inner worlds. But sleep allows Soul to be free for awhile, to explore other dimensions and truths. These realities seep into the consciousness bit by bit. This is why people will often comment that they have a fresh view of a problem or situation after 'sleeping on it'.

In essence, dreams offer a unique view of the inner worlds, as seen through a special portal in the supra-physical body. This is called the sleep window.

Sometimes—though not often—the dreamer will step through the supra-physical sleep window and consciously enter directly into his inner worlds. The dreamer 'awakens' to a heightened sense of reality in his dream, and his experience becomes extraordinarily clear, vivid, and all-encompassing. He has crossed the line into conscious inner-world exploration.

The unconscious dreamer is also technically present in an inner plane as he dreams out some inner drama. But he trails his conscious mind like an umbilical cord. This prevents him from entering completely into the inner arena of the dream. He is there, yet he is not—even though his form can be seen by others in that world.

People who consciously travel the inner worlds have an entirely different appearance from unconscious dreamers. Perhaps you've noticed this at Askleposis. Some of the attendees' bodies seem to glow brightly, as if made of millions of tiny stars. Others are shrouded in a thick mist extending several feet in every direction. It's often hard to even discern their facial features.

This reflects a difference in spiritual maturity. Those who shine bright and clear have well-developed inner bodies. They can travel in full waking consciousness as well as during sleep—even though blockages may cloak their memory of such experiences.

Vague and misty forms house those who are just beginning to use their inner bodies. They are almost always dream travelling unconsciously. Soul has been kissed by the grace of Spirit, and led to an inner class or experience by a spiritual guide.

When an individual consciously enters an inner world, the images he perceives are real. They may also harbor a deeper or wider symbolic meaning or resonance, but the experience remains what it is.

The unconscious dreamer's experiences, on the other hand, are cloaked in symbols. The dream is actually viewed in its entirety by Soul. But the mind reduces the experience to vague images. Contextual insights and much of Soul's understanding is lost in the mind-translation.

If it can, the mind's censor will try to erase the entire dream, symbols and all, from the memory. This is because the mind loves the status quo. Fortunately, the supra-physical body's bio-electric currents often prevent this obliteration.

These supra-physical currents are activated during sleep. They help you remember your inner world experiences. Even if the dream is forgotten, the currents will help you intuitively benefit from a dream's wisdom or insights.

The bio-electric currents establish a connection between the dream experience and the physical consciousness. The better the connection, the more the dreamer remembers his nightly activities, and the greater the benefit they can be. If the currents are strong and true, it's easier to understand dream symbols and relate them to everyday life.

This connection is vital for health and spiritual success. It is maintained for as long as the dream is occurring and remembered. Writing a dream down allows your conscious mind to reflect on its meaning for a longer period of time. Thus a dream journal is an important tool for creating an

318

upward trend or cycle in life. Recording your dreams strengthens and manifests your supra-physical connection to your inner worlds. Subsequent dreams then become more real and useful. You gain more inner-world information, and life improves as you apply it in day-to-day situations.

No matter what the importance or purpose of a dream symbol, its connection to the physical consciousness closes when a dream is forgotten. The subtle bodies's attempt to bring harmony into your physical world is limited. There is no all-important follow-through in the lowest realms of reality.

But let's say you write down a dream as soon as you wake up, even though it makes no sense. Later when you have fully returned to physical consciousness, you read it over and think about what it might mean. A creative insight comes as you brainstorm the beneficial purpose of the dream. You know that each dream is an attempt by Soul or the inner bodies to aid your spiritual growth.

Your daily or weekly dream-review process builds a solid and vital connection between the inner bodies and the physical body. And make no mistake, this connection will grow even if the human consciousness can make absolutely no sense of the warning, advice, or insights in the dream. You are still expanding your communication among the physical and inner bodies in which the dreams took place.

So the purpose of any dream, be it a past-life recall or a warning of future events, facilitates greater harmony among the inner sheaths and the physical body. This connects the physical consciousness to higher states.

This explains the 'spiritual mechanics' of what many of us might take for granted: the ability to remember and potentially interpret our dreams. As I have said, the supra-physical body's functions are so natural, the mechanisms that run them are easily overlooked.

Dreams are a fascinating study. We could continue talking about them for days.

"Does the supra-physical body play a role in insomnia?"
I asked.

Disturbances, imbalances, or inflexibility in the supra-physical body can keep one from falling asleep, yes.

But the inability to sleep can have its root in any of the subtle bodies. The supra-physical body may react to this root cause, magnifying its effects. Then even if the inner cause is resolved, if the supra-physical does not reflect the adjustment, the sleep disorder will not be corrected.

The supra-physical is adept at reflecting. Remember, it manifested itself by reflecting the physical body. Sometimes it may continue to hold an image of a condition long after it has been healed.

This leads me to another point. Supra-physical dysfunctions may hold Soul's consciousness in the physical. It can also befuddle the symbols the mind attaches to dreams, so the individual cannot grasp their meaning.

Supra-physical dysfunctions arise from an improper distribution of energy in the supra-physical body. It may contain pockets of congestion which clog its magnetic flows, and areas of sparse distribution which lead to deficiency and weakness. The technique using wind, heat, and flute music helps loosen blockages in the magnetic particles of this sheath.

A Physical Exercise to Improve Dream Recall

I would also like to give you an exercise that works with physical breath and movement to gently massage the supra-physical sheath.

It will unblock your supra-physical awareness and familiarize you with this body's energies. It will also redistribute energy in the supra-physical body. As a result, dream symbols may be less garbled and dream travel may be easier to remember.

This exercise is not designed to heal the root cause of sleep disorders or other problems. But it may correct supraphysical body dysfunctions that magnify them.

The exercise is performed standing up. Have a chair nearby to hold on to for support. There is a secret to this exercise: Whenever you straighten your arm or leg while exhaling or inhaling, try to imagine you are throwing energy down your limb and into the atmosphere. This visualization is crucial to its success. Let us begin.

Part 1

First, touch the tips of your thumbs to your heart chakra (in the center of your chest). The thumbtips should be touching each other, fingers spread apart and pointing sideways, and palms facing the floor. Your elbows should be lifted so your forearms are parallel to the floor.

Step 1

Inhale while lifting the chin about an inch.

Exhale while returning the chin to its previous position.

Step 2

Inhale as you move your left arm out to the side, and straighten it so that it is level with your shoulders.

Exhale as you bring your arm back to where it was, with the thumbtip placed on the heart chakra.

Step 3

Repeat Step 2.

Hold your breath and let your left arm drop by your side.

Step 4

Inhale as you move your right arm out to the side, and straighten it so that it is level with your shoulders.

Exhale as you bring your arm back to where it was, with the thumbtip placed on the heart chakra.

Step 5

Repeat Step 4.

Hold your breath. Let your right arm drop by your side.

Part 2

Breathe normally and prepare for the next part of the exercise. You may want to hold the back of the chair for support. However, if you can balance yourself, return your thumbtips to the heart chakra and keep them there during Part 2.

Step 1

Inhale as you bend your left leg, lifting your knee enough so your foot rises a few inches off the ground. Your toes should be pointed down. Remember to imagine a flow of supra-physical energy shooting down your leg and out into the atmosphere as you straighten it.

Exhale and straighten your leg, returning your foot to the ground.

Step 2

Inhale, bending your knee again.

Exhale and put your foot down on the floor beneath you.

Step 3

Repeat Steps 1 and 2 with the right leg.

Step 4

If you have been holding your thumbtips to your heart, hold your breath momentarily while dropping your arms to your sides.

Part 3

Perform the same movements that you did in Parts 1 and 2. But this time, reverse the inhales and exhales. In other words, inhale when asked to exhale, and vice versa.

Part 4

Part 4 of this exercise is optional.

Step 1

Inhale as you raise both hands up over your head and stretch your fingers to the ceiling.

Exhale as you bring your arms back down to your sides.

Repeat.

Step 2

Inhale deeply with your arms remaining by your sides.

Exhale as your raise both hands up over your head and stretch your fingers to the ceiling.

Inhale as you bring your arms back down to your side.

Repeat.

Breathe normally.

The inhalations and exhalations correspond to the two magnetic poles of the supra-physical body. Some people will find that throwing energy down the arm or leg while inhaling is easier. Others will discover it easier while exhaling. Neither one is better or worse than the other.

My suggestion would be to practice the exercise until you can easily throw energy during both the inhale and exhale.

For best results, practice this exercise daily for a week or two. Each day that you practice this exercise, keep a record of your dreams. See if you notice anything different about them or about your sleep.

That is all for tonight. Tomorrow I will continue with information about supra-physical energy.

"I look forward to it," I said.

So do I, *replied the Master.* Rest well. And good night.

The weather had cleared. I lingered outside the Tibetan's hut, marveling at the billions of stars that blanketed the midnight-blue sky. They seemed to be singing to me—and all life throughout the universe. I joined in their song by breathing out the universal sound of HU.

Chapter 29

Supra-physical Energy

*T*here are many ways for Soul to transcend the physical consciousness and travel freely throughout the inner worlds. Generally, such travel can be divided into five modes: dreams (which are daily inner adventures), trance, meditation, creative visualization, and direct projection.

All incorporate one or more of the following: the Light of Spirit, the Sound of Spirit, a special feeling or knowingness of Spirit, and the Wayshower. These are the secrets keys that unlock the prison of the Physical Plane.

To employ these keys, one has only to look for, feel, imagine, or think about them. Connecting with the Sound of Spirit is perhaps the easiest of all, for it doesn't require any imagination or inner sight. One can simply sing the word "HU." This word is specially charged to bring awareness and love. Its vibrations harmonize Soul with the highest, the all-encompassing, the Divine One Itself.

Singing HU can free the consciousness from negative situations and the most limiting of conditions. If nothing else, it shifts one to a new perspective, from which answers to life's most intriguing questions can be found.

Direct Soul projection is one of my favorite ways to travel. It's easy (trying too hard simply sabotages the results), and quick. One can be someplace in no time at all, by directly placing the attention there, without the need to 'travel'. By the way, this has nothing to do with the astral projection method, *which is limited to the Astral Plane. Soul projection is a Soul-motivated, Soul-initiated experience, that can take one's awareness anywhere in the lower worlds. Singing HU prepares my consciousness for such 'movement'.*

The HU helps me locate the center of my being. Sometimes I pretend it is a river flowing to the heart of God. I follow the river until I feel synchronized with my center, which is Soul. I rest my attention there. Then as Soul, I instantly shift my awareness so it is completely focused on the inner body I want to use. This becomes my new primary point of reference. I enter that body and begin my exploration—taking care to observe the laws of that world.

Today, I decided to again project directly to the Himalayas for the last of my meetings with the Tibetan Master. I began by singing HU for about a minute. I located my center. Then I pictured the Master's hearth in my mind's eye and said aloud, "Be here now!"

The next thing I knew, I was sitting on the rug across from the Tibetan. He was eating a whole-grain bread shaped somewhat like a doughnut.

Glad you could make it back. Excuse me while I finish my meal. *Soon he wiped his fingers on a napkin and took a long draft of tea.*

This will be the last of our meetings on the topic of the supra-physical body. As I mentioned before, feel free to come back at any time for clarification or expansion on our discussions.

What is supra-physical energy? It is the substance of the supra-physical sheath. It originates in the physical body. Light, in the form of color rays, is drawn to the physical body by its blueprints and its manifested components. As you know, atoms combine into molecules which form cells, organs and the body as a whole. Each of these levels of manifestation draws color rays for nourishment. Blueprints also exist at each of these levels and also attract the color rays.

The Light is drawn in by the magnetic quality of the blueprints and body-components. This magnetism comes from their inherent Sound matrixes. As the Light flows in to fill these matrixes, new rays displace old ones, setting up a reciprocal flow.

The outflowing color rays are on their way back to the Golden Kingdom. They have nourished the physical body and now they are on their way home. But they will collect in the supra-physical body until the individual attains the Second Spiritual Achievement.

Many of the spectrums the body components draw will be different from their blueprint spectrums, *unless* the physical and subtle bodies are in *perfect* health. This, of course, is not possible because of the lessons Soul is learning in the Physical World. Even if the individual achieves balance, the dual nature of the Physical Plane prevents perfection.

Only the healthiest areas naturally attract color-ray spectrums that match their blueprints. Disharmonious zones attract less-than-ideal color-ray spectrums. These same spectrums also outflow into the supra-physical.

If the body was perfectly healthy, its supra-physical form would be a perfect reflection of the physical blueprints. But for most people, the supra-physical body reflects the physical body's disharmonies as well as its strengths.

The blueprints of less-than-healthy areas still ask for healthy spectrums. They always will because blueprints remain forever within the fabric of every molecule, cell, and organ. The healthier the individual, the stronger his blueprint magnetism, and the more of the seven colors he can draw for nourishment.

For most people, lifetimes of karma, accumulations, blockages, and negative thoughts weaken the natural blueprint magnetism. These are reflected in the Sound matrixes of the atoms, molecules, cells, and organs. They distort or cloud the proper ratio of Light so it cannot provide perfect nourishment. The spectrums of Light that actually reach the body are therefore less than ideal. We call these lesser ratios 'functional spectrums'. These imperfect spectrums feed and perpetuate our limited conditions. However they also teach us invaluable lessons.

By the way, some disharmonies experienced by people today even draw disruptive, non-color rays to the body. This was not the case even fifty years ago. Since the dawn of the computer age, more and more electromagnetic radiation is polluting Earth's atmosphere. This pollution is perhaps more dangerous than the atmospheric contaminants perceived by man's physical senses.

Non-color-ray frequencies sometimes replace our life-giving energies or cloud both the blueprint and functional spectrums. Optimal health data becomes less accessible, and the lessons that teach us how to reach that state become less obvious.

This pollution also irritates our functional spectrums—especially those farthest removed from the blueprints. Interestingly, this irritation and discomfort speeds karmic resolution. It encourages us to learn our lessons and move our functional spectrums toward blueprint ratios, if for no other reason than to reduce the non-color-ray irritation.

When replaced by new incoming Light rays of any kind, non-color-rays also outflow to update the supra-physical body reflection.

The vibratory rate of rays flowing out of the physical body is much different from those just coming in. That is a point which you should clearly understand. Inflowing rays are charged with the spark of life; outflowing rays have, ideally, given this spark to the body. They exist in a different electrical state. They are not empty; they have just exchanged their electrical cargo for information.

These rays now carry valuable data about the atoms, molecules, cells, organs, and the physical body as a whole.

This information is imprinted in the supra-physical body to update it and keep it accurate. In this way the supra-physical becomes a vast and sensitive repository of our physical information.

It was these returning rays that originally formed the supra-physical sheath. The collective magnetism of all the cells trapped the light rays and their reflections close to the physical body instead of floating off into the physical atmosphere. Eventually, the amassed light rays created the supra-physical form.

Returning light rays alone do not form the supra-physical body. They needed a glue to hold them together. This glue gives integrity and a unique identity to the supra-physical form. The adhesive that forms the supra-physical is a unique kind of undifferentiated light. Its frequency is simple, basic, and fundamental. Color-rays frequencies are complex in comparison to this light-glue. One way to differentiate among them is to consider their wave lengths. The light waves that glue the supra-physical body together are very short but not irritating. They are in fact of a vibratory rate that is neutral to the human body. They do nothing but reflect.

"Are these waves smaller than microwaves?" I asked.

Yes, indeed they are much smaller.

This light is what you see when you look at all matter. And yet it is not this light that you see. Let me explain. Remember that atoms are not particles of matter, but packages of positive, negative, and neutral energies. The undifferentiated light perfectly reflects or carries information about the substance, character, magnetism, and rhythm of atoms. What you see when you look at a collection of atoms is not the packages of energy they are made of, but a material, manifested object, reflected by this light.

This undifferentiated light can reflect any frequency. And by the way, this is the light carried by a special kind of diamond you are studying called the 'Rallop Diamond'.

Now, I wish to make a point about the development of the supra-physical body.

Let's first look at what happens to the color rays when Soul enters a baby body. Light rays begin to flow in and out of the cells. The color rays outflowing from Soul's new physical body return directly to their source in the Golden Kingdom, bypassing all other inner bodies. In this way, Soul's initial connection to the newborn is established.

A supra-physical sheath begins to form as the body develops its own magnetic field. This occurs soon after birth.

The supra-physical body collects the baby's functional spectrums and reflects its state of health. But it takes much longer than you think for the supra-physical body to mature and become well-defined.

A person could spend an entire lifetime building and defining the supra-physical body. If it matures sufficiently, it can even function independently of the physical body. The supra-physical then becomes a great tool for developing consciousness. It allows one to travel and experience non-physical realities in new ways.

On the other hand, if burdened with enough disharmony, the supra-physical sheath can also become an enemy of sorts. It continually reflects physical disharmonies and negative habits.

Exercises such as the one I described in the last chapter only become useful and necessary when the supra-physical is well-defined. The maturity of the supra-physical form is a landmark in the spiritual evolution of humankind. More people than ever before are enjoying the spiritual benefits of a strong and distinct supra-physical form.

As people develop mature, functional sheaths, technology will take great leaps forward. Laws and principles that once seemed rigid will reveal themselves as more fluid and supple. This has already occurred with once-impossible air travel and once-unthought-of super-conductivity.

Yes, this type of progress is directly tied to man's development of the supra-physical body. This sheath provides an important link to the non-physical planes. With development of this subtle form, the inner worlds become more real and physical laws less confining.

Still, the Supra-physical World is more like the Physical World than any of the inner, non-physical realms. It is so close to the Physical Plane that physical matter can move in and out of it. When you travel in the supra-physical realm, the laws simply become a bit less limiting than in the Physical Plane.

As man develops his supra-physical body he invites a greater awareness of its more flexible states. As people move and explore in this body, the realities of the supra-physical realm can be experienced, acknowledged, understood, researched, accepted as reality, and widely adopted.

Then, just like airplanes opened the skies for travel, other inventions and modes of travel will access the supra-physical realities. The jet revolutionized our concept of movement on the planet. With supra-physical technology such as magnetics, transportation will again leap forward.

But let's get back to the supra-physical body. At a certain point in the individual's spiritual unfoldment, color rays collected in the supra-physical begin to flow outward. An opening is created, allowing light waves in the supra-physical to move closer toward their divine source. This window coincides with the individual's Second Spiritual Achievement.

Light waves from the physical displace light waves in the supra-physical, opening a singular stream from the physical through to the supra-physical body, and on into the astral sheath. This stream provides the astral body with direct and accurate feedback about the consciousness and physical condition of the physical body. It allows the astral sheath to become independently defined and fully functional, like that of the supra-physical and physical bodies.

Heretofore, the astral body received feedback only through the somewhat-remote observation of the physical body. And as you know, what one observes is not necessarily the truth. The emotional sheath also received direct life-system information from the physical body, to relay to the causal sheath. As you recall, life systems knit these inner sheaths together in one seamless vibratory continuum.

When the next spiritual achievement is reached, the return flow of light enters the causal body, providing it with direct feedback not only on the physical and supra-physical bodies but also on the astral body.

With each additional spiritual achievement, this flow comes closer to the Golden Kingdom. At the Fifth Spiritual Achievement, the final connection is made with Soul in the Golden Kingdom. Soul can then receive direct feedback from all of it's lower bodies. This feedback is essential to the experience of Self-Realization—when Soul finally has a complete picture of Itself in the five dimensions of the lower worlds.

This information accompanies a complete restructuring of the individual. Soul evaluates its sheaths and takes action to adjust them in line with Its true spiritual mission.

After each spiritual achievement, any acts of irresponsibility, denial, or ignorance of spiritual laws stops or diminishes the Light rays' return flow. This reduces useful feedback, as well as many benefits and blessings usually afforded the individual.

If one earns the Fifth Spiritual Achievement and then disobeys a spiritual law, the gate closes—temporarily in most cases—for light rays to enter the Golden Kingdom. Instead they stop at any one of the lower bodies. The flow may even recede to the point where it is unable to leave the physical body.

Getting that flow of color-rays back to the Golden Kingdom is difficult, but possible. Whenever light-rays reaccess the area of one's most recent achievement, adjustments again occur in the entire life of the individual.

"What is the difference," I asked, "between the feedback the inner bodies receive from spiritual achievements and that which the life systems normally provide?"

The difference could be compared to voluntary and involuntary muscles. Voluntary muscles, such as those in your arms and legs, respond to your conscious impulses. Involuntary muscles, such as those of the heart and intestines, move independently of one's own free will. They keep the body's life-dependent processes functioning as if on 'automatic'.

The life systems function much like involuntary muscles. The feedback passed from one body to another maintains all of the inner and outer bodies' life-dependent processes.

The feedback earned through spiritual achievements allows the individual to make conscious adjustments in his inner bodies. The individual intuitively stops some actions and amplifies others, to nurture harmony and growth within the inner bodies. For example, thoughts the mind didn't realize caused emotional disharmony would be replaced, based on direct feedback about their ill effects.

The flow of feedback initiated by a new spiritual achievement gradually passes from one body to the next higher one. It always begins as a singular, rather narrow, upward flow. Over time, this flow widens to include increasingly wider and more parallel feedback. The broader this flow, the more information can pass upward for new realizations.

Let me explain. At the Second Spiritual Achievement, for example, a single flow carries present-time, moment-by-moment information about the individual's physical state of consciousness into the astral body. It also brings with it stored information about old issues, unresolved karma, negative energy accumulations, and blockages that may have been collecting in the supra-physical body for untold amounts of time.

When your inner bodies receive these old vibrations, they react to them. This sets a process in motion which allows you to start resolving karma. The inner bodies' responses draw karma-resolving experiences into your life. As you live through these experiences, you have the opportunity to work through the original causes for accumulation in your supra-physical body.

When the karma is resolved, or nearly so, the original single flow widens. Parallel flows are initiated to bring even more karma, additional blockages, and even subtler disharmonies to the attention of the emotional body for resolution.

Let's say in this life you hit someone out of malice. The light rays of that experience bounce off of your atoms and collect in your supra-physical sheath.

One day, you reach a point in your spiritual unfoldment where that stored information is released for processing into the Astral Plane. The astral body will then arouse your emotions in some way that will allow you to burn off the anger and hurt of the original blow.

Perhaps you will be hit by the person you injured, or by a reincarnation of that Soul. Sometimes a different person will help you repay your debt. Or you may not be hit by a person at all. A falling tree branch may glance your cheek, or you may slam your finger in a door. Who knows? But the experience of being hit sends its own spectrum of light rays into the supra-physical body. If this spectrum cancels out the one associated with the original blow, the cycle is completed. Information about the stored experience is released and the karma is resolved.

Of course, there is an easier way, though few Souls have discovered it. That is to sing the oft-mentioned word, 'HU'. It can help you release or streamline the resolution of these karmic debts.

If one dies before all the supra-physical disharmonies are cleared, a special process is initiated so Soul is not cheated of any of Its lessons. The collected and unresolved accumulations and blockages themselves fade from the dissolving supra-physical form. But their existence is recorded into matrixes and stored in the astral body.

When Soul takes on its next physical body, it transfers these matrixes from the astral body to the newly developing supra-physical body. This information shapes the individual's new physical and supra-physical forms.

And so the body develops under the direction of the supra-physical matrixes, which were earned in previous lifetimes. Eventually the light waves that collect in the new supra-physical body will reflect the same unresolved issues and blockages of previous lifetimes. This allows Soul to grow and unfold with some semblance of continuity.

Interesting, don't you think? In this way, all karmic debts stay with you until you take full responsibility for them. Only then will their matrixes be resolved and released.

If your astral body is also dropped when your physical body dies, then information about both the supra-physical and astral bodies is collected into the causal body.

"Sire," I queried, "the energies of gemstones have a special affinity with the energies of the inner bodies, especially the supra-physical. Can gemstones also assist in the process of releasing and resolving one's 'old stuff'?

Some gemstones can, and of course their spherical form would be most effective.

As I mentioned earlier, the concern when applying the crystalline form of gemstones to the aura is that they have the potential to release blockages stored in the supra-physical body, but in a rather uncontrollable manner. If more accumulation is released than the individual is ready to let go of, more karma arises than a person can resolve at one time. His life may become imbalanced. Ironically, if he acts out of this imbalanced state, he may end up creating even more extensive debts.

Of course, one can clear the supra-physical aura without physically-manifested tools. This can be done as I said by singing certain sacred words or practicing spiritual exercises. They also prepare the individual for the Second Spiritual Achievement. This is indeed a blessed event, when light waves are finally released from the supra-physical body, and the journey of the resolution of the past is begun.

Now don't get me wrong. It is possible to resolve karma long before a supra-physical opening is established through the Second Spiritual Achievement. Hitting someone can easily be paid back through the experience of being hit in return. The light waves that record those experiences will cancel each other out.

This process is similar to what occurs when gemstone spheres are worn. Gemstones do not take on, or take away, your karma. They just ease its resolution. The wave pictures of some gemstones are broadcast into the aura to cancel out the light waves of needless disharmonies. Others metabolize accumulations which would prevent certain experiences from both entering your life and canceling out the wave-pictures of undesired conditions.

"Do you mean to say that accumulation in the supra-physical body will inhibit the resolution of karma?" I asked.

Yes, and it is unfortunate. Using our example, let's say you hit someone and eventually get hit back. The return hit would normally resolve the karma. But accumulations can prevent the return hit from canceling out the first blow. As a result, you might attract other experiences in which you get hit again and again. Eventually there is a break in the clouds of accumulation, and the return hit is finally recorded.

I want to mention that individuals with similar functional spectrums will also be attracted to each other. This is why children of any species have a particular affinity to their parents and especially with their mother. People are drawn to others with similar color-ray deficiencies or excesses. They feel comfortable when the rhythm and magnetism of their spectrums is compatible or in harmony with those of another.

Attraction between two individuals can also occur symbiotically. One person may be deficient in a particular color ray that another has in excess.

Now, I want to present a final technique that will teach you to perceive your supra-physical aura. It will also help you mend any holes and weaknesses you identify in it. The method of presentation will be different than anything you have experienced.

Let's begin by singing 'HU'.

We closed our eyes and sang one long HU. The Master's deep voice was music to my ears. In the silence that followed, the air became magically still. I prepared myself for anything that might occur.

Then the Master spoke in a calm, yet determined voice that sounded almost like an order, Be here now! Know it now!

For a split second I experienced a consciousness expansion of incomparable enormity. It was accompanied by a brilliant flash of light and a voluminous eruption of sound. As soon as it happened, it disappeared. I was bursting with new knowledge. I will try to express some of what I learned:

Knowledge from the inner worlds isn't always given in discourses or classes. Nor does it always take a great deal of time and effort to receive it. Occasionally, individuals are blessed with the ability to accept whole blocks of information outside the framework of time.

During such an experience, it's as if your consciousness is placed in the spotlight of Spirit. Within seconds, a body of knowledge is 'downloaded' into your aura. You can know facts, think thoughts, feel feelings, and construct information about the topic. You can also receive true understanding and wisdom. Downloads tend to come unexpectedly, but usually when one is open and receptive to them.

It was through this process that I received the following technique:

How to Perceive the Supra-physical Body, and Mend Holes in the Supra-physical Aura

Part 1

Begin by studying your hand. Notice its shape.

Now close your eyes and feel the skin surrounding your hand. It defines the parameters of your physical hand.

Now expand these parameters. With your imagination, feel your hand growing. Watch it unfold like the budding of a flower in time-lapse photography.

Let it expand to about six inches. You may be surprised to find this is not difficult to imagine. Your supra-physical hand actually extends several inches around your physical one.

Open your eyes and dare to perceive your hand as more than what is contained in your skin. See it as an energetic form that extends about six inches in all directions.

The next step is to repeat the entire procedure with a greater portion of your body. Start with your whole arm, then try it with the upper part of your body. Move on to your entire physical body.

Once you have a good sense of the supra-physical aura, at least around your hand, proceed to Part 2.

Part 2

Hold your hand a few feet away from an object such as a tabletop or a pillow. Very slowly and gradually, bring your hand toward the tabletop.

When your hand is about four to six inches away from it, gently move your hand up and down, toward and away from the tabletop, with small bouncing movements. See if you can

338

detect a cushion of energy between your physical hand and the table. This is where your supra-physical 'skin' meets the table-top.

Now slowly move your hand in a circular motion as if caressing the tabletop. You are tuning in to the senses of your supra-physical body.

Do the same with some part of a physical body—yours, a friend's, or even an animal's.

Note the difference between sensing the supra-physical aspects of living and non-living forms. It should be much easier to feel the supra-physical aura of living beings.

Part 3

Now practice sensing inconsistencies within a person's supra-physical aura. To ensure that the inconsistencies you identify aren't simply differences in magnetic attraction, you must first 'de-polarize' your hands.

Hold your hands in front of you with palms facing each other, about two feet apart. Gradually bring them closer together. Use all your sensitivity to feel them make contact at about twelve inches apart.

Now move them together and away from each other in very slight movements. Try to feel the magnetic field developing between your hands. After a minute or so, the cushion of energy between your hands will magnify.

Your right hand holds a north-pole polarity. The left is oriented toward the south. Normally, they would be drawn to each other—and other areas of the body that hold an opposite charge. Your right hand has an affinity for organs holding a south-pole orientation, and your left is magnetized toward those with a northerly-charge.

Holding your hands in proximity in this way will de-individualize their polarities. As each hand gradually stops canceling the other's energy, it becomes more sensitive to supra-physical energies.

Part 4

Hold one palm at a time about two feet from your body, over an area of your choice. Slowly move it closer. When it is about six inches away, begin to bounce it on the layer of supra-physical energy that exists there. Now circle your palm over the area. Practice this with both hands over various parts of the body.

Let's say an area draws your hand in and you don't feel the supra-physical cushion of energy. It may indicate a weakness in that area of the physical body. To determine if a debilitation is indeed present, check the area with your other hand. If both hands are drawn to the same spot, there is probably a lapse or inconsistency in the energy in that portion of the supra-physical body.

Such a gap usually indicates an absence of life force flowing through the area. Life-force deficiencies can become holes, through which negative energies can flow. If these energies, which include environmental and atmospheric disturbances, are allowed to flow through they can cause even greater disharmony in the physical body.

Other layers of the aura also defend against certain outside negativity. But the supra-physical is the last outpost that protects the physical body from environmental hazards.

It is possible to help mend the weakness using the palms of your hands. Bounce the palms of your hands between about six and two inches from the physical body where the weakness is detected. Do this first with your right hand, then your left. Then try it with both hands together, thumbs side-by-side.

Repeat this sequence several times. This bouncing has an energizing, pumping effect that draws the body's energy to the area, to help mend it.

I opened my eyes and looked up at Rebezar. He nodded his head, letting me know I had translated the information correctly.

Tomorrow you will begin the next leg of your journey, *he announced.* I will guide you to the Master who will present your next discourse.

Go home and prepare for it. *The Master raised his hand in salutation.* With love, May the blessings be. And good night.

"Good night," I replied.

Again using direct Soul projection, I instantly transported myself back home. I arrived in my supra-physical body just outside the house. I circled the yard to make sure everything was alright, checked on my sleeping children, and then reentered my physical body resting comfortably on the couch.

Chapter 30

Spiritual Gifts

*T*onight *when I closed my eyes to contemplate, I didn't have an urge to go anywhere. I was content to listen to the quiet sound of HU endlessly rolling throughout the Physical World and all eternity. I decided to enjoy the HU for a while before traveling back to the Himalayas.*

Suddenly, Rebazar Tarz appeared on the empty screen of my inner vision. He was dressed in his traditional short-sleeved, knee-length maroon tunic and brown scandals.

I thought I would come to you this time, *he said smiling.* I am here to escort you to the spiritual city of Agam Des. The Guardian of this city will discuss several pertinent topics, including gemstones. This should help with your study of their spiritual significance.

"Thank you, sire," I replied.

We direct-projected to a rugged area of the mountains, where only sparse patches of grasses lived between the rocks. Snow-capped mountain peaks loomed majestically nearby. As I scanned the familiar landscape, I recognized our location: we were on the opposite side of the city I had visited less than a week ago.

Then I realized I had arrived here without picturing our destination. I just went with the Master. Skilled spiritual travelers can take someone along who either doesn't know how to travel or exactly where to go. In the past, several different Masters had helped me explore this way.

The Golden Being who had met me at this city before was waiting for us. This time he looked less celestial, in a floor-length maroon robe.

The Tibetan introduced him to me.

You can call me the Nameless One, *the Guardian said.* You need not record what is said, for the pure expression of Spirit in any form—be it words, music, thought, or deeds—is enough to impact and uplift the world.

I would like to record your words anyway, if that's alright. Then I could offer what you have to say as a gift to fellow Souls on the path of Light and Sound.

Very well, *he replied.*

People often come to Agam Des in their dream states. Many wish to learn of their future and of their past. They take this information and apply it to who they are today. Knowledge and understanding of the past and future enriches the moment of now.

The nameless one turned to the Tibetan, and the two Masters spoke quietly for a few moments. The wind took their words away so I could not hear them. I watched and waited as they conversed.

Rebazar stopped talking and pointed skyward. I looked up and saw the lights of Aurora Borealis dancing above the horizon. The colorful phenomenon grew until it covered almost one third of the heavens. It was astonishingly beautiful.

It seems as if the sky is laughing, *he said.*

Spirit itself is dancing to the tune of it's own music, *concurred the Nameless One. We enjoyed the display for several minutes.*

Now, shall we get on with our discourse? *asked the Tibetan.*

We each sat on a nearby rock, forming a triangle. I was wondering about the "we" part of the discourse. "Are you both going to speak?" I asked.

I'm only here to observe and to listen, *Rebazar replied.*

And to provide moral support, *added the Nameless One with a grin.*

They both chuckled.

Laugh with us, *the Nameless One invited.* Life doesn't have to be so serious. You see, even the sky has been laughing. *He too pointed to the Aurora Borealis, which flared with activity.*

I took a deep breath and managed a smile. I had always regarded this Master as a solemn, disciplined, serious being. Seeing him so relaxed made me feel more at ease and broke my limiting concepts.

Let's continue, *the Nameless One announced.* His voice resumed the dignified tone I had known him for. But now I understood that he wasn't always solemn—rather, he was ernestly devoted to Spirit.

That which divides the future from the past is the same as that which separates the inner from the outer. For example, just as the inner bodies are inside of you—for in essence you 'go within' to find them—they also manifest outside of you. Specifically, they manifest as the layers of energy which surround your physical body and which comprise what is called the aura.

So little is known about the aura. Many have felt it or seen it. With the recent development of Kirlean photography, the auras of some plants and people have been photographed. But only the supra-physical aura is detected on the film.

The aura extends many feet around the body. Some say it extends into infinity, but I realize that concept may be hard to grasp. So we define the aura-proper as several layers which extend about five total feet from the physical sheath. Each layer corresponds to an inner body.

The link between past and future, manifested substance and unmanifested essence, inner and outer dimensions: this

345

is one of life's spiritual mysteries. However, this link can be observed and probed through an understanding of the spiritual nature of atoms and their components.

Living beings—plants, animals and human beings—manifest this spiritual connection by their very existence. You might like to know that gemstones also manifest this link because they too have a life energy that flows through them.

I speak of gemstones because they are containers of Light and Sound present in the Physical and all other lower worlds. They are unadulterated by any lower sheath or lower-plane vibration.

A gemstone is like a jar filled in the pure Golden Kingdom itself. Its lid is then sealed, and the jar placed in the Physical World. To keep the jar's lid and contents intact, the molecules of the jar form a strong crystalline matrix. This crystalline matrix is the only container—with one exception—strong enough to hold such a pure expression of Spiritual Light and Sound in the Physical World.

The one exception is your physical body, which houses Soul. It is also a container for pure spiritual essence—or it can be. A gemstone expresses the Light and Sound of Spirit because that is its nature. Unlike a gemstone, you must become aware of what lies inside you before that pure essence can be expressed.

The Soul-awakened being radiates pure spiritual essence just as the gemstone. In other words, if you can operate in daily life from the Soul state of consciousness you are like a gemstone.

Make it your goal to be like the faceted gemstone. It is its nature to uncontrollably express Light and Sound. It radiates it freely with no inhibitions, blockages, patterns, or accumulations holding it back. For the gemstone has none of these. Its inclusions do not obscure its purity. They are present only because in the gemstone's infancy, the Physical World resisted the presence of these flawless containers.

Spiritual exercises also help you learn to express Light and Sound freely like a gem does. The technique I will share later is designed specifically for this.

One can use the physically manifested forms of gemstones as well as their inner-world counterparts to help you achieve this goal. Faceted gems are especially good for this. Certain faceted stones can also speed awakening.

"I thought that hastening the unfoldment of consciousness was dangerous," I commented. *"If I open to Spirit too quickly, am I destined to fall? I don't want to reach the spiritual heights only to plunge back into physical unconsciousness to complete unfinished business, so to speak. Perhaps I would have to repeat cycles that were not completed because I grew too quickly away from them?"*

If you are sitting still, enmeshed in darkness, only good can result from a helping hand shining a flashlight at the door. It is up to you to run and open the door, and cross the threshold. The gemstone's energy is one such a light in the lower worlds.

If you work with the Sound and Light you will not skip ground. You will simply cover it more quickly. The Sound and Light come to Soul only in the most efficient and economical way.

The very existence of gemstones is a gift of Spirit. That they are present in the coarse vibrations of this Physical Universe is a miracle. Therefore, whether one receives an inner gem from a Master as a symbol of something greater, or procures one in the physical or inner worlds, one is truly blessed.

To receive a gemstone in the inner worlds, one must earn it with a giving heart. To have a giving heart, one must be open for a continual inflow and outflow of love, and be strong enough to maintain it. Physically manifested gems must also be earned. It is only the nature of the Physical Universe that one's earning is measured in coin.

There are many concepts held by people today about poverty and wealth. Here are a few thoughts on the matter:

There is no virtue in being poor unless one is also spiritually rich. For then poverty is only a state in which others perceive you.

When one is spiritually rich, one has enough. Does it really matter how others measure the standard of enough?

One who is spiritually rich can have nothing, and yet all his needs are fulfilled.

Regardless of how much money you might have, if you feel you are poor or lacking in any way, you are deficient of spiritual riches.

If you are unable to receive spiritual gifts or afford the physical things you think you need, then do what you must physically and inwardly to change your circumstances. Start by looking within. Practice the spiritual exercises in this discourse series. They will help you attain inner-body mastership. This is a key to all the richness that life has to offer.

It is Spirit's plan that all Souls receive what they need. But they must earn the right to have these needs fulfilled.

When Soul learns to use all Spirit's gifts, the journey home reaches new heights. Life unfolds its true meaning and abundance. Soul then exists in these lower worlds but truly is not of them. It is here and yet It is apart from all that is here. The tools of life are used to work more closely with the Divine.

As a co-worker with God, life becomes so abundant no amount of coins could match it. Living this life from the consciousness of Soul—in this world but not of it—the lessons change. One is no longer earning, recognizing, and mastering tools. One uses tools based on the spiritual Law of Economy. In fact one's entire life revolves around this law.

When working with the Law of Economy, ask yourself: Which tools do I really need? How much attention should be kept in the Physical World, at the expense of the spiritual worlds or Soul Consciousness? How much time is needed to exercise each of the sheaths so they remain well-toned?

These are some of the conscious choices Soul must exercise. When I speak of Soul, I do not mean an unconscious part of you. I speak of that part that can become conscious of Itself. And when this Self-Consciousness is obtained, all I am saying makes perfect sense.

When one lives from Soul Consciousness, everything one does and learns anchors on one point: How can I align my life more closely to God? How can I open my heart more fully to Spirit? How can every action express more fully the love of Spirit, God, and the Wayshower?

In one's quest for Soul Consciousness, an equilibrium develops unlike any other. It is a harmony, cooperation, and interconnectedness among and between one's seven major centers of energy. These are known in Eastern teachings as the Chakras. Each is associated with a division of lessons, expression, or quality of experience.

Each physical chakra corresponds to an energy center in each of the subtle sheaths. Balance must be struck in three ways: within every energy center in each body, among the seven chakras of each sheath, and among the corresponding centers in all of Soul's lower bodies.

When this balance is achieved, all knowledge is available as you need it. You simply access information in the inner worlds, which become open for exploration. Inner travel becomes a lucid experience of awareness. Abilities develop to help you fulfill your life's work.

The first steps toward this three-fold chakra balance involve a series of spiritual awakenings. These open the individual's eyes to life. They are not spiritual achievements. Awakenings occur throughout one's existence. Like beams of sunlight shining through the dark clouds, they come and go. Often they are forgotten. But when the individual is spiritually ripe, the sun's rays spark a spiritual fire in the heart. Eventually Spirit guides him to the Wayshower to earn his First Spiritual Achievement.

For the first time in Soul's journey, the many chakras become aware of each other. Heretofore, it would be impossible to approach alignment in these energy centers. They did not even know of each other's full existence.

The First Spiritual Achievement provides this awareness. Nothing can take it away—even if all interest in spiritual matters is renounced and Soul reverts to a life of utter physicalness. The awareness remains. In fact, reverting to a life submerged in the physical may be just what is required. More color-ray adjustments will allow a new and higher balance to emerge.

One may attain high spiritual achievements and suddenly choose to re-submerge in the physical reality. But beware! An apparent fall from spiritual grace may not be what it appears. Hold back all criticism of the fallen and keep your heart open. The apparent fall may be exactly what is required to attain a steady balance in each color-ray, in each chakra, and in each body.

Chakra centers should be aligned directly above each other throughout the aura. When misaligned, one might be to the left and another to the right, or higher or lower than it should be. Ideal chakra positioning is determined in the subconscious body, which is nearest to Soul.

For thousands of years, the physical body's chakra centers have been misaligned. Most often the warping occurs in the sacral, stomach, and heart chakras. Only recently have the chakra centers of the entire population begun moving into their proper places. This has occurred because enough people have risen in spiritual awareness to earn the First Spiritual Achievement.

Thousands have reached this achievement level. Yet many have not continued on their spiritual quests. They await a resolution of certain color-ray imbalances before reaching once again outside the physical consciousness. Eventually they will look toward Soul and progress to further spiritual achievements.

To remain in the physical consciousness until these imbalances are righted is a blessing that others may not fully appreciate. Why does Spirit direct Soul to further incarnations in the darkness of physical reality, when it has won the First Spiritual Achievement? It is a blessing, which allows one to fully complete cycles within the physical consciousness. Completing these cycles now will save time in the long run. Soul will not have to revert to these lower states again to correct certain imbalances.

The extra-long sojourn in physical reality allows people to completely resolve the Physical Plane cycle. When they eventually reach high spiritual achievements, they will not have to apparently fall back into spiritual oblivion to complete unfinished business. They are indeed truly blessed.

Cycles are cousins to Time. Both are made of the fabric of the universe. As you have learned, universal fabric differs from the fabric which clothes Soul in manifested sheaths. The difference lies in the Light and Sound frequencies which formed them.

Cycles are made of non-color-ray fabric. The lower bodies, on the other hand, are woven of all seven color rays. Every cycle that affects an individual, however, is associated with a color. This color links certain cycles to people's lives.

"This must be why color-ray-bearing gemstone spheres can help people work through cycles!" I exclaimed. "Gemstones are close in substance to universal fabric, yet their spherical form harmonizes with living beings. Now I also understand why Therapeutic Diamonds which carry color rays can work directly with our blueprint and functional spectrums. Their carbon substance resonates with living cells."

I'm glad this is now clear to you.

351

That which drives the spiritual seeker homeward to God enlivens the lowliest cricket, empowers tornadoes, ripens apples, and gives your physical body life. This is the living expression of Spirit. It lies in the heart of the Wayshower, and is present within the heart of all living things. It is also manifested in the gemstone.

This is objective truth. If you publish this statement, many will struggle with it. They are struggling with their own past experiences when gemstone energy was misused. You see, it is the very nature of the Physical Universe that anything that can be used for good can also be misused.

There is only one who stands above the laws of the lower worlds: the Wayshower. The Wayshower exists on every plane to guide us into the pure spiritual worlds and beyond. He reminds those Souls who are ready of their true spiritual heritage.

Those who have served as the Wayshower exist in a state of consciousness beyond one's concept. The Wayshower's heart is linked to the very heart of God. The strength required to maintain this connection with the Divine in the midst of the lower worlds is staggering.

One of the duties of the Wayshower is to adjust the flow of Spirit into the Physical Universe. When chakras start moving into alignment after the First Spiritual Achievement, individuals will release an abundance of negativity. To counteract this negativity, the positive flow into the lower worlds must be readjusted. The Wayshower sees to this, continually checking and maintaining the lower worlds though his own love.

It is influx of positive flow that helps balance the chakras. This re-balancing awakens those who have been sleeping physical consciousness, to realize their true nature.

A staggering positive force is required to balance the negative energies released by newly awakening Souls. These energies result from the burn-off of karmic debts, the release of limiting states of consciousness, and the movement away from old, non-life-giving habits. The Wayshower's consciousness needs no protection from this release of negativity. But his physical molecules are constantly tested. A cadre of perfectly dedicated Souls surrounds the Wayshower. Their hearts are centered in Spirit, lending strength and protection to his physical form.

If you are awakening, do not try to hold back this negative release out of newfound love for the Wayshower. It is a gift to let it out. This is not an offer to express negativity, however. The release occurs in the natural course of unfoldment. Besides, the individual must take responsibility for all his actions, thoughts, and feelings. Ultimately, this release gives the positive force an opportunity to make an even greater stand in the Physical World.

The negativity released by newly awakening Souls is actually an invitation for more positive flow to enter the Physical Universe via the Wayshower.

Newly awakening Souls partake of this positive force to fill the vacuum created by released dross. In turn, new and different forms of spiritual energy are also allowed to flow from the Astral Plane to the Supra-physical and Physical Worlds. New technologies evolve from this flow. Individuals who are inwardly trained in these new inventions are able to bring them forth on Earth.

The negative force is simply a doorway for the positive force, in this grand picture I have painted. This also occurs in the small picture of an individual's life. Every mistake you make, every crime you commit, everything that you do wrong is a blessing. Though you must take responsibility for repayment, there is also an unparalleled opportunity for growth. You could not gain this growth without learning from and stumbling into mistakes.

How many times have you tried to reach God and failed? Let me tell you a secret. In general, the higher one's position in the spiritual hierarchy, the more he has tried for God and failed. Consequently, he has also made many more mistakes.

But there is a difference between a Spiritual Master's mistakes and those of others'. Like everyone else, the Master learns from the mistake and grows from the experience. But he also makes subtle-body adjustments via spiritual techniques (many of which are shared in these discourses), to ensure the circumstances leading up to the mistake do not occur again. These exercises also help ease the karma, or repayment incurred by a mistake. They transform negative energies directly into Light and Sound for the upliftment of all.

You see, mastery of Spirit is something which must be achieved over and over again. One does not attain mastery in any final sense, as if graduating from school. It is an ongoing process.

The Second Spiritual Achievement is a mark which cannot be erased regardless of how many lifetimes one experiences thereafter. On the other hand, spiritual mastery is not a permanent attainment. It is tested at every turn, at every decision, at every cycle. Eventually one's love for the Divine becomes so strong the tests are unlike anything experienced by a spiritual seeker.

Spiritual masters live in a world apart from the seeker's. They do not just 'live in this world but not of it'. They live in their own special world.

Spiritual masters are like gemstones in that their bodies become containers of pure spiritual essence. This sets them apart, in a realm with its own laws, so to speak. Its tests and trials would be fruitless to try to explain, since this is a reality apart from your own. And yet, the rewards, the gifts, the richness of life in that state is beyond words. It makes the trials of expanding one's consciousness worthwhile.

When a spiritual master gives a gift to someone, it is usually a gift of consciousness. In turn, Spirit blesses him with more than what was given. In a life-giving, beautiful, and awe-inspiring way, this compels one to give even more.

The ongoing test is to refocus where gifts are to be given. Sometimes the gift of attention must be bestowed on family or friends. Other times one's own physical sheath must be nurtured to maintain personal balance. One of the keenest tests of mastery is to constantly place oneself where the greatest spiritual gains are to be made.

It is incorrect to think the spiritual master gives selflessly to everyone except himself. Let me speak from my own experience, for I was once under that misconception. As a result, my physical body and those of my family members died. But Spirit was kind and we eventually reincarnated into the same family.

I learned something important between my incarnations in those families. I discovered the true meaning of giving 'selflessly' and the responsibility Soul has for 'owning' lower bodies. It is the Spiritual Master, as Soul, who acts as a distributor for the gifts of Spirit.

To maintain balance, one's gifts must be given not only to all of the spiritually starved people of the Earth or of the lower worlds, but also to one's own lower bodies, and one's family. Giving selflessly takes on a whole new meaning.

Still, only so much can be given to one's lower bodies. The amount given is, within the Law of Economy, only enough to satisfy balance. It is important to also prevent the *need* to give. When we feel obliged to give, there is no spontaneous, loving outflow. The gift is marred, and Spirit stops replenishing that which was given. As soon as that happens, Mastery fades and one re-enters the consciousness of the spiritual seeker. Having lost the endless flow, Soul is compelled to search for it within Itself and through its lower bodies.

Maintaining the balance of Mastery is a very delicate task. It is walking what has been called the Razor's Edge—the perfect balance point in each moment.

I remembered a question I had been yearning to ask for some time. This was my moment. "Do spiritual masters use gemstones?" I asked.

I once used them to balance my chakra centers. Now they serve to remind me of my commitment to the Divine. My ongoing goal is to be like the gemstone, the unconditional and eternal giver of spiritual essence.

There are many ways to express the concepts I have been discussing. But I think a central image to hold is that of being a clear vehicle for Spirit—just as the gemstone is an uninhibited expresser of its energies.

Be Like a Gemstone: Experience What it's Like to Naturally Express the Sound and Light

To help you experience this concept for yourself, I would like to share a technique called 'Be Like a Gemstone'.

Cup the palms of your hands together, with your fingertips and wrists touching each other.

Imagine them enveloping a star that shines with piercing brightness through the cracks of your fingers. It also sings with a hauntingly beautiful music.

Know this star is a manifestation of Spirit itself. Now allow it to grow in size. Cup your hands more to accommodate it, but keep your finger tips and wrists touching.

Resist the star's desire to expand. Contain the star's growth; struggle against it. Use all your strength to keep the star within your hands. As the conflict escalates to its highest degree, let the crystalline structure of a faceted diamond manifest.

I choose the diamond because it has the strongest crystalline structure known on Earth. It can therefore contain more Light and Sound than any other gem.

356

Feel the smoothness of the diamond's facets and the precision of its edges. See within the diamond, flashing like flames of a fire, all seven colors of the rainbow. A golden light surrounds the singing stone.

Then, part your fingers as you surrender to the still-increasing pressure of the star within the diamond. Watch the diamond and the star within it grow, and open your hands in order to continue holding the expanding gem.

The first few times you do this exercise, you may be filled with so much spiritual energy your diamond stops growing at six to twelve inches in diameter.

Continue to practice this exercise daily, until you can allow the diamond to grow about three or four feet in diameter. At this point, your arms will be filled with the radiant gem.

Now step through your hands and into the diamond. You can do this in your imagination or with physical movements. Allow the star of Light and Sound within the diamond to find a home in your heart. Feel what it is like to naturally express the Light and Sound of Spirit.

With this awareness and feeling, get up and do something. Play with your child, cook a meal, draw a picture, or place a business call. What you give in any of these activities will be replaced by Spirit in abundance.

Practice keeping the diamond and star in your heart as you go about your day. You might even forget about it. No matter. When you repeat the technique, you will just be adding a new star and a new gem into your being, overlaying the one that already exists there. Day by day, your state of consciousness will begin to reflect the unlimited giving of the diamond and star.

I know my discourse has left many questions unanswered—and perhaps raised many more. But questions are good. They indicate you are reaching out of the morass of physical consciousness. Your questions will lead to answers.

Posing questions to Spirit is like throwing a baited fishing line into the river of life. Spirit will guide the fish to the fisherman. It might lead him into the water itself or to a new place on the riverbank, but eventually he will have his answer.

I have enjoyed this little chat, one-sided though it may have been. In you, I see myself as I once was—and that's meant to be a happy recognition. I leave you now in the hands of Spirit, for It will guide you to your next destination.

With the love of God, may the blessings be.

The Nameless one raised his right hand as he spoke his final words. Then he rose and walked back toward the white-domed spiritual city.

The Tibetan looked at me and asked if I was ready for my next and last interview.

"Tonight?" I replied.

Spirit always completes that which it has started. But It works in balance with you, your work, and your family.

When the student is ready, Spirit will respond. And I see that you are not quite ready. Perhaps tomorrow or the day after?

It was true, my cup was full. These almost daily interviews had been a rigorous exercise. My state of consciousness struggled to accept and incorporate all I was learning.

The Master surprised me with a quick yet warm embrace.

Goodnight, *he said. Then his form disappeared.*

I ambled alone across the barren terrain, thinking deeply about what I had just learned. My attention was fixed on the ground as I stepped carefully to avoid twisting an ankle among the cragged lava rocks.

As the Master's words settled into my consciousness, a new view of life emerged. Soon my feet were no longer avoiding the sharp rocks, but the fragile life that grew between them.

These little plants were everywhere, in hundreds of varieties. Some even had tiny flowers among their leaves. How frail they looked, yet how strong they must be to survive here.

I felt a special kinship with them and sent out all the love I had within my heart. The diamond star within it glowed. It gave and it received.

Chapter 31

Love and Power

All afternoon I had been sensing the presence of several other people in the house. Finally after dinner I asked my husband, Michael, if he felt them too. He said he did.

Our first reaction was to clear the entities from the house. After all, we didn't know who they were. And as far as we knew, they were uninvited. Michael and I sang HU together in each room and kindly asked the entities to leave in the name of the Wayshower.

This is a powerful technique for clearing negative energies of any kind from one's space. Surprisingly, the exercise didn't work. We wondered why, and sat down to investigate. We closed our eyes and began to study the visitors.

First we examined the way they made us feel. The beings were neutral. They didn't seem to have any malicious intent. Then, I began to see them. Except for their varied styles of dress and the light that radiated from their bodies, they all looked like normal people.

More and more of them materialized from nowhere, filling our house. They entered through walls, windows, and doors. Perplexed and somewhat frustrated, I decided to ask one of them why they were coming.

I left my physical body and in my supra-physical form, I went up to a person standing by himself near a window.

"Excuse me, why are you in our house?" I demanded.

Undaunted by my tone of voice he replied, "I was invited to attend a meeting."

"By whom?" I sputtered.

He pointed to a woman talking to a few others across the room. She was rather short, with light-blond hair twisted in a pile on top of her head. She had a definite air of authority about her; perhaps she was indeed in charge.

Determined to find out what was going on, I marched up to the woman. Her face lighted the second she saw me—as if she recognized me as a friend. "Why have you invited these people into my house?" I demanded.

Her expression changed. She studied my face and then the aura that surrounded me, with a quizzical look on her face. Finally she said carefully, I am acting under the orders of the Spiritual Masters. It was my duty to organize this meeting and invite these people here.

I stood speechless. How strange it was. Who had the right, even Spiritual Masters, to invite people into somebody else's house?

Then she seemed to realize something. Perhaps it is only your physical consciousness that was unaware of the meeting and of the invitation set forth. *A note of understanding had entered her voice.* Your inner forms definitely took part in the planning of this event.

I nodded to the woman, who immediately continued giving directions and answering others' questions. I wondered what kind of an agenda I had helped organize. And come to think of it, what other activities did my inner bodies participate in, that my physical consciousness might never grasp?

I walked back into our bedroom. Michael, now sitting in a circle with several of our guests, was still singing HU. The others had joined him. The song was so beautiful, the gathering of strangers united in a bond of love. The holiness of the experience almost moved me to tears.

The guests were still arriving. Glancing out the window, I saw many of them approaching from all directions. They moved on glowing supra-physical lines of liquid gold. I projected above the roof of our house to watch the spectacle. Gradually the movement of these beings towards us slowed. They overflowed the house and gathered on the lawn. Some even hovered in the air surrounding our home.

Michael's HU song spread among the visitors, until everyone was enjoying this love song to God.

A strong gust of wind swept through the calm autumn air. It blew across the treetops, through the walls of our house and into our bodies. It tugged at my attention until I was brought instantly to the Golden Kingdom.

I stood in the throne room before the great Sat Nam, who was majestically seated on his golden throne. Michael and our guests were gathered about fifty feet behind me.

Now, tell me again: What is power, and what is love? *Sat Nam asked in a compassionate tone.*

My thoughts raced through the discourses I had received. I hadn't realized any obvious connection between their information and the distinction between power and love. Perhaps the understanding was born of the experiences of these discourses and the exercises I had been given.

Sat Nam waited as if I had a million years to formulate my words. Finally I drew a deep breath and said, "I have learned that the lower worlds exist because of love. The love that the Divine has for each individual Soul.

"Like a father provides his best for his children, God manifests the lower worlds through Spirit. They exist to help Soul reach a greater understanding of Itself and awaken to its true relationship with the Divine.

"In the worlds of God, love and power are one. Only in the lower worlds does the human consciousness separate them, and sometimes express them negatively.

"Power seems to be a point of view. It seems to take precedence over love when the lower states of consciousness fool an individual. He starts thinking Soul is in command, when in reality the mind, the emotions, or the physical state of consciousness is ruling his world.

"The physical state of consciousness is puny when compared to any of the other sheaths—not to mention the Soul awareness. And yet, the greatest expression of negative power comes when the human consciousness raises itself above all else. Sometimes it thinks of itself as the only reality. Other times, it simply wants to be in control."

The words stopped flowing, so I stood silently.

You have answered well and from your own experience, *Sat Nam said.*

Understanding Love and Power

Sat Nam continued, Many times during Soul's journey to the Golden Kingdom and beyond, Soul is asked this same question: What is love and what is power? Soul's answer is a reflection of it's growth and state of consciousness.

There is no judgement upon the answer. The answer simply manifests one's state of consciousness.

Therefore, from time to time, ask yourself, 'What is power and what is love?'

By manifesting the answer in your dream journal or diary, you help solidify any spiritual growth achieved. Do this periodically, and look back at your answers several weeks, months, and years from now. I can promise you will be amazed as you see growth chronicled before your eyes.

Gradual unfoldment allows for a balanced awakening to Soul's spiritual destiny.

Looking back at your viewpoints of love and power that you recorded in your journal is an easier way to recognize your own unfoldment than reading through your dreams or spiritual experiences.

Dreams show experiences and can offer guidance. But the actual unfoldment can be better recognized by your evolving answers to the question I have posed.

Spiritual awareness should unfold continuously, with periodic great awakenings to speed you along. During an awakening, you may feel almost out of control. Yet your life is held together by the love of Spirit—as long as your heart remains on the spiritual path.

Sometimes you may feel you have failed all your lessons and made mistake after mistake. Ponder the question of power vs. love, let Spirit show you the rightness amidst the wrong. You have indeed learned something of great value. As you listen, It will suggest a reason and a way for God's presence to enter more fully into your life.

You have been shown the invaluable growth opportunity of mistakes already, but it bears repeating.

The guardian of the Golden Wisdom Temple of this plane is here to meet you. Go now and receive the wisdom he has to share. *Sat Nam held up a golden hand in a timeless salutation:* May the blessings and the love of Spirit be with you.

The vision of the throne room dissolved into a whirlwind of golden light. My husband and the guests also disappeared. In the center I stood alone with Sat Nam, waiting to see what would happen next.

Chapter 32

Soul's Destiny

*S*at Nam and I remained in the calm center of the swirling golden whirlwind. We didn't seem to move or travel anywhere. But after a time, the whirlwind slowed and a vision of a Temple and its gardens materialized around us.

The Temple seemed more like a column of light than a building. Its rooftop reached into the heavens—if there was indeed a sky in this realm. Faceted gems of enormous proportions—some three feet wide—rested among the flowers. Their crystalline matrixes were almost transparent. Yet they were vortexes of concentrated Light and Sound, shining like stars in the vastness of space.

A man in flowing robes of white light appeared at the temple door and walked towards us. He had short, curly, light-brown hair and bright, baby-blue eyes. He bowed to us in greeting, and we returned the gesture.

The Guardian of the Temple, *Sat Nam announced.*

The three of us walked up the temple steps. By entering into this Temple, *noted the Guardian,* one learns what is required to take the next spiritual step. Wisdom here is ever alive and growing, a Living Word. Therefore the Book of Golden Wisdom in this Temple does not contain printed words. The unchangeable nature of printed words would limit the ever-evolving wisdom of the Golden Book. *The Guardian's soft voice was echoed by a rushing sound of soft flutes in the atmosphere.*

367

We will remain just outside this holy place. This way, words can be used to impart some knowledge. True wisdom is beyond words. Though, it can be born when the experience of words becomes firmly planted in your consciousness. Words can grow into ideas, understanding, realization, and finally, knowingness.

We reached the top of the stairs and walked a short way across a large, white marble patio that separated the steps from the temple. I turned to face the Guardian and saw Michael and our guests following silently behind.

We all sat down on the terrace except the Guardian, who stood so all could see and hear him. This must have been the meeting the guests anticipated. Our household had merely been a waystation for their arrival.

The Guardian waited until everyone was seated comfortably. Soul's destiny, *he said,* does not end in the lower worlds. Although from the Golden Kingdom, they seem so trivial and temporary, these worlds are essential.

Without them, Soul would exist in a state of convoluted beingness. Its attention would be upon Itself so much, It would turn inside out. By constantly turning inward, Soul would separate from Spirit and burden It. It is practically impossible to describe such a state, which does not occur anyway.

But you are here to learn of Soul's destiny. People want to know why they have problems, why there is so much disease, pain, and suffering. Even those who've achieved spiritual awareness can't help but wonder why they must remain in the lower worlds.

When will they be free of their lower sheaths to enjoy the richness and eternal bliss of the heavenly kingdoms?

It seems hard and uncaring to simply say that the purpose of all illness and pain is to teach spiritual lessons. Ultimately it is true, but that knowledge alone doesn't take pain away.

Lessons can be shrouded in accumulation and blockage, or intricately interwoven with other spiritual lessons to converge in a wave-pattern of experience. Unlocking these experiences releases long-held disharmonies and reveals life-altering lessons. But the process can be so overwhelming that one cries for help to get through it.

You have been provided with a special knowledge. It unfolds every time you study at Askleposis or take part in life's daily experiences. You are learning how to work directly with the Spiritual Essence. In the lower worlds It takes on the twin aspects of all creation—the Light and Sound.

Knowledge of how to work with the Light and Sound comes through practice of spiritual exercises, living life creatively, and recognizing these twin threads within all physically manifested objects.

You have learned that many diamonds and gemstones are strong containers of this Light and Sound. Some may be used for healing. In this function, diamonds differ from gemstones. Physical differences aside, diamonds do not impart a personality into their expression of Light and Sound as gemstones do. This is why every gemstone, regardless of its form, expresses Light and Sound in a unique way characteristic of that gem.

As instruments of change, each gemstone satisfies certain needs more than others. The diamond has no such personality. It simply presents a state that lies beyond limitations.

Diamonds appropriate for therapy express the color rays—that part of Spirit which forms the sheaths of Soul. There are many other frequencies of Light and Sound which comprise the lower planes. But only the color-ray frequencies make up healthy lower bodies. Non-color-ray vibrations can prove very harmful when presented to the bodies. This is especially true when the carriers of these vibrations are the non-therapeutic, non-color-ray-bearing diamonds.

Spiritual truth can be misused. Of course, there is a penalty and it is known as karma. The individual pays for misdeeds and digressions from the path.

Individuals will also suffer the consequences of misusing information such as knowledge of Diamond Therapy. Therapeutic Diamonds are powerful tools and must be used responsibly and correctly.

The greater one's understanding of spiritual laws, the more deeply negative expressions of power can affect him. The individual becomes vulnerable when he loses his balance in life and stops focusing on the heart of the Divine.

There are many who are suffering in the lower worlds. They want to know the reasons for their pain and how to be free of it. Others simply cry, 'why me?' The answer is: There are unlimited tools for spiritual unfoldment. There are the spiritual exercises you have been given. There is the sacred HU, which uplifts Soul.

These help you climb out of your despair and reach into the joy of life. The first step out of your misery is to begin using the tools at your fingertips for healing—any tools. Diamonds and gemstones are of particular interest to you, but they are not the only tools.

The next step is to find a path that is comfortable for you—any path. For a ship that does not choose its course and destination can get lost upon the seas. There are myriad paths, in practically every direction you turn. There is also the direct path provided by the Wayshower.

The Wayshower focuses Soul's attention beyond the mind, straight into the heart of God. The mind knows not of Soul's future. It can only guess and complain that the future has not come soon enough. Soul's destiny is not what the mind thinks it might be.

The Guardian pointed to the sky of golden mist. It parted as a beam of white light created a rectangular shape over our heads.

This is a window into the world above the Golden Kingdom, *he explained.* Just as there are planes in the lower worlds, so too there are subtle divisions in the higher worlds of God.

The Golden Kingdom is an area of transition, similar to the transitory areas between each of the lower worlds. Souls must pass though here from the higher planes to the lower planes, and back again.

We will remain looking through this window, but will not pass through it. Know, however, that the planes beyond are accessible. Those who reach the next realm are met by a representative of the spiritual hierarchy of co-workers. This spiritual agent will lead you to a region of awakening, where two things occur.

First you will be given an opportunity for consciousness expansion. Second, you will be tested in your ability to incorporate this expansion throughout all your lower bodies.

If the tests are passed, you are given an assignment. The assignment may be clear, direct, and definite such as 'Go here and speak to so and so'. Or it could be vague and open to one's own definition: 'Look for the balance in all things', or 'Today more than any other day, live the Law of Economy to the fullest of your ability'.

Carry out the assignment with the utmost of creativity. This is the true reward for completing the task. Creativity is the mark of the spiritually open being—one who is attentive to the guiding whispers of Spirit. And Spirit, as I and others have said, is the voice of the Divine Itself. It is the Word of God. Look for It as It speaks or expresses Itself in Light and Sound.

This is the difference between the individual who has attained Soul consciousness and one who is reaching beyond, into the consciousness of the Divine Itself: The first lives life by the direction of Soul, while the second follows the direction of Spirit. 'If Spirit so wills, then shall I be. If Spirit so wills,

371

then shall I do'. These are the words written in the heart. Nay, they are embedded in the heart of the one whose destiny lies beyond the Golden Kingdom.

To many it is enough to return to the Golden Kingdom. Only a handful recognize that there is more and step toward it. They are driven to glimpse the Divine Itself.

These individuals travel a different path, though it may appear no different than others'. They too may wonder, When will I be free of the lower worlds? Of course, the exact amount of time differs for each individual.

But for those striving for God-consciousness, the word 'when' is just another word in the dictionary. They understand that there will always be another step into the heart of God. Always another challenge. The rewards for having met and accomplished a challenge are beyond description.

An endless journey, however, is not a fruitless one. Rewards abound. But they are not the reason for the journey or for accepting the challenges. Gifts are received with gratitude. But instead of reveling in them, the individual turns his sight toward the next challenge.

Experiencing life fully in the lower sheaths is one of the greatest gifts Soul can receive. Yes, the lower bodies malfunction and cause great pain and grief. Yet if you knew of the thousands upon thousands of Souls awaiting the opportunity to incarnate—not just physically but even into mental, causal, or emotional sheaths—gratitude would engulf you. Perhaps that thought will ease the pain, as you realize how blessed your incarnation truly is.

Having a physical body is paramount to returning home to the Golden Kingdom and beyond. Soul must learn how to negotiate both the positive and negative forces. It must live in harmony with all frequency-manifestations of Spirit while being aware of Itself as Soul.

The physical incarnation is a golden opportunity to read a part of the Divine Story which is otherwise inaccessible.

Physically manifested sentences and paragraphs of the Word of God can only be understood if one can read them. They can only be read when one is linked to a physical body. Yes, I am speaking poetically, but my point is that the physical body is Soul's most precious possession. It allows Soul to experience a full spectrum of the vibratory rates of Spirit.

With this understanding, many of the functions of the other sheaths make more sense. For example, why do the inner bodies manifest as an aura that surrounds the physical body? Mainly this is to protect it. The mental aura is able to protect the physical body from the mental-body emanations of other people. No other sheath can do this. The causal aura guards against foreign causal emanations. The emotional aura does likewise. It protects the physical body from the emotional miasmas surrounding Soul.

There is no better way that I know of to gain spiritual strength and stamina than in the midst of the most challenging conditions. Without intending insult to those who live there, such conditions are found in the Physical World.

My thoughts returned momentarily to the Physical World and the supra-physical beings who were with me listening to this discourse. Their thoughts were clear: many of them wished they too had physical bodies.

Back here now, *said the Guardian, calling my attention to return.* There is more I wish to share.

The purpose of life for those who have attained the First Spiritual Achievement is simply to grow in substance, to fill the inner sheaths with experiences. It seems as if each Soul must have a certain quota of experiences before It is eligible for the Second Spiritual Achievement.

After this blessed occasion, the purpose of life becomes a quest to realize the existence of the lower bodies. Soul must discover the more subtle aspects of the physical and inner forms and master them. During this time, one learns how to work and live in Spirit, as per the Word of God.

At each spiritual turning point, life refocuses around one central mission: how to respond more fully to Spirit. How to put aside one's personal desires, and live, act, be, speak, and do all in the name of Spirit.

One soon recognizes the presence of Soul within the physical sheath of every person on the planet and in the lower worlds. Then, one also becomes aware of the presence of the Word of God Itself enlivening these sheaths.

Spirit is the essence which keeps Soul in the body. It decides when Soul's sojourn in a particular body is over. It also guides Soul's attention among the bodies for inner-world exploration. Recognize Spirit—not just Soul—in your fellow human beings, and do all things for Spirit. This is how one's life becomes dedicated to service and growth.

In a spiritual sense, the best way to serve others is to be as creative as possible—doing whatever is required for Spirit to flow through you at Its maximum potential. Spirit flows at Its height, and creativity is manifested in its fullness, when you do what you love. So focus on what gives you joy, happiness, and fills your heart with gratitude for being alive.

If you want to live to serve others and recognize Spirit within them, open your own flow of Spirit first. Then others will recognize It in you. They, in turn, will be sparked to serve all life. Not just human beings and living things, but all manifestations—for Spirit exists everywhere, even in the fabric of the universe itself.

The Guardian gazed through the white rectangular window into the heaven-worlds of God above. His bright blue eyes sparkled with an abounding love for the Divine.

There are worlds upon worlds beyond this Golden Kingdom yet to be explored, *he said.* Where do you set your sights? Where do you place your spiritual goals? The nearer to the center of God's heart that you can possibly place your goal, the quicker your unfoldment will be, and the greater the momentum established in your life.

Your goal is like an anchor thrown from a boat into the water. It can only fly as far as your strength can hurl it. Your goal can only be planted as far as your state of consciousness can imagine it. So reestablish your goal periodically and search ever inward to find where that divine center is.

This is the last advice I can give you. Go now, seeing others not just as Soul, but as Spirit also. In quiet contemplation, see if you can find this difference in yourself as well.

Soul is the part of you that has consciousness. Spirit is the part of you that allows you to exist. It's the part of you that comprises not only your physical body and all your inner sheaths, but your Soul body as well. By 'Soul body' I mean that form in which your Soul consciousness exists.

The sheaths are only the manifestation of Spirit. They are not Spirit Itself. Just like capturing the Living Word into writing limits Its life, manifesting Spirit limits and confines It.

Spirit is confined within your sheaths. But It is also present in you in an unconfined, limitless way. The best way to identify this spiritual essence—the Living Word within—is to listen to It. Doing so can take you beyond the light, past the often dazzling and brilliant illusions of lower-world manifestation, and into the heart of the Divine Itself.

Moving Beyond the Light

Part 1

To experience what lies beyond the light, close your eyes in quiet contemplation. Then use any of the techniques that help you become aware of yourself as Soul.

One technique is to imagine walking through a series of doors. The first door can be the screen behind your forehead or at the top of your head. Go either forward or upward through the door.

Each subsequent door leads into the world in which the next inner sheath exists.

First open the door of your physical body. Pass through and listen to the sound of the door closing. Hear the latch.

Approach the next door to the astral body. Open the door with feeling. This will help; feel the handle and then the door shutting tightly behind you as you release your hand from the knob.

The next door will be that of the Causal Plane. As you approach this door, pay attention to the rhythm of your footsteps, your breathing, or your heartbeat. Attention to rhythm is a key to opening the door. Open the door, pass through, and close it in time with your chosen rhythm.

The fourth door is that of the mind. Imagine this door has a symbol with special meaning painted on it. The faculty of perceiving color, design, and symbols is a mental function. It engages your mind in a positive way. Don't try to think. That is a trap. The design is the key to open this door, which is also painted a particular color. Note the color of the door as you pass through it.

Finally you will enter a hallway. At the end is a wall with seven doors, each a different color. Choose the color that matches the one you just passed through. You will enter into the Golden Kingdom.

You could practice this technique seven times, and see a different color each time. Don't worry about it. Just go through the door that corresponds to the one on the Mental Plane.

Everything in the Golden Kingdom is wrapped in a golden mist. Landscape and objects manifest only to provide rest for your consciousness. This is so you can comprehend or relate to this world of unmanifested essence.

Part 2

Find someplace to sit—perhaps a smooth rock or even a plush rocking chair. Make whatever forms you wish out of the golden mist. Sit down and contemplate your surroundings. Fill yourself with the Light. Then, reach into it. Plunge your consciousness into the golden mist.

You are enveloped by the Sound. Listen for music that sounds like a soft, resonant flute or singing violins. They will play a single note and yet it will be a note that contains all notes. It will be hauntingly beautiful, completely fulfilling, and divinely beautiful.

Listen for several minutes.

If you cannot see or hear this, take heart in knowing that just by reading this exercise, Soul has taken the journey. If you are willing and desire this experience, Soul will travel through these doors and into the Kingdom of Gold to hear the voice of Spirit.

Accompany this voice by singing the word HU. Let its vibration blend in with the celestial sounds around you.

When you are ready to open your eyes to the Physical World, continue to sing the HU. Now let its vibration blend in with the celestial sounds that manifest in such things as traffic noises, refrigerator hums, and people's voices.

As you go about your daily life, practice keeping your ears open to the sounds of Spirit. Go beyond the light that you see reflecting off the manifestations of people, plants, animals, the Earth itself, and the stars in the heavens.

Listen to the Word of God everywhere. For indeed it is everywhere!

No other topic could end this series of discourses better.

May the blessings be!

Conclusion

The Temple Guardian bowed to me and walked with Sat Nam toward the gathering of our guests.

Peddar appeared at my side.

Come with me now, *he said.*

We left the group and the Golden Kingdom and sped through the borders of several worlds. Soon we were welcomed by the familiar fresh, crisp air of the Astral Plane.

We arrived at the top of the steps, near the front doors of the main university building at Askleposis. I took in its view of the ocean and the city across the bay. The sky was particularly clear today. I could see higher up the previously-shrouded mountain peaks behind the city than ever before.

As I contemplated their towering heights, I recognized a familiar feeling in my heart. A cycle was over. This series of discourses on the subtle bodies had ended.

Well, what do you think? *Peddar asked.*

"No school teacher ever gave me an assignment like this," *I replied with a smile.*

He laughed.

"But it seems I have only touched the surface."

Indeed you have, *he replied.* You have painted a framework. Many questions are yet to be answered. Many stories are yet to unfold. The whole picture is incomplete. But it is not meant to be complete, for it can never be. Even the

Souls who choose to rest eternally in the Golden Kingdom find their unfoldment is not finished.

The Masters who spoke with you did so under the direction of Spirit. Now your task is to translate the recorded experiences into readable English and research any concepts you didn't understand.

I am here to help if asked, for that is the law of Spirit. During writing class, in the wee hours of the morning, we can discuss your progress. Your dream body will communicate with your physical consciousness. Record your dreams and Soul will speak with you.

Do you have any questions?

"No, not now," I replied.

Very well. I will leave you to your other responsibilities. And yet I will always be with you.

May the Blessings Be!

Peddar winked and smiled. Then turned and entered the building.

Michael was waiting as I returned to physical consciousness. The guests were already starting to disband. As I looked around the house, their supra-physical forms seemed much clearer and easier to see. Several gave Michael and me flowers. I wondered in passing if supra-physical flowers needed water.

After everyone left the house, we still felt someone's presence. I looked out the window. Four armed sentinels, each at least twelve feet tall, guarded the corners of our property. They stood like statues with arms crossed and feet apart. I knew they were there to protect us. Negative energy might try to fill the void as the high-intensity spiritual vibrations slowly drained from our house. I sent them gratitude and love.

"The house is going to seem empty without our guests," Michael said. I agreed.

We sat in silence on the couch, each reflecting on the experiences received.

I felt the way I feel after I've read a good book. I never want it to end. But the time was right.

And so I say to you, dear friend, good night, and may the blessings be.

Products and Services
From Golden Age Publishing

Dear Reader:

You have just completed the account of one of the most fascinating journeys ever published. If you would like to share your experiences with this book, or the exercises it contains, please write; the author would like to hear from you.

Those who would like to know more about Diamond and Gemstone Therapy will find Golden Age Publishing offers an ever-growing library of informative resources. Descriptions of several publications, plus an order form, are printed on the following pages. Of special interest is the Golden Age Journal. This is a free newsletter available to all on our mailing list. It is an excellent way to network with individuals working with Therapeutic Diamonds and Gemstones. Here you can learn how others have benefited from Diamond and Gemstone Therapy, as well as read articles and updates on Golden Age's books, training tools, products, and services.

Please join us in our efforts to spread the news of Diamond and Gemstone Therapy and the effects of these powerful healing tools. If you know someone who may be interested, please offer them a brochure or a copy of the Golden Age Journal. Refer to the ordering information at the back of this book to receive extra copies of brochures and Journals.

Yours in Service,
—The Golden Age Staff

Diamond Therapy

Revolutionizing the Art & Science of Healing

Diamond Therapy: Revolutionizing the Art & Science of Healing

Therapeutic Diamonds awaken and enliven the very blueprints of our being—the intelligent information about optimal health within each of us.

At the same time, they reprogram the patterns, remove the accumulation, and resolve the blockages that prevent blueprint information from manifesting physical, emotional, causal, mental, and spiritual health, balance, and well-being.

This brochure presents an overview of the vast and exciting information available on this remarkable new science which is compatible with all other healing modalities. Learn how you can take the first steps toward using Therapeutic Diamonds to recharge your own health, treat family and friends, or incorporate these amazing therapy tools into your own healing practice.

Therapeutic Diamonds

Before a diamond can be considered therapeutic, it is carefully studied by Ginny and Michael Katz to ensure it meets extensive and specific physical and energetic criteria. Only a very small percentage pass these tests. Certified Therapeutic Diamonds are available from Golden Age, or your own diamonds can be evaluated for potential certification.

Diamond Therapy Manual

(258 pp., 81/2 x 11)

How to Apply One and Two Therapeutic Diamonds

This invaluable reference is available to those who own a Therapeutic Diamond certified by Golden Age. It contains fully illustrated, step-by-step information necessary to perform basic Diamond Therapy. Learn how to determine which application to use, and, just as important, how *not* to apply these powerful tools.

Therapies are described with detailed, clearly-written, step-by-step instructions with headings that include: 'When to Apply', 'Where to Apply', 'Effects', and 'Time Guidelines'.

This easy-to-use manual includes everything you need to put Diamond Therapy to work in your life today!

Diamond Therapy Videos: Coming Spring 1992!

Diamond Therapy is both an art and science. These videotapes are an excellent accompaniment to written training materials. They let you see for yourself how therapies should be performed, and help refine your application technique.

The first volume of The Golden Age Diamond Therapy Video Library is scheduled for release in Spring 1992. It is a training tape available to Therapeutic Diamond owners.

Additional videos will explore new, and more advanced methods for using one, two, and several Therapeutic Diamonds.

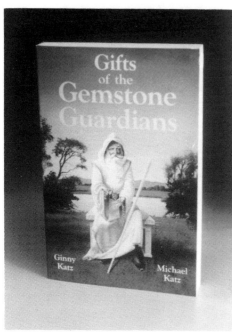

Gifts of the Gemstone Guardians

by Michael Katz
and Ginny Katz

(374 pp., 6 x 9, $12.95)

Gemstones are the strongest, most concentrated containers of the healing force on this planet—and this book tells you why and how they work!

Gifts of the Gemstone Guardians is the true account of Ginny and Michael Katz's conversations with the spiritual caretakers of thirty different healing gemstones. The Guardians' discourses are a treasure-trove of insights about the origins and effects of these healing gemstones and their role in human evolution. Perhaps the most important new fact the Guardians reveal is that for people today, the most effective gemstone form is not the crystal, but the sphere.

Each chapter in the book focuses on a different gemstone. It recounts the gemstone's history; describes its purpose and effects on humans (including specific therapies), and then gives a glimpse of what we may expect from that gemstone in the future.

The rays of hope, encouragement, and love showered by the Guardians on the reader of this fascinating book are a healing experience in themselves. The Guardians shine light on virtually every facet of human life and how it can be uplifted by gemstones—from the most subtle aspect of our inner lives and our physical health to our true roles and responsibilities as inhabitants of the Earth.

Free Brochure

Diamond Spheroids: Empowering Therapeutic Gemstone Necklaces

With current technology, diamonds cannot be cut into perfectly smooth, round spheres like gemstones can. But, they can be cut into spheroidal shapes covered with many tiny facets.

With just one Therapeutic Diamond Spheroid, a gemstone necklace's effects can far surpass the effects of the gemstones by themselves.

Learn how these amazing carriers of the seven life-building color rays heal and uplift, as well as catapult a Gemstone Necklace's effects far and deep into the fabric of our being.

Find out how a single Therapeutic Spheroid Diamond can transform your Therapeutic Gemstone Necklaces, and bring the healing Light and Sound of Diamond into your life!

Free Quarterly Newsletter: The Golden Age Journal

The *Golden Age Journal* is packed with stories of readers' personal healing experiences with Therapeutic Diamonds and Gemstones, articles on Gemstone and Diamond Therapy, and updates on Golden Age's fascinating books, training tools, products, and services.

Order your free subscription today!

Home Study Course: Gemstone Therapy 1

(One year of study, twelve lessons, 8 1/2 x 11, $145.00)

This exciting home study course offers you a wave of new, advanced information from the Guardians who brought you *Gifts of the Gemstone Guardians*. It is a natural next step for readers who wish to work toward becoming gemstone therapists—or those who simply desire greater knowledge of gemstones for self-application.

In the course, twelve Gemstone Guardians go more deeply into the way their gemstones work—and how they can benefit one's physical, emotional, causal, mental, and spiritual aspects.

Therapies included in the course range from simple to complex; however, step-by-step instructions on when, where, and how to apply each one are provided so that anyone can learn to perform them. For example, learn how to:

- Awaken the body's healing energies
- Cleanse and renew the mind and body
- Align, clear, and balance the chakra centers
- Relax tight, stiff, and congested areas
- Clear disharmony from the eyes, sinuses, & brain
- Sooth traumatized areas following surgery or injury
- Improve the relationship between the physical and subtle bodies—for clearer Soul awareness

The course is divided into twelve monthly lessons—giving one ample time to digest the material and practice the therapies presented. Get started on Lesson One today!

To Order Call: 1-800-727-8877 or (503) 241-3642

Title	Qty	Price		Total
Beyond the Light		x	$14.95	=
Gifts of the Gemstone Guardians		x	$12.95	=
Gemstone Therapy I Home Study Course		x	$145.00	=
The Golden Age Journal		Free		-
Diamond Therapy Brochure		Free		-
Spheroid Diamond Brochure		Free		-
Gemstone Therapy 1 Study Course Brochure		Free		-

Subtotal

Total Shipping & Handling (See box below)

Total Amount enclosed (USA funds only)

Shipping and Handling (1st Class mail)				
Title	U.S.A.		Canada/Mexico	
	1st item	Ea. Add'l	1st item	Ea. Add'l
Books	$3.00	$1.50	$4.50	$2.50
Gemstone Therapy I Home Study Course	No Charge		$10.00	
Brochures	Single copies no charge. $1 per 10 copies.			
The Golden Age Journal	Single copies no charge. $3 per 10 copies.			
Other Countries please write to Golden Age Publishing for a shipping quote.				

Please charge this order to my: ☐ Visa ☐ Mastercard

Make checks payable to Golden Age.

Number :_____

Signature :_____Exp. :_____

Prices subject to change.

Name :_____Phone : (   )_____

Street :_____

City :_____State :_____Zip :_____Country :_____

Mail to:
Golden Age, 2066 N.W. Irving #1, Portland, Oregon 97209 USA

To Order Call: 1-800-727-8877 or (503) 241-3642

Title	Qty	Price	Total
Beyond the Light		x $14.95	=
Gifts of the Gemstone Guardians		x $12.95	=
Gemstone Therapy I Home Study Course		x $145.00	=
The Golden Age Journal		Free	-
Diamond Therapy Brochure		Free	-
Spheroid Diamond Brochure		Free	-
Gemstone Therapy 1 Study Course Brochure		Free	-

Subtotal	
Total Shipping & Handling (See box below)	
Total Amount enclosed (USA funds only)	

Shipping and Handling (1st Class mail)

Title	U.S.A.		Canada/Mexico	
	1st item	Ea. Add'l	1st item	Ea. Add'l
Books	$3.00	$1.50	$4.50	$2.50
Gemstone Therapy I Home Study Course	No Charge		$10.00	
Brochures	Single copies no charge. $1 per 10 copies.			
The Golden Age Journal	Single copies no charge. $3 per 10 copies.			
Other Countries please write to Golden Age Publishing for a shipping quote.				

Please charge this order to my: ❏ Visa ❏ Mastercard

Number :_____

Signature :_____Exp. :_____

Make checks payable to Golden Age.

Prices subject to change.

Name :_____Phone : (   )_____

Street :_____

City :_____State :_____Zip :_____Country :_____

Mail to:
Golden Age, 2066 N.W. Irving #1, Portland, Oregon 97209 USA